Management meets Nietzsche

A Leadership Philosophy

by Steffen Reckert

Introduction	3
Philosophy of Work	6
Part I	14
Zarathustra's Prologue	14
Zarathustra's Discourses	29
The Three Metamorphoses	29
The Academic Chairs of Virtue	41
Backworldsman	45
The Despisers of the Body	50
Joys and Passions	56
The Pale Criminal	62
Reading and Writing	73
The Tree on the Hill	80
The Preachers of Death	84
War and Warriors	89
The new Idol	95
The Flies in The Marketplace	109
Chastity	120
The Friend	130
The Thousand and One Goals	136
Neighbor-Love	142
The Way of the Creating One	147
Old and Young Women	152
The Bite of the Adder	156
Child and Marriage	161
Voluntary Death	166
The Bestowing Virtue	171
Part II	185
The Child with the Mirror	185
In the Happy Isles	192
The Pitiful	197
The Priests	202
The Virtuous	206
The Rabble	210

The Tarantulas	218
The Famous Wise Ones	225
The Night Song	228
The Dance Song	233
The Grave Song	240
Self-Surpassing	245
The Sublime Ones	250
The Land of Culture	254
Immaculate Perception	260
Scholars	266
Poets	271
Great Events	276
The Soothsayer	279
Redemption	282
Manly Prudence	291
The Stillest Hour	294
The End	**298**
Note of Thanks	301
Principles	302
Literature	310

Introduction

One must still have chaos in oneself to be able to give birth to a dancing star.
- Friedrich Nietzsche

My partner is one of the most influential people in my life and she loves memes and quotes. One day she showed me the above quote by Friedrich Nietzsche, and I was left speechless. I love space and science. And in my eyes the natural basis for all science and knowledge is philosophy.

Nietzsche's words triggered all sorts of thoughts about quantum physics, chaos theory and how important chaos itself is for us. I wanted to find out more about this crazy guy. Being an avid reader, I decided to buy his, "Thus Spoke Zarathustra." The insights it contained were all the more impressive when you see that he wrote it in 1883. At that time, I enjoyed listening to audio books and fortunately the narrator of the German version (Peter Wapnewski) reads as if he is the real Zarathustra.

On first hearing the book, I was confused. Nietzsche writes in parables, and you have to think carefully, sometimes repeatedly, about almost every sentence. Even then you still may not understand. So I decided to read a Wiki article and listen to the book again. And again, and again. Intrigued, I felt like with each hearing, I understood more and more. Like a puzzle building to its final state, piece by piece. I came across many messages that I think are still valid today, especially for my current job. However, listening to an audiobook has the disadvantage that you can't easily slow down or stop to reread a complicated sentence to let it sink in or think about it further. Ever helpful, my partner pulled a paperback version of the book from our bookshelf, so I decided to read it again in written form.

During this fifth reading, I thought of taking notes and applying the lessons to past and present situations at work and in life in general. I also decided to write down what happened and what I learned from it. I used these insights in conversations with my managers, and eventually noticed that they were using them with their managers as well. There was some kind of general and resonant application emerging.

During dinner with three of my managers, we found ourselves discussing different leadership styles. They told me that they were elated with the company culture we had built and that my unusual leadership style was a critical component of this success. They asked me who or what had influenced me in developing this leadership style, but I was momentarily stumped. I mean, there was so much.... conversations, situations and experiences (good and bad), feedback received and given, books and even movies. But as I thought about it, it was Nietzsche's book - or more specifically, my interpretation of it. I decided to bring order to the chaos of my notes and see if it could become a book. And here we are.

A short disclaimer;

I am NOT going to philosophically analyze Zarathustra or give deeper insights into Nietzsche's thinking or try to reinvent philosophy! Books inspire me. In my experience, the most influential sentences in the books I read are usually subordinate clauses or otherwise tangential to the main story. I steal wisdom from others, enrich it with my own experience, and then summarize it as a rationale for the way I lead.

Have you ever read something and thought, "Wow, what a cool sentence!" or "Damn, that's well worded!"? When I read these standout sentences, I store them firmly in my long-term memory, perhaps by writing them down or memorizing them. Many of Nietzsche's sentences express exactly how I feel. This relevancy was surprisingly greater than that of the well-known management literature I'd been reading. I don't remember the core messages of most management books I read. There are exceptions, like Jack Welch's book, Winning, or others that I am happy to recommend upon request, but most revolve around the same themes.

I don't suggest that you impose Nietzsche's thinking on your management style. We'll see later that this could lead to serious problems, since the 19th century, for example, was not exactly known for its strong culture of diversity and inclusion. The point is to take Zarathustra's story, his path to success, his teachings and growth, and explain how that can inspire you to grow, learn and build a successful career.

Philosophy of Work

After years of managing people and projects in different companies, I came to realize the importance of authenticity in inspiring people to follow you. If you can't inspire the people around you, you are definitely in the wrong role. You may not be an idiot or a bad manager, but you are not maximizing your value. A manager's job is to get people to perform at their best to maximize value to the organization.

To be authentic, you must have your own "working philosophy". And yes, I intentionally chose the word philosophy. Personal values, principles and beliefs shape a great leader. People need to feel that they can learn from their leader. The employee must feel the personal benefits of working for the company beyond the paycheck. This is one of the core principles emerging from this book. Engagement is the key to success - always!

Developing one's own, authentic work philosophy is the hardest but most fundamental goal in becoming a great leader. It requires one thing above all: Time. The aim of this book is to follow Zarathustra's personal journey to create his philosophy and use it to craft our own philosophy. Together we will learn about a basic development process based on Zarathustra (the three metamorphoses of the spirit) and derive the most helpful principles from it. Everything will be summarized at the end of the book.

Very important: developing your own philosophy of work doesn't mean reading some well-known management bestseller and parroting the beautifully polished phrases in every appropriate situation. Your employees develop an incredible sense of bullshit detection over time - regardless of level. You feel it when someone else's sentences bubble out of your mouth instead of your own words. You've seen it when an insecure person tries to elevate themselves with an inflated vocabulary that just doesn't quite fit. In this situation, you think "where did that come from"...? Have you ever googled "bullshit bingo"?

I'm not saying to stop reading books or watching Ted Talks. Your mind needs external inputs to learn. You must experience as much as you can yourself and mix that with those external inputs to develop your own style. You need to constantly challenge yourself and incorporate the feedback you receive. Be self-reflective and never assume that you are already at the end. The point is that learning takes time, and if you try to jump ahead, people will know you are faking it.

The philosophers of the world, great and small, have constantly revised their philosophy and changed their outlook, sometimes dramatically, over the course of their lives. Some would say, "Consistency over correctness," but that only applies to a limited area of management decisions and certainly not when it comes to building something great, new and disruptive. History shows so many examples where inflexibility led great companies into irrelevance or vaporized vast amounts of money. Politicians would often rather stay wrong than be accused of "flip-flopping", and this is one reason we don't like them. Many managers (or politicians) are trapped in situations or systems that are inherently inflexible. The only question is whether or not you accept the situation or system. If you authentically accept the situation as it is, then you stick to it, but if things have changed, then you must change too. Are you authentically putting all your effort into evaluating the situation? And if so, if you accept defeat, are you at least creating the best possible work environment for the people who rely on you? Engagement is the key!

My personal version of hell would be working under a supervisor who doesn't care about my development, constantly skips conversations, or doesn't support my ideas. Engagement is the core component of any good work philosophy. Engagement is based on two main pillars:

1. the employee identifies with the company and/or

2. the employee identifies with their supervisor.

If the company you work for has a good reputation, always pays on time, has a trusted sustainability agenda, or whatever else makes you proud, you'll be extra engaged. In other words: If the company's philosophy is authentic, you'll love working for it. You will identify with the company. A great company has engaged employees.

The same is true for your supervisor. "Emma is a great leader, she is always responsive and takes my feedback into consideration. She is trustworthy and I feel valued by her. She is a pleasure to work for. When I have problems, she usually has good advice that gets me back on track, and I feel good after our conversations."

Fantastic Emma, you nailed it. This employee will go the extra mile for you. If asked to put in extra effort, the employee will most likely tackle it without grumbling. So, identification with the manager is the second important building block for engagement.

When you identify with both the company and with the leader - it's a clear bull's eye. If you remove one of these two pillars, you may still have an engaged employee, but the risk of turnover may be high. If you don't meet either, then your employees are almost certainly disengaged.

So, engagement is a key part of any work philosophy. It underlies employee satisfaction and is an absolute key to success. There's also a wealth of research on engagement that shows the overwhelming benefits of employee engagement at all levels (I refer in particular to the most recent Gallup study[1]). The Gallup study shows that engaged employees have:

- ❖ 41% lower quality defects
- ❖ 64% lower safety incidents
- ❖ 28% lower theft rate
- ❖ 81% lower absenteeism

---

[1] https://www.gallup.com/

- ❖ 14% higher productivity
- ❖ 23% higher profitability

than disengaged employees. Any manager who ignores these facts, shouldn't lead people.

Our working world is changing drastically from a primary focus on profit to a search for meaning. I stole this sentence from Richard David Precht, an author and philosopher who is one of the brightest minds of our time and whose books have inspired me. What is meant by this is that in the future people will no longer work mainly for money. These generations will be primarily concerned with fulfillment, doing what they think will enhance their personal well-being. To date, in our Western world, this has primarily been money. Money has been our main driver and motivator. If you have enough money, you can achieve all of your goals. But this is changing. More and more people realize that money cannot buy everything. And when this becomes clearer, the benefits of engagement become even more important.

I am a child of the 90s and consider myself lucky. I grew up safe and well cared-for in Germany. But my grandparents' generation had suffered greatly in the war. They knew what it meant to starve. My grandmother had come to Germany as a war refugee as a small child and lived with many other refugees in an old castle. They had no running water, no money and nothing apart from each other. They couldn't build wealth, as a whole generation first had to rebuild a destroyed Europe. Work was a means of survival, not fulfillment. To build a fortune was unthinkable for most people.

So, my parents' generation did not receive large inheritances. Interest rates for home purchases were about 9%. Owning a small house or a condo required a job, most likely for both parents. I grew up with two families and eight people in a two-room apartment in a lumber yard. But both my parents got an education that led to good jobs. There was a rapid economic upswing after the war. But still, very few people were rich. Vacations were simple retreats in relatively pleasant places, not too far away, where families could send some time together, away from work. Especially for families who lived in the socialist part of Germany, jetting off to an exclusive tropical resort was out of the question.

We benefit greatly from what our parents and grandparents built up and from the first small fortunes they accumulated. Nevertheless, we have to work - at least in my case - to have the things we want.

But my children's generation, the famous Generation Z and even more Generation α, will benefit even more from what we have built for them. They can live in established apartments or houses with relatively low rents. They likely receive much more financial support from their parents. I am not talking about every person but rather, the statistical average. On average, since 2000, the wealth per adult in the USA has more than doubled[2] according to the Central Bank of America (FED) .

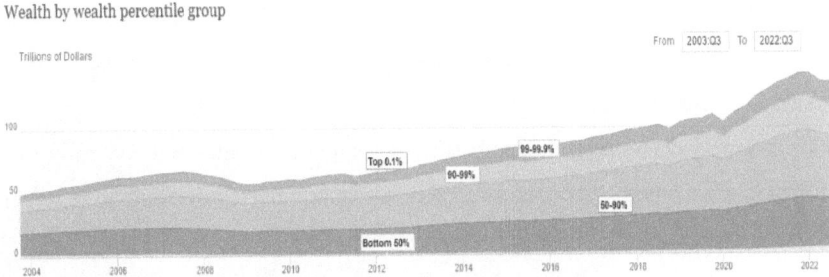

In other words, our children's generation will no longer have to work primarily for money. Softer factors will play an increasingly important role in motivating them to work. Soft factors will be things like the working atmosphere, non-monetary benefits, the behavior of superiors, flexible hours, and vacation times. I know that this does not apply to everyone, of course; this is more of a statistical look at Western society. The accumulation of wealth has been historically unfair, particularly among populations of color who have suffered

---

[2] https://www.federalreserve.gov/

from a legacy of discrimination, but even the historically disadvantaged are striving to build wealth, which will hopefully come. Although there's a wide range of wealth and access to opportunity, work is changing, and the work environment will be increasingly important. This brings us back to the importance of engagement.

I am writing this book in a time of great uncertainty. The leading media are obsessively covering the "big quit" as many workers are leaving their jobs - mainly because of an unattractive work environment. *"[...] low pay (63%), no opportunities for advancement (63%) and feeling disrespected at work (57%)"* were cited as the top reasons for quitting in 2021/22 by a study from Kim Parker and Juliana Menasce Horowitz of the Pew Research Center[3]. It has also become insanely difficult to recruit new talent. There are enough applicants, but applicants today are increasingly interested in soft factors, not just salary. This changing world may require adjustments to my work philosophy, but I am certain that those who implement a relevant work philosophy will succeed. I hope that each of you will feel animated to develop your own ideas. Take from me what fits you best. This is the only way.

It is time for a second short disclaimer! Some of you may not share my views. That's fine. Please send me your feedback! My personal credo is "Challenge drives Innovation", and I'm pretty sure your feedback could help me develop my philosophy of work. Since Nietzsche is controversial in today's world like few other philosophers, I would like to point out that the interpretations I draw from the texts are seen differently by many other readers of his works. I have read in the research in countless articles, books and scientific works such an extremely wide range of opinions and interpretations that I would never claim to have found out Nietzsche's motives behind it. In some passages it is clearer in others not. If someone thinks that I am completely wrong, let me know. I am looking forward to feedback.

---

[3] PEW Research Center https://pewrsr.ch/3hVWMfr

Nobody should just copy my views and assume they will work for them. It worked for me, but that doesn't mean it will work for you. I am very extroverted and therefore handle situations very differently than an introvert, for example. Take the best from this book and develop your own style. Steal with pride but be selective.

The subtitle of Nietzsche's book is: A Book for All and None. That's what this book is too. I hope many people read it and it inspires them to improve the way they manage their employees. I'm not saying you're a bad manager, but we can all improve - always. And finally, if you find yourself in strong disagreement with the book, you have at least spent time thinking about and improving your management style, and what to avoid. Before we get started, a quick word about my methodology. Nietzsche's book has four parts. In the first part Zarathustra works out his philosophy as a hermit and tries to share it, with rather moderate success. In the second part we accompany him on his second attempt to convince people of an ideal. For me, the first two parts represent the personal development of the fictional character Zarathustra. If you will, the first years on the way to becoming a great leader. To accompany Zarathustra on his way is like watching my managers on their way today. He struggles, he celebrates successes, he suffers setbacks, and he is tossed to and fro on the sea of his knowledge. Just as it happens to so many newcomers to the profession or people in new fields of activity. That is why I have based this book on these first two parts as both a structure and guide. We accompany Zarathustra on his way and learn from his examples, enriched with situations that I was allowed to experience, a philosophy that is still in the camp to be a guide to a great leader. In the second two parts of Nietzsche's book, Zarathustra is searching for the ideal people. Eventually he more or less finds what he was searching for.

The quotations that I include at the beginning and end of each chapter flank the framework of our investigation. All texts are original texts from "Thus spoke Zarathustra" and were provided by The Project Gutenberg eBook of Thus

Spake Zarathustra. Available at: www.gutenberg.org. Since the text is written more in the style of William Shakespeare and thus for non-native speakers partly very difficult to understand, I have taken the liberty to simplify it where I found it necessary.

I encourage every reader to also read the original book, maybe alongside my book or afterwards. It's a great piece of art. But now, let's kick it off.

Part I

Zarathustra's Prologue

Behold, I am weary of my wisdom, like the bee that has gathered too much honey; I need outstretched hands to take it. I would like to hand out and distribute, until the wise become joyful again in their folly and the poor happy in their riches.

Zarathustra was thirty years old when he became a hermit. For ten years thereafter, he worked on his philosophy in complete solitude, finally deciding that it was time to share it with any who would listen. No sooner said than done, Zarathustra sets out motivated on his way back to the people. On his way back, however, he first met another hermit, albeit a rather pessimistic one. He tries to convince Zarathustra that he should remain in his solitude, since people don't deserve his wisdom. But Zarathustra is convinced that he can do something good for humanity and continues his journey. He is certain about his quest and is anxious to finally meet his future followers.

Optimism is a key element of a good philosophy of work and also of life. If you're surrounded by cynical, pessimistic people, you need to change those surroundings. Don't get distracted by people telling you all the things you can't or shouldn't do. Follow through and learn from every obstacle. Building your own work philosophy is something that will take you many years. There is no shortcut to experience... unfortunately. Or perhaps fortunately. There is great satisfaction in mastering a skill with time and owning it. However, you will be running against the wall for some time. And now it comes down to how you handle these seemingly impossible situations. You know you have to deal with it, but you don't know how. This is where the pessimist has no chance. You need optimism in difficult situations. Success is not impossible but could be incredibly painful. You should choose your companions on this journey wisely and try to minimize negativity.

However, having super positivity as the only criteria for membership in your team is not the best strategy. You also need diversity of thought, and experience. You need people to ground you. The visit to the other hermit helped Zarathustra reflect on his journey and assess his preparedness for his future audience. A touchstone for all of us. When I write a whitepaper, I check it with two or three smart people who will question my mission and challenge it hard. I am not looking for bootlickers or affirmation, but rather, real improvement. The touchstones are the walls we build ourselves to run against. We challenge ourselves to be better prepared to meet the next challenges.

Some pessimists always tend to focus on the downside of things. They share their concerns and then obsess over the negative aspects. Let's call them the real pessimists. We can use this kind of constructive pessimism to help us see the problems ahead. As we know, a medal has three sides, the front, the back and the surrounding edge. While real pessimists can be very useful in various teams, there is another very special type of pessimist we will call poison pessimists. They not only focus on the negative, but also try to convert other people to a negative mindset. They need you to see it their way. These people are poison to any engaging environment and work culture. Just like Zarathustra quickly decides to leave the other hermit after a few short sentences, you should do the same. From these poison pessimists, you learn what not to think.

Martin E. P. Seligman, a psychology professor and author, describes in his book "Authentic Happiness" that the best lawyers are pessimists, and that pessimism is considered an advantage among lawyers because they are more likely to find the best strategy if they are not too optimistic about winning every case.

I have seen many managers spend much of their valuable time trying to "cure" pessimists and get them on the "bright side of life" or simply trying to get rid of them quickly, which is both wrong and a tremendous waste of resources. As mentioned earlier, pessimism is not synonymous with badness, lack of efficiency, or a burden. Being cautious, challenging ideas with a different perspective, or providing critical feedback is a great asset to any project work or team. Use it. However, if you find that these people are actively hindering your team, yourself, or other colleagues, try to get rid of them. Remember that statistically, your health improves when you're optimistic, and that's central to everything that follows including, by the way, being perceived as an authentic leader. Realistic optimists still need to understand the challenges ahead.

In the conversation with the hermit, Zarathustra tries to understand his motivations to remain isolated. He finds out that the hermit is happy where he is because he has found God and that is all he needs. When asked what he does alone in the forest, the old man replies:

"I make hymns and sing them; and in making hymns I laugh and weep and mumble: thus do I praise God. With singing, weeping, laughing, and mumbling do I praise the God who is my God."

Zarathustra is convinced that this is a waste of a lifetime and wonders why the old hermit still believes in God. This is the place where Nietzsche's famous (usually misquoted) quote - "God is dead!" - comes from. Originally it says:

"Could it be possible! This old saint in the forest had not yet heard of it, that god is dead!"

Let's not get into religion here. But I must mention this because it's what people think about when they think about Nietzsche. Everyone can believe whatever they want. It doesn't matter if their god is called Jesus, Krishna, or Greenback. I have seen people who have received tremendous energy "from" their god(s), and others who have been hamstrung by their beliefs. In the end, everyone is the architect of their own happiness and if your faith prevents you from developing your full potential and you knowingly accept that as the cost of your salvation, that's absolutely okay.

To my point though, cultural awareness is another key to success. Globalization, open borders, and high demand for talent have caused many bright minds to migrate from their culture to another, and teams, especially in larger companies, tend to be quite diverse. Studies suggest that more diverse teams are more productive. A 2015 published study by Max Nathan & Neil Lee named: Cultural Diversity, Innovation, and Entrepreneurship: Firm-level Evidence from London[4] found that, *"First, companies with diverse management are more likely to introduce new product innovations than are those with homogeneous "top teams." Second, diversity is particularly important for reaching international markets and serving London's cosmopolitan population. Third, migrant status has positive links to entrepreneurship. Overall, the results provide some support for claims that diversity is an economic asset, as well as a social benefit."*

But that's only half the truth. A diverse team only unleashes its benefits if the leader is aware of its advantages and leverages them to motivate the team accordingly. I know I'm lightly mixing religion and culture here, but they intertwine and often depend on one other. A formulaic guide on how to deal with Muslims vs Hindus vs Christians would come across as stereotypical and bigoted. But you should absolutely show interest! Especially if you are also religious. Read books, talk to people with an open mind. Get in touch and take in the good things about the person you are talking to or the book you are reading. Let me share a personal example.

I once thought it was a great idea to read every book someone recommended to me, even if I first thought it was garbage. I was chatting with another manager about his favorite books. He was from India and recommended that I read "Autobiography of a Yogi" by Paramahansa Yogananda. He said the book had

---

[4] Max Nathan & Neil Lee (2013) Cultural Diversity, Innovation, and Entrepreneurship: Firm-level Evidence from London, Economic Geography, 89:4, 367-394, DOI: 10.1111/ecge.12016

helped him a lot and could help me too. Admittedly biased, I never-the-less read the introduction. I spend my time reading about the religious awakening of someone from the other side of the world.... WTF. But stick to your rules. I bought it and read it of course. It wasn't easy to read and it took me some time to get through it. Eventually I got over my bias and got something out of it for my work philosophy. But what is most important was what happened during my next conversation with the manager who had recommended the book. His eyebrows went up when I told him I was reading it. He was surprised that someone like me had followed his recommendation. Even more so because this book is far from my culture. We excitedly discussed the book together. He shared how he uses the wisdom of the book in his current work. It was a great conversation, and you could feel his engagement growing during that conversation. I also felt that he was so much more open in all conversations from then on because he simply felt valued, and his culture respected. His opinion mattered and he had influence. And that's the main point I want to make here. You don't have to agree with him on everything, but by showing genuine interest and being open-minded, you can win hearts and build an engaged team. Nearly everyone has an interesting story to tell, so listen to them. That's our job as leaders. We need to understand our employees to best meet their needs and align them with the needs of the business.

Back to the words of Zarathustra mentioned above:

"[...] *until the wise have once more become joyous in their folly, and the poor happy in their riches"*.

What could this possibly mean? Nietzsche comes back to this point again and again throughout the rest of the book. The prologue itself can really be seen as a kind of summary of the book. It simply means: think differently!

You hear these phrases like "out of the box" or "think differently" all the time, but do we really understand what that means? Abandoning known habits and entering new territory is very difficult.

Henry Ford said, *"If you always do what you've always done, you'll always get what you've always gotten."*

It's not just about thinking differently, it's about DOING something differently. If you don't gather new knowledge, how can you develop new ideas? Your neurons like to follow well-trodden paths, and the more often they use those paths, the better they work. Now, if you ask them to leave their paths and try something new, they will resist. Do everything you can to expand your mind. Read books, talk to people, travel, eat differently - never stop learning new things. Knowledge is an output! It grows with its inputs, and so thinking differently or thinking outside the box is naturally followed by acting differently, which cannot be achieved by thinking differently alone.

When you come across a task, whether at work or at home, try doing it differently. Read about a new technique you can use to make conversations with your co-workers more engaging? Try it out! You'll get the feedback you need to determine whether or not this new approach was a good one. Keep improving. Keep going from here until you find the right technique for you AND the people you're talking to. But always be aware that you are not the center of the universe. You can always learn. And if you're good at anchoring new ideas with an open mind, don't think it ends here. Start sharing your ideas. Inspire others so that they are able to inspire even more people. It doesn't end with you.

When Zarathustra left the pessimistic hermit and finally reached a town, he found its inhabitants in the market waiting for a tightrope walker to perform his craft. The crowd was already waiting but there was no artist to be seen. Zarathustra sees a great opportunity to speak. He climbs figuratively on the prepared stage and starts to preach his wisdom to the people. He lays out all the knowledge and wisdom he has acquired in ten years of hard intellectual work. He gives a very engaging speech with real fire and the crowd and is enthusiastic. He tells them how to achieve the next, the better version of humanity, or as he calls it the superhuman. You can really feel him pouring his wisdom over the audience and the passion he has for it. Here is a small excerpt from Zarathustra's speech:

Man is something that is to be overcome. What have you done to overcome him?

What is a monkey for a man? A laughter or a painful shame. And this is what man shall be for the superman: a laughter or a painful shame.

You have made the way from worm to man, and much is still worm in you. Once you were monkeys, and even now man is more monkey than any monkey.

But who is the wisest of you, he is also only a dichotomy and hermaphrodite of plant and ghost. But do I make you become ghosts or plants?

Look, I teach you the superhuman!

The Superman is the meaning of the earth. Let your will say: The Superman SHALL BE the meaning of the earth!"

The whole speech is longer, of course, but as you can see, it's quite dramatic. And what happened when he finished? Nobody cared. Just nobody. Maybe people just don't like being told that they are nothing more than worms and monkeys, but the truth hurts, as we all know. The crowd replies:

"We have now heard enough of the rope-dancer; it is time now for us to see him!" And all the people laughed at Zarathustra.

He tries again and changes his way of speaking, using other stylistic devices. But still, no one understood. He tries a third time to get his message across and now, even worse, they have completely misunderstood him. Zarathustra does not understand what is happening and sadness overcomes him and his heart sinks.

"They understand me not: I am not the mouth for these ears."

He learned it the hard way.... He sat in his cave for a decade, developed a great idea and philosophy, prepared the speech of a lifetime for the people he wanted to inspire, and then he went on stage and flopped. There you are building your life's work, going to the performance full of anticipation, and wham, all you get is negative reviews. Worse, you may be made out to be an idiot and laughed at. But it gets worse. The tightrope walker who eventually comes on stage was attacked by a buffoon during his performance and fell off the rope. As he lay dying, there was no one to help him. Zarathustra goes to him and promises the tightrope walker to find him a grave and bury him. He carries him out of the city and through the night, during a long and exhausting march, he talks to him and laments his sorrow. Of course, he gets no answer, as he knows that the tightrope walker is dead. He puts him in a hollow tree and falls asleep.

When he wakes up, he realizes two important things:

1. *"I need companions—living ones"* and
2. *"Not any more will I discourse unto the people; for the last time have I spoken unto the dead."*

We combine both into the principle: **Don't speak to the dead**.

There are always people out there who don't want to understand you and people who can't understand you. The former are driven by conscious or unconscious prejudices and the latter are held back by either their abilities to understand, or your abilities to explain. The question now is how much time you spend talking to them. How much time and energy do you invest in convincing them of an idea or an argument? Avoid obsessing over converting the obviously unwilling, like the mob in the marketplace. There are ears for your mouth, either you find them, or you change your language. This decision is up to you and is best made wisely. Value your time and energy and optimize its use. We are coming full circle. Choosing your companions wisely and the importance of positivity is exactly what Zarathustra is learning now.

You need companions. You will most likely not win on your own. You can have the greatest business idea, but the likelihood that you can execute it all by yourself is pretty slim. Even Jeff Bezos or Steve Jobs always needed real companions around them. They needed people to support them with the initial money to fund their business, or with advice and support to make their dream a reality.

When I started my career, I had no idea what to do. I was hired directly after leaving the university in a field in which I had no professional experience. I had to lead people and make important decisions that directly impacted their lives and the lives of their families. I was lucky because I had great colleagues who would become real friends. We supported each other through difficult times, and we always had each other's backs. Without them, I would never have been here to write this book. My first cohort of friends and colleagues have all had good careers and achieved our professional goals quite quickly, while others have had to struggle as lone warriors. We all face tough times in life, it doesn't matter who you are. Without great companions by your side, success is much harder. But as important as your needs are, you will find people who need your help even more often. The question now is how you find the right balance between giving and accepting help.

If Zarathustra had proofread his speech just once before he climbed on stage in the marketplace, he surely could have spared himself this first total flop. Someone could have told him some important details about his audience. Understanding your audience is critical to every form of effective communication. Someone could have told him that this audience were neither interested in, or able to understand his message. They came for something else.

While Zarathustra realizes that he has completely failed, he gets up and recommits himself. And he finds a fundamental truth for himself. No matter what you do, you will never convince everyone. You'll also never please everyone. It's impossible. This is where he learned his hardest lesson, and it's among the most important.

Be prepared for your job to be tough. Today we are coached about non-aggressive communication, non-judgmental feedback, and microaggressions. The goal of all these sensitivity training is to create an environment where no one has to feel anxious about anything, especially about other people. While we all do our best to be nice supervisors and good colleagues, there seem to be a lot of people out there who haven't learned from the latest sensitivity or anti-aggression training. As a supervisor, you have to be prepared for the fact that not everyone is inclined to join the "fluffy teddy bear club." There are people who seem to be born to cause conflict. That is their only goal in life. This behavior may well then extend to entire groups. If you are prepared for it, these folks won't be able to surprise you.

However, it is similar to the two kinds of pessimism. It can also be an added value to accept the challenge to deal with these kinds of people. Constructive conflict is a driver of positive change. I remember several instances where a conflict over a key performance indicator (KPI) with stakeholders caused me to dive deep to demonstrate that they were wrong. As a result, I improved the environment for many. Without this conflict, I would not have challenged myself to examine the data, and the wrong behavior would have continued to harm the company.

When I once took over a corporate department in a new company, the success or failure of this business unit was measured by a single KPI. It was a quality metric. My team and I were challenged on this metric every week in the weekly business review. We set up an action plan with many tasks for us and implemented them in the following weeks. But in fact, the quality metric did not change significantly. My statement was now that the main drivers must be somewhere else. My statement was taken as an excuse, and I continued to be driven to think up and implement more actions in my department.

I sat down and started an extensive deep dive with my team in which we looked at every single quality case and tried to figure out what was causing it. This was a huge task and took us a lot of time. However, we were able to determine and now also prove with data that most likely only 20% of the KPIs were influenced in our department and the majority of the rest were the responsibility of other external stakeholders. It was now possible for the company to identify the real cause and to influence the KPIs in a positive way for the benefit of our customers.

Don't get me wrong: If there is a person creating a toxic work environment, you need to act quickly to remove them from the company. But we often mislabeled people with disruptive ideas as troublemakers. People who have a great idea and fight for it are often perceived as too disruptive. But disruptive people with a vision are your gold dust. The smartest people are the hardest to lead, and that's why many managers despair when they're asked to lead them. This leads to frustration on both sides, but more importantly, great missed opportunities for the company. Great employees fight for good ideas. Back them up with data and lay out why they are good and, most importantly, why they are beneficial to the team. And if your company doesn't value ideas, it will lose its best people! The market is desperate for good people. And good people are often disruptive.

And that's true for Zarathustra, too. He realizes that his approach is wrong. He could give up now and climb back up his mountain and spend another ten years thinking about a better method to satisfy the masses. He has gotten feedback and could improve it. But he is convinced of his idea, and now understands that some people may not like it - fine. He wants to change the world but needs a new strategy.

"A light dawned on me: Zarathustra does not speak to the people, but to companions! Zarathustra shall not become the shepherd and dog of a herd!
To lure many away from the herd - that is what I came to do. People and herd shall be angry with me: Zarathustra wants to call the shepherd robbers.
Shepherds I say, but they call themselves the good and just. Shepherds I say: but they call themselves the faithful of the right faith.
Behold the good and the righteous! Whom do they hate the most? The one who breaks their tablets of value, the breaker, the criminal: but this is the creator.
Behold the believers of all faiths! Whom do they hate the most? The one who breaks their tablets of value, the breaker, the criminal: - but this is the creator.
The creator seeks companions and not corpses, and also not armies and believers. The creator seeks the co-creators, those who write new values on new tablets."

Many management books harp on how best to behave in an ideal environment. But these books usually don't take into account that most readers are in the process of climbing the ladder. They are not yet in a real position of power. So, most are not yet in an ideal environment. And that means conflict, hard work, difficult decisions, sleepless nights, and tears. There are few books that deal with this side of the coin. "The Hard Things about Hard Things" from Ben Horowitz is an exception that I recommend.

I have witnessed countless managers crying or hiding their red eyes. Struggle is unavoidable for creators. And yes, struggle is the best word to describe how we navigate through difficult situations. And if you're not prepared for struggle because you believe - like Zarathustra in the beginning - that everyone is just waiting for you and your opinion, you're in for a rude awakening. The challenging situations a manager faces are incredibly varied.

For example, at the beginning of my career I was working as a division manager, with a great employee on my team. A high performer and very friendly and well-liked person. After a while, however, I noticed open sores on his arms and legs. A colleague tipped me off that this could be from heroin abuse. I read about it and decided that I had to do something. I spoke with him and after some small talk I asked him directly if he had a drug problem. Of course, not with a sledgehammer, I was careful and diplomatic. I told a story from my youth from a good school friend. He went with me from the 8th to the 10th grade together in the same class. He started taking drugs and at first, I experimented with him, but I quickly got away from it. It was just not for me. However, he slipped further and further and finally he just disappeared. That was a drastic experience for me, and I told him that I was afraid that this would happen again here at work. I have him as one of my best employees and a person I really like to have in my team, and I observe the same behavior and physical signs.

My good relationship with him led me to think I could be direct. His mood immediately changed, and he became angry. He, of course, refused and fought back. I accepted and mentioned that as a company we had several programs running that offered professional help. The company even recognized drug addiction as a disease and offered paid leave for treatment. He didn't want to hear about it and was upset at my accusations.

The next day he did not show up for work. I was sad but didn't want to harass him for calling in sick. Calling in sick is a normal avoidance strategy and an expression of rebellion for many employees in Germany where I worked at this time. So, I didn't give it a second thought. I had a hundred other employees to take care of.

Two days later, his girlfriend showed up at work in the morning to tell us that she had found him dead in his apartment. He had died of an overdose.

Had I pushed him to kill himself? Or would all this have happened anyway? Could I have saved him if I had reacted earlier? No one will be able to answer these questions, but the point is that your experiences in life change you. They are unpredictable, and sometimes awful. Leading people means experiencing critical situations. It depends on you how you move on. This event both saddened and strengthened me. It encouraged me to greatly improve my conversation skills and carefully adjust my communication style to fit each situation. I learned about how to watch for signs of addiction. I learned about company policies. Ultimately, it taught me how to help other employees. I was totally unprepared for this, and I talked through it with my colleagues, who helped me cope with the situation. We need companions along the way. At no university did I learn how to deal with anything like this. These are (painful) things that you will learn if you work together with humans and go through these situations together with them.

"Thus began Zarathustra's down-going."

Zarathustra's Discourses

The Three Metamorphoses

"I will tell you three transformations of the spirit: how the spirit becomes a camel, and the camel a lion, and the lion a child."

Becoming a good leader is a long process. No one is born a great leader. This chapter provides an analogy for that hard road. The camel - lion - child transformation. At the very beginning of your career, you will bear the heaviest burdens. You must first learn the hardest lesson.

You must accept that this world does not revolve around you. The company you work for wasn't created to facilitate your career, and it won't be in chaos when you're gone, by the way. The people around you were not hired to become the rungs for your career ladder. It's not your boss's top priority to promote you. And believe it or not, companies usually do extensive research on fair compensation packages, and it's not their diabolical goal to pay you as little as possible. Your salary is most likely fair! (Most likely…there are exceptions.) It is shocking how many employees come into a company with ridiculously inflated expectations.

I once had a conversation with a young manager who asked me for a feedback session to get my opinion on a topic. I love to develop people and talking to each other is crucial so of course I agreed. He briefly explained to me how happy he is at the company and that he has never had such a warm welcome. Great atmosphere, etc., etc... And then he said, *"I've been here eight months and I'm confident I've done a good job, so I think I'm ready for my promotion. What else can I do to make sure I get promoted in the next review cycle."*

I was a bit taken aback and didn't quite know how to respond, so I told the story about the three transformations of the spirit from the book. I finally asked him what state he thought his mind was in right now in this analogy. He smiled at me and understood the message. When he left, I remembered my attitude when I came out of university and started my first real job. Then I got goosebumps. I remembered having a similar discussion with my HR business partner six months later and asking her basically the same question. Looking back, I have to admit that I was very impatient. And my hubris didn't necessarily help me. But I was like the camel described. And Nietzsche did not use camel as a synonym for a stupid burden bearer.

The camel stands for the first steps to becoming a great leader. It stands for the first steps in life. It stands symbolically for the accumulation of knowledge that one acquires, for example, in school or during training. The knowledge that one acquires by reading books, watching movies and living life. With every piece of information, you carry something more with you. It also stands for the sum of the experiences one collects along the way, good and bad. All the crap you go through and the associated lessons that you draw from it. So, with every bit you learn and experience, you pile more on your back, like a camel. Much of it becomes a burden and little will really be very useful to you, but a camel is strong.

In summary, the camel walks the hard path. It carries the heavy load that many people try to avoid. And if you have never done that, you cannot transform into a lion. Heavy burden is not exclusively physical. It includes heavy psychological burdens. The heavy burden of responsibility and the hardest of all, admitting your own failures and mistakes. You must carry this special burden alone, as this is your experience and can't be shared. To overcome the camel stage, you must experience it alone.

"But in the loneliest desert the second transformation happens: here the spirit becomes a lion, he wants to capture freedom and be master in his own desert.

He seeks his last lord here: he wants to become an enemy to him and his last god, he wants to wrestle for victory with the great dragon."

In Nietzsche's book, the second transformation is marked by a battle against a golden dragon. The spirit transforms into a lion and this lion comes to a dragon lying in the sun and its scales shine golden. On each of these scales is written: Thou shalt! The dragon is of the opinion that all good values have already been created and there are no more new ones to discover. Therefore, the world no longer needs creative people, but only those who live under the already created values. The golden dragon is a metaphor for "going with the flow" and obeying. The lion is the epitome of courage, pride and will to fight. So, the next stage of development is one that a carrying beast of burden could not endure. It is the fight against that golden dragon. The dragon that tells us what to do and how far we are allowed to go (any reference to your parents come to mind? Or the behavior of the media?).

"What is the great dragon that the spirit no longer likes to call Lord and God? "You-shall" is the name of the great dragon. But the spirit of the lion says "I will".

"Thou shalt" lies in his way, sparkling gold, a beast of scales, and on every scale shines golden "Thou shalt!"

Thousands of years of value shine on these scales, and thus the mightiest of all dragons speaks, "All value of things - that shines on me.

"All value was already created, and all created value - that is me. Verily, there shall be no more "I will"!" Thus spoke the dragon."

The average person does not have the backbone to stand up to the dragon. In today's "yes culture," it is uncomfortable to say "no". We try to avoid conflict. We want to live and work in a comfortable environment because we feel safe there. The average person will always stay in the camel phase.

Have you ever watched a movie you hated just because your partner thought it was great? Often, it's not a problem, but for example, taking on another assignment when you are already pushed to the max, just because you can't say no leads to failure, and perhaps even serious health problems. But if you want to create something new, you have to break the table on which the values stand and create new values. You have to become a creator. Rise up against the golden dragon. And when the shitstorm comes, it separates the wheat from the chaff. And by that I don't mean you drove drunk, got caught, and are now in the line of fire - if that is the case, you deserve to go down. I mean you're standing up to people with their "we've always done it this way" attitude.

You fight for the project idea that you brought in. You don't stop to reiterate on a rejected project idea that you think is great. Sure, you may not win every time, but that's no excuse for not advocating hard for what you think is important. Standing up for your ideas also means getting negative feedback. People don't always like what you've come up with. It is even possible that some of your ideas are not as good as you think they are. Going back to what was said above: Don't be foolish, letting pride get the better of you. Take the feedback seriously, process it, and come back stronger. Challenge drives innovation. The lion says, "I do" and thus creates new value.

Now you are the fighter, the lion - loud and proud. There is nothing to be afraid of anymore. Everything you carried as a camel which you are not able to delegate is still there, but your strength makes it easier to carry. You also retain all that you learned that enabled you to become the lion. This is a stage marked by behavior. At a certain stage, you act strong and confident. You collect recognition not for its own sake, but rather, because you are kicking ass, and doing great things. A lion is already a leader. And mostly even a good leader. They can attack but also protect. They can roar loudly and state their opinion, and they are heard. They separate from the mass and are counted into the pool of the creators. They don't accept that something needs to be done as it has always been done and are able to think outside the box. They lead to new lands and conquer new worlds.

The person in the lion phase might be a good leader but will never be a great one. The lion phase is the phase in which the majority of managers get stuck. As they believe that it does not get better, there is nothing more to strive for. However, this is also the phase you have to be most careful.

I have seen many managers yelling, insulting and cursing in meetings. Managers who believed that aggression was the answer to everything. So many people in high management positions (whether male or female) become bad managers, but more on that later.

The lion phase is characterized by your own successes. The phase in which you realize that you can finally apply all that you have learned and that it really makes a difference. Your years at university have finally paid off, and you are earning a good salary. But you don't rise to your position so that you can rest. The status has to be defended and many people start to worry about what will happen if they lose their status. Fear mixes with pride and this becomes explosive. This fighting mode is not the last stage. It is the midpoint in becoming a great leader.

Now that you know how to fight, you are ready to evolve to the next level.

I would like to share with you my "eureka" moment on this topic. I was working for a pan-European project management group and was responsible for the re-launch of a project related to the implementation of routines for managers and the supporting data behind it, which had failed the year before. We decided that the way to increase adoption was to justify the project with more data to clarify the gains we envisioned. The project was about routines for managers. The downside was that it could be perceived as a reduction in autonomy, and nobody likes less freedom, especially managers. However, the hypothesis was that our managers waste a lot of time on non-value-added tasks, and that we might have a problem with stress and impossible workloads, increasing sick leave, turnover, and other mental health issues. An interesting trade-off.

We hired consultants to conduct a time study. We put a consultant next to every manager across Europe and had them document every single task - minute by minute. The database this gave us was amazing. For example, we determined the average overtime worked by managers by country, evaluated the time spent on non-value-added tasks versus value-added tasks, and much more. The database was used by various departments for years after it was created. We were really proud. And then came the day when we presented the project paper to the European leadership team. We stated that "based on a time study" we had found clear evidence of this and that and were convinced that the project was necessary. We knew exactly where to attack the inefficiencies we had uncovered. Again, we were bursting with pride.

After a short period of silence in the room, our vice president got up - super lion style - and loudly told us what a huge waste of time and resources we were, that we were wasting so much money trying to find something we already knew. We could have saved two months and hundreds of thousands of dollars if we had just followed his original guide. He went into a long monologue about how stupid and useless we were. And I looked at him and thought, "You stupid a-hole.... What's wrong with you? How can you talk to people like that? And I felt the heat rising inside me. My lion was ready for a fight.

But at that moment, some kind of light bulb lit up in my head. I realized that I was actually just using the above five words, "based on a time study", to condense all we had learned from the great data analysis that would render tremendous benefit to tons of other projects. How the heck is he even supposed to know all the great stuff we found? How is he supposed to evaluate the benefits of our great work? How was he ever going to have the same sense of accomplishment that we did? You should never assume that the details that you know to be true, nested inside your head, are obvious to everyone else. Such assumptions can lead to "studies show…" statements that don't explain sources or findings. It wasn't his failure (although I deeply believe that people who swear in a meeting, belittle or insult people in front of others should not be in any leadership position - ever).

I'm not coming to the defense of any bad manager, but what I want to say is that I realized at that moment that it was my fault, solely my fault. No excuses. Maybe I'm not the incredibly cool and all-knowing manager. Fighting for my mistake would be absolutely worthless. Instead of complaining and bitching, I picked myself up and got super motivated to rephrase the paper. The team and I rewrote the paper and highlighted the actual value. In the next round the paper got the recognition it deserved, and we were able to start implementing one of the biggest projects that existed at that time in my company. The point here is that usually after a (very) negative feedback you are very disengaged and need time to get back on your feet. Since that moment, however, I literally draw energy from feedback, whether positive or negative. It drives me and motivates me.

From that moment on, I forced myself to always think first about my responsibility in every situation. It's a difficult balance, because usually you can almost always find something - if you honestly look. And it takes time, because overcoming your vanity is one of the hardest things to do and takes a lot of practice. This is part of overcoming the lion stage. As you jettison your vanity, your pride and your aggressiveness, your transformation into the child begins.

Most people in the lion stage strive for something that no child strives for - at least not as long as it has not been thought differently by their parents - recognition. Of course, recognition and appreciation are important in raising children, but not for the sake of recognition. Children learn whether their behavior corresponds to society's idea of good or bad. Recognition is different from admiration or other exaggerated forms of recognition. For many in the Leo phase, admiration by others is the most important thing.

Ayn Rand, in her novel Fountainhead, calls these people "second handers" because they live second-hand lives. They live for the approval of others, and without admirers, their lives have no meaning. They don't create for themselves. Their art chases the whims of others rather than expressing anything meaningful. They drive expensive and fast cars not to feel free or have fun, but to be seen in them. The child plays, paints, sings - not for recognition but for fun. The empty pursuit of recognition for its own sake is the purest form of arrogance.

The managers in the lion stage may not yet understand this. A truly great leader does not work to please others, to gain recognition, or to win praise. The only real drive of great leaders is to make great ideas real, to build great things, to create great environments, to explore new things and discover new worlds - for their sake. A great leader shares credit for accomplishments and takes responsibility for failures. Like the child, it's all about the thing, the principle. A wheel rolling on its own, not needing admiration as fuel to roll. The manager who does not strive for recognition by others, does not need these others either. Children can excellently deal with themselves. Second handers can't move forward because they never set their own course. Their compass is not based on the magnetic field of the Earth but on the flag in the wind.

The child even goes one step further here. It doesn't need a compass, it just goes, driven by pure curiosity and the urge to explore. Wherever it will take it.

When you reach this stage, you will feel how lonely it gets around you, because now you develop a very good sense of people who are not yet ready. They are overconfident and arrogant, scrambling to jump ahead without going through each stage of development. You will immediately recognize them and must distance yourself from them. And then you'll see that it gets pretty lonely around you.

One of the main intents behind this book is to guide you on this way. It's time to transform your spirit into a child.

"But tell me, my brothers, what else can the child do that even the lion could not do? What does the robbing lion also have to become a child?

Innocence is the child and forgetting, a new beginning, a game, a wheel rolling out of itself, a first movement, a holy yes-saying."

It is important to note that these changes are not active or on a schedule. It's more like you're doing your normal work and suddenly realize you've been doing a familiar task differently. And you think back and then realize that even on the last few occasions you've done it, your way of working and your behavior has already changed. It's a long and silent process. Changes in attitude take a lot of time and need to be remembered over and over again.

So what is the final phase? What does it mean to transform your mind into a child? There may be alternative explanations but for me it is an analogy for the transformation of authority.

We can categorize authority into four types:

Functional Authority - the authority you get from the role you hold. If you are the mayor of a city or the vice president, your authority stems from that role. This says nothing about you or your abilities (except that you were granted a title).

Aggressive Authority - this type of authority is based on physical characteristics or behavior that is perceived to make people afraid, for example. Typical would be dictators or other people who lead through fear.

Epistemic Authority - based on knowledge, experience, or wisdom. People usually follow these authorities because they trust them and feel protected by their knowledge. Great teachers might be a good example here. They lead through example.

Natural Authority - This is pure charisma. People like to follow because these people give them the pure feeling that it is right to follow them. These people are perceived as natural leaders. Everything good of the former authority types are combined here.

To me, the three metamorphoses of the spirit are just that, the normal progression toward natural authority. When your mind reaches the state of the child, you have this pure and natural leadership where, for example, anger is no longer a quality that others would attribute to you. You stand rock solid in your field because of your knowledge and experience. You have your own work philosophy and know how to lead people. You usually get good feedback and achieve great results. The people who work for you trust you - what a dream. But what does this have to do with the child? Children have this natural eagerness to learn, this curiosity. They haven't yet been corrupted by society. Children want to do things out of natural impulse and will do so as long as no one slows them down. They can because they want to and don't know shame. They freely make mistakes and love learning from them.

The moment you enter the child phase you will find the fine distinction between all the burdens you bore as a camel from the aspirations that fulfill you. You will know exactly what you need and what you don't. You will throw away all the unnecessary ballast. You will free yourself and carry exactly what you need, not to show off, but to be happy.

A Chinese proverb says, "It is better to be a warrior in the garden than a gardener in the war!" I love that phrase because the best managers I've encountered over my career have been calm, kind, generous and reserved, not fearful, aggressive and violent. But you could really feel their strength and competence. They are the warriors in the garden. While for the other kind of managers, you feel that they lack something. They are the gardeners in war. But even worse, they pretend to be the greatest elite soldiers of all. They are in the lion stage but are unlikely to ever make it to the last and most important step.

Tim Urban wrote a long blog post about Elon Musk on his website waitbutwhy.com in 2015. The blog is divided into four stories whereby the fourth is called "The Cook and the Chef: Musk's Secret Sauce". He is explaining the key to success for Musk and while reading it, the last metamorphosis kept coming back to my mind again and again. Urban is using a metaphor for success which is the difference between a cook and a chef.

He states: *"what all of these cooks have in common is their starting point is something that already exists. Even the innovative cook is still making an iteration of a burger, a pizza, and a cake.*

At the very end of the spectrum, you have the chef. A chef might make good food or terrible food, but whatever she makes, it's a result of her own reasoning process, from the selection of raw ingredients at the bottom to the finished dish at the top.

In the culinary world, there's nothing wrong with being a cook. Most people are cooks because for most people, inventing recipes isn't a goal of theirs.

But in life—when it comes to the reasoning "recipes" we use to churn out a decision—we may want to think twice about where we are on the cook-chef spectrum."

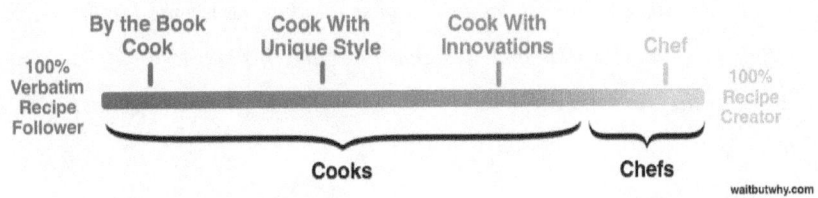

It is a great analogy for the camel-lion-child metamorphosis. In the beginning you learn all your tasks "by the cookbook" and the moment you realize that you are actually quite good at it, you might start experimenting. You will become more creative and start also serving for friends and family. But still, you are a cook and no chef. Only when you advance into the child stage, you enable yourself to really create something new. You throw off the cookbook chains and invent your own dishes.

A manager in the lion stage might still be a good manager, as the cook might still be a good cook, but won't be a great one - they won't be chefs. From my experience, the vast majority of managers get stuck there and don't develop further which is the main cause for having so many managers in high leadership positions who are not great. Maybe good, but not great.

The three metamorphoses form the basis of the philosophy of leadership presented in this book, and we will continue to refer to it. Every manager must be aware of the stage they are currently in so that they can find out what needs to be done next to move forward.

It is of course also incredibly helpful to realize that there is always more to accomplish, regardless of where you are.

The Academic Chairs of Virtue

"When Zarathustra heard the wise man speak thus, he laughed in his heart: for a light had dawned upon him. And thus he said to his heart:
A fool is this wise man with his forty thoughts: but I believe that he knows how to sleep.
[...]
His wisdom is to watch in order to sleep well. And truly, if life had no meaning and I had to choose nonsense, this would also be the nonsense most worth choosing for me.
Now I understand clearly what was once sought above all when one sought teachers of virtue. Good sleep was sought and poppy virtues in addition!"

After his speech on the three metamorphoses of the spirit, Zarathustra heard about a wise and virtuous person. He went to him and saw him sitting in front of his chair with his students and talking about how to get the best sleep ever. His solution was simple: do what you're told, don't question the status quo, and never break the rules of the game. Obey! That will give you a great night's sleep. Zarathustra laughs out loud after hearing the "wisdom" of this teacher.

Humans usually choose the easy way which means following the rules and don't shake the foundations of the system around you. We were raised in school and even before that by our parents to do just that. "Don't touch that!" / "Be careful, it's hot!" / "Don't drink too much Coke!" / "Don't climb that tree, you might fall down!" We all experienced this from our parents. Parents want their children to be safe and healthy. The main reason behind this is hardwired within us and we can hardly do anything about it unless we are aware of it. The root cause is in the so-called mirror neurons. Mirror neurons cause the same pattern of activity in the brain when you watch something as when you actually do something.

Imagine seeing someone standing on a cliff by the sea. The person seems to be watching waves roll out to sea and a strong, cold wind blow. The person is only four steps away from the edge of the cliff. And at that very moment, the person takes another step toward the cliff. It's only three small steps and the strong wind is shaking him. You want to shout to him not to go so close to the edge, but because of the wind he can't hear you. And at that moment, the person takes another step. You stand there as if rooted to the spot. And the person takes another step. Just one more step and he falls off the cliff. The wind seems to push and pull him at the same time. He spreads his arms, and the wind shakes him back and forth. His hair flies and he looks up at the sky. He doesn't seem afraid and takes another step, but fortunately backwards. The person falls to his knees and laughs.

Did you feel the urgency of the moment? Those are the mirror neurons. Impressive - and they are the reason why most parents forbid their children from participating in risky situations. They usually have experience with the pain of doing so. And so, the mirror neurons force them to inhibit the experimenting child. That is often a good thing. One of the greatest achievements of our time in developed countries is the precipitous drop in infant mortality. That's mostly thanks to scientific progress, of course, but also to parents with the resources and knowledge to provide greater care (for example, access to drugs, or child seats in cars). But it also sets the society up to avoid every dangerous situation. Disruptive environments are unfortunately exactly that: dangerous.

So, you can say that the wise man instilled in his students exactly what our schools do today. To nip entrepreneurship, creativity and willingness to take risks to produce a broad adapted mass with the same, standardized factory settings. This safe mediocrity satisfies the respective required labor market demand as effectively as possible. We are products of this persistent concept, whether we like it or not. There are always exceptions who break this vicious circle and are still willing to take risks and write new values on new boards. Unfortunately, these same creative people are perceived as different, not adapted and thus somehow subversive.

Our education systems need a thorough overhaul to enable our children to meet the challenges of the future.

Nietzsche says the same thing in this chapter, and don't forget that the book dates from 1883! What he is really saying is that people who want to be creators cannot care about the virtues of today, just as a child is uninhibited by social norms. No child knows political correctness or cares about social class. They don't worry about the correct pronoun, income inequality, or gender equality. They don't worry about money, pensions, or filing taxes for years. They have the time to create their own world until adults step in and shape it. Pablo Picasso expressed, "Every child is an artist. The problem is how to remain an artist once we grow up." Many of the social norms make perfect sense, and the prosperity of our nations is based on them. But that prosperity was not built on what we have always done. Today's prosperity comes from breakthrough technologies and world-changing companies that required people who thought outside the box. Make the impossible possible. You can't if you are locked into society's norms. As the wise man teaches his students, the main focus should be on how to get the best sleep - the best synonym for a pious, authoritarian, risk-averse conformist.

It's critically important to consciously examine this reality. Free yourself from all the burdens that your upbringing placed upon you. Not everything your parents and teachers taught you was bad, but it was naturally channeled through their mindset, belief framework, and political motivations. You certainly know people who are best described by the word individualist. People who go against the norm, not in an aggressive way, but in a creative, intelligent way. People with whom you notice that they consciously play with these norms and have fun doing so. You don't need waving flags, thundering guns or other violence to make other people feel that norms are something that doesn't limit you.

I had a wonderful professor who wore various stunning Peaky Blinders-style suits - years before Katie Swindon produced the first BBC series - and he had a great sense of humor. He had kept his rough edges under control with a keen sense of how far he was allowed to go in terms of political correctness as an employee of a state university. He taught innovation management, among other things, and his style alone enhances his teaching because it was so incredibly credible. But these people are rare. My point is... If you really want to think and act disruptively, you must first disrupt your thought process. Free yourself from all these norms that create boundaries - at least in thinking. They need to write new virtues on new tables. This will not be possible if you only care about how to put yourself in the safest position possible by trusting the sleep preachers.

After all, being a great leader isn't about sleep and conformity, it's about how to wake up most effectively and make the best use of your time. It's about how to wake up all the sleeping dreamers and get them excited about ideas, and you can't do that by talking to them about how to sleep best. Our energy must be focused on the day, because that is the time when we can positively influence the people around us and the world as a whole. Life is the day. Or as the famous philosopher Arthur Schopenhauer once said, "Every day is a little life - every waking and rising a little birth, every fresh morning a little youth, and every going to bed and falling asleep a little death."

"Even at present, to be sure, there are some like this preacher of virtue, and not always so honorable: but their time is past. And not much longer do they stand: there they already lie.

Blessed are those drowsy ones: for they shall soon nod to sleep."

Backworldsman

"Suffering was it and incapacity - that created all back worlds; and that short madness of happiness, which only the most suffering experiences.
Fatigue, which wants to go to the last with one leap, with one death leap, a poor ignorant fatigue, which doesn't even want to anymore: that created all gods and back worlds."

My partner has a habit that annoys me from time to time. Every time I use an excuse, she quotes a famous German proverb that translates as, "Do you know why the devil killed his grandmother?" It's a rhetorical question because people (at least from our area) all know the answer, "Because he ran out of excuses."

Since she's been using this trick for as long as we've known each other, she's already trained me so that I usually don't give her excuses anymore. And if I do, I know she'll notice anyway. She can decipher my attempts to hide them and ask the question. It's awkward, so I just try to avoid excuses altogether. The lesson I learned was amazing for my career. Take responsibility and don't push it on someone or something else. Taking responsibility is hard because we have to accept that we are not perfect and there is no higher authority to blame for our mistakes. It's not the traffic or the weather that's responsible for you being late to the meeting, it's you! You didn't plan for these contingencies. The "idiots" in government are not responsible for the chaos around you, because you elected them (or did not participate in the election). And if you want to change something and your superiors or politicians can't handle it, join a party or start one and learn how hard it is to make real change. But stop telling everyone that someone else is responsible. And also stop using God or Gods as an excuse. It wasn't God's will that you were stuck in a bad job, it's your inertia. Find a better one! Imagine someone missing the deadline for a critical project, and they explained, "It was God's will." You would be right to question their mental state.

We humans love excuses. According to the Bible, when Adam and Eve ate from the forbidden tree of knowledge, their first reaction to God's anger was to look for excuses. Adam blamed Eve, and Eve says it was the serpent's fault. So, we have a long tradition of shifting responsibility away from ourselves.

We often confuse excuses with explanations, and there is a very fine line between the two. The most important difference is the internal attitude. An excuse usually comes in the form of an apology and has emotional aspects. Another characteristic of excuses is that they do not indicate shame or guilt. The intention behind excuses is absolution by others. The feelings of guilt are reduced by having others being inclined that it wasn't our fault. An excuse will never make you feel that the person really feels guilty.

An explanation is informing about the circumstances and your own behavior in an unemotional way. It does not try to convince others. An explanation shows that you take responsibility.

Have you ever heard the excuse from people who are a few minutes late to a call and say that another meeting ran over (and yes, I've used that a lot too...)? No! They didn't leave the other meeting on time. That was, after all, a deliberate decision. Why should you apologize for that? Perhaps the other meeting was more important. But then you don't say that the other meeting "ran over". It wasn't the meeting's fault. Instead, you could say that another meeting was a higher priority and you preferred to stay there to get all the information you needed. Because that's the truth - it was your decision. Not a blame game, but a statement of clear conscience. People who talk like this are seen as better leaders because it builds trust. I know I can trust someone who doesn't blame others for mistakes.

Accept that you and only you are responsible for your position. This is another important cornerstone of any good leader's work philosophy.

"My ego taught me a new pride, which I now teach to men: - no longer to bury the head in the sand of heavenly things, but to carry it freely, an earth-head, which creates sense for the earth!

A new will I teach to men: to want this way, which man has gone blindly, and to approve it and no longer to creep aside from it, like the sick and dying!"

Never shirk responsibility. If you do, you have not even gone through the first metamorphosis and are not even past the "camel" stage. How could you ever become a lion?

As you work your way up the career ladder, and therefore the ladder of responsibility, the focus shifts from tactical to strategic. Tactics are specific steps, while strategies involve long-term visions. While you start out being responsible for smaller projects or teams, this gets bigger as you move up the ladder. It is not a bad thing to consider strategies early, but unless you are in a position of authority, you still need to do your job, even if you have a plan of your own.

When I became general manager and was given full responsibility for a fairly large team and budget, I have to admit I was even a little scared. To be well prepared, I asked friends with experience about their biggest challenges and pitfalls. One stood out. A good friend from Poland told me (paraphrasing),

"The most important thing you need to understand is that no one will do exactly what you want. It doesn't matter how well you explain it, they will never do what you expect."

I laughed when he said that, but now I have seen it so many times throughout my career. I'll always remember the phrase and his good humor. However, I would like to modify his phrase a bit based on my experience:

"The people who work for you will never do exactly what you expect them to do, and that's your fault."

Sounds bold and pretty depressing, doesn't it? But if we take a closer look at the why, it becomes pretty clear. It's rooted in the sender-receiver model (or Shannon-Weaver model)[5]. Shannon and Weaver originally developed the model to improve telephone communication. Later, sociologist Stuart Hall, psychologist Friedemann Schulz von Thun (e.g., the four sides model[6]), and communication scientist Paul Watzlawick, among others, picked it up and developed it further. In a nutshell, it says that in communication, there is always a sender and a receiver. To get information from the sender to the receiver, the sender must encode it and the receiver must decode and interpret it. For example, to communicate, your thoughts must be converted into words (along with gestures, tone of voice, and much more), and those words travel via sound waves to the receiver, for example, me. I now have to decode these words into thoughts and interpret them. As you can imagine, there is a lot of room for error in this process. Every second, about 11 million sensory impressions are processed in our brain. However, we only consciously perceive about 40 of them (0.0004%). The fact that your words arrive in your counterpart's brain the way you intended is nothing short of a miracle. Therefore, it is no wonder they don't deliver exactly what you intended. There

[5] Shannon, C. E., & Weaver, W. (1949). *The mathematical theory of communication.* University of Illinois Press. https://psycnet.apa.org/record/1950-04584-000
[6] Four Sides modell (Schulz von Thun 1981)

is a great book by Ben Kimura-Gross called "How We Connect" if you want to dive deeper into this topic. I found the book difficult to read as it is very scientific, but it is well worth the effort. To summarize it:

- ❖ It doesn't matter what you say, it only matters what the receiver hears.
- ❖ It doesn't matter what you do, it only matters what the receiver sees.

In other words: If something doesn't go the way you intend, always ask yourself first if you explained it correctly. And here's the kicker: You can't answer that, because you don't know the decoding software that the receiver's brain is using. So, you must assume that you didn't code your explanation with the proper decoding software - it was your fault. Don't blame it on someone else, because - as we have already learned - that is just an excuse.

As Florence Nightingale the famous British nurse and statistician and founder of modern Western nursing once said, *"I owe my success to one thing - I have never made or accepted excuses."*

The Despisers of the Body

""Body I am and soul" - that's how the child talks. And why should one not speak like the children?
But the awakened, the knowing one says: Body I am completely, and nothing besides; and soul is only a word for something in the body."

Nietzsche had a quite "unromantic" vision of the dualism of body and soul. For him there was no separation, but they were one and the same. Everything is the body. There is no such thing as a soul that could be separated from the body, or even a life after the death of the body. This is quite pragmatic and also contrary to many people, especially in the 19th century, who believe in higher beings, spheres, gods and the like. We still cannot prove whether there is a soul or not, and even if we could, there are a variety of views about what a soul is. Today it is mostly said that the summary of our feelings and mental processes could be the soul or, in other words, the psyche. But all of these feelings and mental processes originate in the brain, part of the body.

Despite this vast body of work on the philosophical and religious views of the soul, this book is about work and management, not religion. Nietzsche claims that people who believe in a soul, in turn, despise their bodies; they don't pay enough attention to their bodies. This brings to mind a discussion of health in general and its relation to mental health. A healthy body is the basic requirement for high level performance. It doesn't matter if there is a soul in it or not - or as a great Latin saying goes, shortened from the satires of the Roman poet Juvenal, "Mens sana in corpore sano", or "a sound mind in a sound body".

It doesn't matter if it's work, personal life or anything in between. You can't win Olympic gold with a bad cold.

One great executive I met early in my career was perceived as one of the most dedicated managers we had. He was always at work and there for us. His example was the foundation for one of the cornerstones of my work philosophy: engagement is key. But one day he came to work sick. We told him to go home and get better, but he refused. The cold got worse and eventually developed into heart muscle inflammation (Where the heart is strained by illness, and then pushed beyond its abilities by additional stress). He was immediately hospitalized. During his extended hospital stay, he developed painful disc damage in his neck that forced him to take another three months to recover and return to work. Fortunately for him, he had no serious long-term effects. Others I know have not been so lucky.

But what happened at work was even worse. During his long absence, his position was given to someone else, so he had to move to a specially created job. In the financial sector, this is hugely expensive in terms of fixed labor costs.... and therefore, deeply unpopular for any company that controls its costs very closely. Senior managers treated him as a traitor, and assigned tasks that no one else wanted to do. Eventually, he became increasingly unmotivated. He lost his inspirational drive and left the company.

How many leaders could have helped this person develop? How much value could he have added? The happy ending to this story is that he bounced back after getting his health in order and joining a new company. He now performs at that level again and has a positive influence on many managers. But that small cold and the misinterpretation of his loyalty wasted years for him. How loyal was the company to him in the end?

Take care of your body. You don't need to look like those crazy fitness TikTok stars. And this is not the place for crazy dieting tips. But it bears repeating that a healthy body is the foundation of your performance. Additionally, a healthy appearance is the first thing people see about you. I know we're all working toward a prejudice-free environment, but subconscious prejudice, by definition, can't be eliminated by our longing for a perfect world. People see what they see, and how they interpret it will vary, and may not conform to your ideals.

A severely overweight person might be perceived as undisciplined. A person's bad teeth might diminish perceptions of their speaking abilities, regardless of their rhetorical mastery. It doesn't matter if these perceptions are conscious or unconscious, fair or unfair. Some people will have an uphill battle ahead of them to get to the top, for which they are already handicapped. The starting line is different for everybody. No excuses. You can still win.

Another great example of this is a co-worker I met early in my career. We were opening a new warehouse and hiring employees en masse. During these events, we hired a regular shop floor clerk. His excellent performance earned him a promotion to team leader. He demonstrated high commitment, good attendance, quality work and a very proactive attitude. After a year or so of success as a team leader, he applied for a department manager position and was interviewed. On paper, the decision was pretty clear based on his skills. He was perfect but for one problem: All of his front teeth were reduced to little broken stumps. So, he seldom smiled and carried an unnatural facial expression. The panel argued that staff would not take him seriously, would make fun of him, and that his appearance might inhibit him from difficult conversations out of fear. The question was also raised about whether his teeth were an indication of drug problems or whether the staff might suspect this and not accept him as a leader. I decided to end this speculation and discussion. He passed the panel, and we promoted him. I talked to him and gave him the feedback and concerns.

It turned out that he did not have a drug or alcohol problem, but just before he was hired, he had a serious bicycle accident where he had almost completely lost his teeth. He had to spend three years rebuilding his jaws and teeth. These "broken stumps" had been implants that would later support his dentures. So, it wouldn't have been long before his teeth were fully restored. I was ashamed of myself for having participated in the speculation about the reasons for his appearance. Drugs or alcohol, violence or just an unsanitary lifestyle. None of us considered a "positive" explanation. We all thought the worst. Such is the power of perception. Now, you could say that he got the job despite his disability, but it was a tough discussion, and it could have gone either way. There are people who try very hard to be unbiased, but that won't always help you. Others don't even care. Even if supervisors are as unbiased as possible, other employees in a manufacturing environment are not and probably never will be.

But it's not just about outward appearance. Mental health issues are on the rise. A study published in 2021[7] states that:

The number of US adults with MDD increased by 12.9%, from 15.5 to 17.5 million, between 2010 and 2018, whereas the proportion of adults with MDD aged 18–34 years increased from 34.6 to 47.5%. Over this period, the incremental economic burden of adults with MDD increased by 37.9% from $US 236.6 billion to 326.2 billion (year 2020 values)

For a long time, I was skeptical of this burnout "bullshit." I interpreted it as work avoidance. These people are just too lazy and have now been given a great argument by doctors to relax at home while we work our asses off filling in for them. Then I had three cases of serious illness in my close circle. No cheating, no relaxation at home, these were cases of severe suffering that extended to their whole families. So, it is not only the body that needs to be taken care of, but also the psyche. Whether you consider the body and mind to be one or separate, you should never lose sight of either to be happy.

But what does "being happy" actually mean and why is this important? There are many ideas, like the hedonism theory[8], the desire theory[9], or the objective

---

[7] Greenberg, P.E., Fournier, AA., Sisitsky, T. *et al.* The Economic Burden of Adults with Major Depressive Disorder in the United States (2010 and 2018). *PharmacoEconomics* 39, 653–665 (2021). https://doi.org/10.1007/s40273-021-01019-4

[8] Moore, Andrew, "Hedonism", *The Stanford Encyclopedia of Philosophy* (Winter 2019 Edition), Edward N. Zalta (ed.)

[9] The Three Traditional Theories - Authentic Happiness By Martin E. P. Seligman and Ed Royzman; July 2003

list theory, just to name three of them, and that's an old debate. I know that I can't solve this problem here. In my opinion, happiness is undefinable because every individual defines happiness differently. I am talking about the influencing factors of happiness, and especially the local references to where you are, whether in your professional or personal life.

If you are not happy where you are, your brain will seek avoidance strategies to keep you from going where you are not happy. Why would you want to be in a place that makes you depressed? This creates a cognitive dissonance. That is, a discrepancy between what is expected and what actually happens. Your brain cannot resolve this discrepancy for the time being, and slowly goes into defense mode. Every brain deals with this differently, and some start a real fight. And now, you're in a mess. That's why it's so important to take care of your mental health by seeking happiness where you are. I know that's easy to say when you have a choice.... Be honest with yourself: If your life depended on it, would you be able to change jobs? If your life depended on it, would you end a toxic relationship?

Guess what? Your life depends on it! So do it. No excuses. Take charge of your life, take charge of your body, or you won't be able to rise above. And also keep a healthy distance from people who let themselves go.

I do not go your way, you despisers of the body! You are no bridges to the superhuman for me!

Joys and Passions

"My brother, if you have a virtue, and it is your virtue, you have it in common with no one.
Of course, you want to call it by name and caress it; you want to pluck it by the ear and amuse yourself with it.
And behold! Now you have her name in common with the people and have become people and flock with your virtue!"

What is a virtue? A virtue is generally understood to be an outstanding quality or an exemplary attitude. When you think about virtues, a lot comes to mind. There is the traditional canon of the seven virtues, consisting of the three divine virtues of faith, love and hope and the ancient Platonic cardinal virtues of prudence, justice, fortitude and temperance. In addition to the theological virtues, however, there are also quite normal civic virtues such as neatness, punctuality, cleanliness or frugality. I am pretty sure that every reader could add at least one more virtue. If you ask Google, you get at least 79 different virtues.

Zarathustra makes three important points in this speech:
- ❖ Don't brag about your virtues, live them and that's it.
- ❖ Virtues arise from yourself (from your passions) and are not dictated from outside (e.g., by a god).
- ❖ Being a role model, living by your virtues, is a damn tough job.

On the first point, nobody likes a braggart. How do we react to braggarts? As my partner says .... With a big boo.

There are rare occasions when you can mention your virtues, like when you want to challenge yourself on something, telling everyone to watch you closely. But that's an exception and I would tend not to recommend it. The better way is to define and prioritize your virtues for yourself.

Zarathustra even mentions that you should have only one virtue, and even this is almost too much for most people. Decide your main virtue and pursue it. I decided 12 years ago to live straight edge - to live a clean life. No more alcohol, smoking, coffee, or drugs for example. My reasons are relevant to me, and I could explain them if we were to meet in person, but that's not important here. I have challenged myself, and if we look closely, we can also define a virtue as a challenge. We live in a world where living a virtuous life has become quite difficult. Everyone has a smartphone and can take pictures of you on your cheat day....

I am proud to be meeting my challenge but who cares? This is for me, not you. If you decide to live a mindful life, it's for you, not for others. If you say that you want to be on time from today on, and never miss a deadline or appointment again, you may think that it's to respect other people's time, but it's not. The point is that you want to be perceived as a trustworthy partner, colleague or employee. You are not doing it for others but for yourself. Don't talk about it, be on time and that's it.

Challenge yourself and improve yourself through that challenge. Everyone knows that it is difficult to overcome your weaknesses (how many of your New Year's resolutions came true?). We fail for many reasons. Perhaps our resolutions were not made concretely, but rather vaguely, or that we didn't really want to follow them, but were influenced by peer pressure. Everything is doomed to failure. Or as Oscar Wilde put it: "Good intentions are useless attempts to interfere with scientific laws. Their origin is pure vanity. Their result is absolutely nil."

But some people make it. People who achieve their goals. Who quit smoking or exercise hard. If your will is strong enough, you can achieve difficult things, because virtues are personal choices. This is not comparable to playing professional football, which most people probably could never do, especially after age 40, even if they wanted it badly enough. I'm also aware of how difficult addictions are to overcome, and I believe drug addicts when they say they couldn't do it on their own. Overcoming heroin addiction is a lot more difficult than losing 10 pounds, but in both cases, the drive to succeed must come from you.

My dad smoked two packs a day and liked to party. Once on New Year's Eve, as a kid, I teased him that he would never be able to quit. He was drunk and made a joke of it, but he said he would quit. I didn't expect him to remember it the next day, but he did. His wife continued to smoke and once I heard her say to him, after we were in bed, "Go ahead and have one...the kids won't see it." But he pulled through and never again touched another cigarette. This story always comes to my mind when I make up my mind to do something. My father was lazy in some respects, and I never expected him to succeed. But he surprised me. I always tell myself that if he could do it, anyone can - especially me.

Pick the virtue that is the highest priority for you and stick the hell to it. Once you've accomplished that and are holding it, choose the next one. Become the role model you've always wanted by simply living it.

"So speak and say: "This is my good, this is what I love, this is how I like it completely, this is how I want the good.

I do not want it as a God's law, I do not want it as a man's statute and necessity: no signpost is it for me for the higher earth and paradise."

The important thing is that you choose your virtue for yourself and no one else. Do not choose one that society, religion, your mother or your boss demands of you. Social norms change, and different religions have different priorities. Your whole life and career will change several times, and expectations will be different. Nietzsche's point in this speech is about the hereafter compared to the here and now. From his point of view, we should only live here and not focus on the hereafter (as religion does). The superman lives entirely in this world. She is engaged in every moment of his life. And so, virtues arise from our inner self. You should not concentrate on a virtue because it would give you a place at the great table of the Almighty Spaghetti Monster or a place next to the great warriors in Valhalla. Focus on what you need here and now, that will pave the way to a better life. I agree with Nietzsche here. This book offers ideas on how to become a better leader, not how to access some otherworldly place. Virtue is a leadership strategy.

But how do you develop great virtues? Zarathustra suggests that you turn your passion into a virtue. This reminded me of something I read in a book by Jack Welch, "Winning 2". I recommend that you read it. Welch states that you have to find your area of destiny. He describes how his son was unhappy in a well-paying job. After quitting to focus on his passion he becomes even more successful. The field of destiny analysis is now part of the management consulting business built on Welch's books, and from the feedback I've heard, a pretty successful tool.

Passion, especially in Nietzsche's day, was scorned by religious leaders. Basically, virtue could never come from passion. Passion was about lust, frivolity, and sin. Nietzsche, known for his confrontational style, took the complete opposite view. He said that the best virtues you can acquire must arise from within you, and the strongest driving forces within you are the passions.

Therefore, if you could transform your passion into a virtue, it would increase the likelihood of that virtue sticking and would perfectly suit you as a person. You would automatically become the embodiment of that virtue. If, on the other hand, you want or, even worse, have to commit to a virtue that has been imposed on you or that you have been forced to do, then it won't work. And here I agree wholeheartedly.

<u>You need to build your own philosophy of work. This philosophy must be built on your virtues. It will only be credibly represented by you if you are passionate about what you do. Logically, then, your passion supports your</u>

virtues. And people will follow your philosophy only if they see you embodying the virtues or pillars of that philosophy.

One of my favorite quotes is from Augustine Aurelius: "In you must burn what you wish to kindle in others." or sometimes, "What you wish to kindle in others must first burn in yourself."

A great leader can only be great if you see that person burning for what they do every day. The person can only credibly convince others of the idea if they share it themselves. Here we come full circle to the topic of happiness. If you are at some point high up on the career ladder, that means of course that many people below you are dependent on your qualities of advocacy. You have to embody the company's goal; you have to burn for it. Otherwise, you are not credible, and your employees will not follow you with the zeal they need to build a world-class company. If you do not burn for it, you will not be successful and sooner or later you will be unhappy with the consequences discussed above.

"It is excellent to have many virtues, but a hard lot; and many a man went into the desert and killed himself because he was tired of being the battle and battleground of virtues.

My brother, is war and battle evil? But necessarily is this evil, necessarily is the envy and the distrust and the slander among your virtues.

See how each of your virtues is desirous of the highest: it wants your whole spirit to be its herald, it wants all your power in anger, hatred and love."

Our last point was that being a role model is a damn tough job. When I searched for a good quote on this phrase, I found tons of quotes from celebrities who claimed to be role models themselves. It makes you laugh your ass off when you see the names behind the quotes. One can only think, how dare you claim to be a role model? I would never call myself a role model. My BMI is less than optimal, my workload could be considered unhealthy, and my diet consists of at least one ice cream sundae a day. I'm sure there are other sides to me that I'm very proud of, but is that enough to be considered a role model? I don't think so.

But if you think about it twice, it's not so easy to say what a role model actually is. My daughter, for example, looks up to people who bring to my mind a facepalm emoji buzz. The requirements for a role model are constantly changing and writing it down in a book would probably make the book look dated after just a few months.

So, I'd rather point out how hard it is to achieve that ideal state. I often hear the saying about the decline of virtues these days. But it is not a decline, but a dilution. In the past, there were a few virtues that society expected people to follow. Today, we recognize a wide variety of virtues, and a general shift. For example, being a good mother or father is something completely different today than it was in the 1950s. In the past, the mother was expected to stay at home and take care of the house and the children. The father supported the family financially. Nowadays, the father is expected to do his share of housework, and childcare, and the mother works outside the home (at least in Western countries).

So, you have to choose the virtues that best fit your work philosophy (and life philosophy). And then tackle one at a time. If you focus on too many things, you will fail. And many of these virtues work against each other. Take frugality and generosity, for example. After all, you could never get the most out of both at the same time. You could balance them somehow, but that will already require your full attention. So, make sure you have a plan, prioritize which areas you really want to invest your time in. Which ones are important to those around you? What appeals most to the people around you. If you try to reach too many, you will fail at too many and thus get bad feedback. This bad feedback will demotivate you and start a vicious cycle that you will most likely get sucked into. People sense that you are not yourself and pretend to be someone else by copying virtues or trying to adopt virtues that do not suit you.

The Pale Criminal

"Once the doubt was evil and the will to the self. At that time, the sick man became a heretic and a witch: as a heretic and a witch, he suffered and wanted to make suffer.

But this does not want to enter your ears: it harms your good, you tell me. But what do I care about your good ones!

Many things about your good ones disgust me, and certainly not their evil. I wish they had a madness that would destroy them, like this pale criminal!"

When Zarathustra speaks of madness in this chapter, he means the perception of madness by society. If someone shakes the foundations of the doctrine and the faith, this person is called crazy by most. And this continues until success is achieved. Then a madman usually becomes a genius. If you read the biographies about the people who are considered the great geniuses of humanity, you will often find adjectives like "crazy" or "strange" or worse.

Have you ever heard of the Gaussian curve or the normal distribution? There's one below. The source is Mensa, the largest and oldest society for highly gifted people in the world. The aim of Mensa is: "to create a society that is non-political and free from all racial or religious distinctions. "Mensa" means "table" in Latin, and the organization was so named because Mensa is a round-table society where ethnicity, color, creed, national origin, age, politics, educational and social background are all completely irrelevant. The only relevant qualification for membership is scoring within the upper 2% of the general population on an approved intelligence test."

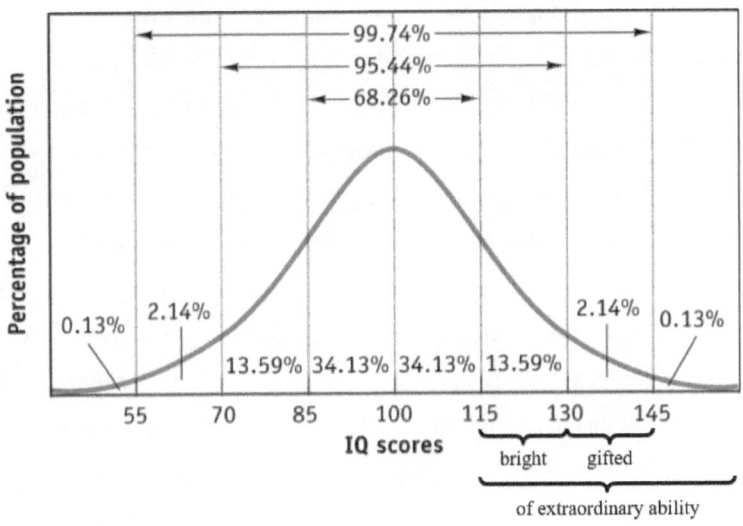

If we look at the distribution of IQ, we find that only 2% of an age group have an extremely high IQ (above 130). If we assume that it takes a bright mind to achieve exceptional results, we can already assume that the vast majority of people (84%) will have a harder time achieving this goal for this reason alone. I'm not saying it's impossible, just that these people will have to fight much harder than the few who just get it. For some people who are even further to the left in the normal distribution, the chances are particularly bad. Pure statistics, I know, and the chances are never 0, you just have to be ready to fight much harder.

All this talk of "you can achieve anything if you just try hard enough" is just plain nonsense. However, you don't have to have a high IQ to be successful. It takes more than a high IQ to succeed in the workforce. There are a lot more qualities like willingness to take risks, hard-headedness, or empathy. A specific test only quantifies the attributes that were tested. Attributes such as "people skills", artistic abilities, or even physical appearance can influence leadership abilities, and may not be reflected in the test. Often, a high IQ is an obstacle for highly gifted people, because it can be difficult for them to relate to others.

Many of those who have a very high IQ are often rather risk-averse, which, for example, makes it much more difficult to start a business, which is usually associated with high risk. If one were to take courage as the sole criterion for success, we would see that courage is normally distributed too, just as intelligence is, but a person could find themselves in the middle of the intelligence distribution, but within the far right tail of the courage distribution. Only a very few people are courageous enough to bring their idea to life and found a new startup. More importantly, of those few people who have founded a startup, only a very few are actually good (or lucky) enough to become successful. Courageous and stupid, after all, is not a winning combination.

Think of it like a matrix, you take each trait that correlates with professional success and give it a value from 1-10 on a scale. Most traits fall in the middle, reflecting the hump in the middle of a normal distribution, with narrowing tails on each end. Then you rate how high the value is for you (or someone else) and plot it. It might then look like the table below. The higher than the average value of all traits, the higher the chance to be successful. I know that this is an extremely simplified representation, but I hope it clarifies what I want to say. You can be super intelligent (in our picture a 10) but an absolute coward (1 for courage), then the chance to be successful is much lower than someone who is not so intelligent but just has the courage to go through with it. It is difficult to succeed if any of the requirements for success are in the 1 or 2 range, but if you are aware of your deficiencies, you have a better chance of compensating for them. The table can be greatly expanded, and each trait may be positively or negatively correlated with other traits (for example, empathy is positively correlated with kindness, and negatively correlated with the ability to fire people).

Trait	1	2	3	4	5	6	7	8	9	10	Result
Intelligence									X		9
Courage								X			8
Hardiness			X								3
Empathy				X							4
											mean=6

The point of this chapter is to say that the craziness required by Zarathustra is not present in most people. They have settled in the large mass near the center under the Gauss curve and are very content there. There will always be only a few who will have either the intelligence, courage, or creativity that is needed.

When we started Terum, the environmental social network, it was a hard road and we had to go "all in". Since we couldn't find an investor initially, we funded it with our personal savings. I had nothing left in my bank account and even asked my mother for a loan just so we could keep the programmers working for us for a few more days. My co-founder and CEO Julia quit her great job as CTO in a prestigious German company and joined our team, adding all her personal savings. We had to kick out the programming company we had been working with, which caused additional costs. At one point, it would have been possible to launch the app, but without marketing or troubleshooting. At the very last moment, we found an investor who backed us, and the venture succeeded. Success in this case was dependent on belief in our project, the financial resources to support it, and a willingness to risk everything we had. Friends and family called us crazy for putting so much money and effort into an idea that was guaranteed not to pay off. But we believed in it.

Zarathustra points out that you should never be ashamed of your craziness. Shame or timidity prevents you from achieving great things. That leads back to the first quote:

"You must still have chaos within you to give birth to a dancing star."

Apply this to launching a startup or pushing through a great idea, inventing a breakthrough product or establishing a groundbreaking theory. Basically, you give birth to a dancing star. But to do that, you need sufficient chaos (or insanity or whatever you want to call it) in you.

Now the question is, do you want to be one of the 2% or one of the 98%... or asked the other way around, what does it take to be among the 2%? As mentioned earlier, according to Jack Welch, it's all about finding your destiny zone. I agree with that, but it takes some effort to find out what your own area of destiny is and if you can be good at it.

I will never be an Olympic swimmer. I am simply too unathletic for that, but I do like to swim. However, if I had really burned for it, I could make it to the pool several times a week and train. If I train enough, my athleticism will increase, and maybe I could compete in the senior age group. Well, maybe for fun. Things like that are not impossible. I once participated in the Dodentocht Kadee in Belgium: a 62-mile (100km) trail run. I talked to a woman at the start, and she told me that she was almost 80 years old. Her husband had died a few years ago and she didn't know what to do with herself and went for a walk. Then she started to walk farther and farther and found out that this can also be done as a sport discipline. She started to participate in ultra runs and enjoyed them. I will never forget this woman, because she was already wearing so many badges on her backpack for so many different ultra runs that I could only marvel in awe. She cheerfully overtook me a few miles before the finish.

To return to Nietzsche; it's about passion. Passion that is free of shame. At first glance, most people would wonder why anyone should be ashamed of their passion, but social norms, prejudices, expectations from peers, family or children can all plant seeds of caution or shame. There are so many different things that can create conscious or even unconscious pressure to prefer to abandon your passion or destiny. How many other women or men in their retirement club would be persuaded to participate in an ultra-run? The couch is more comfortable.

According to a Gallup study[10], only 36% of full-time employees in the United States (US) are engaged in their jobs. Worldwide, that number is only 20%!

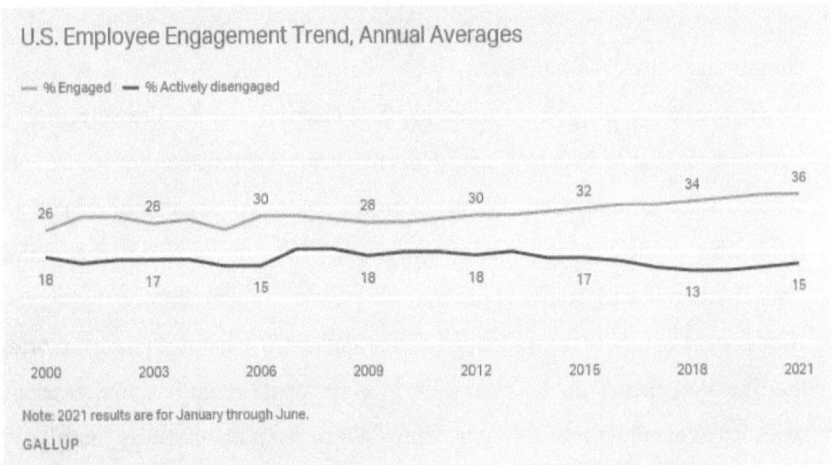

That's just crazy. Even though it's been improving, all the alarm bells should be ringing. Not only for all managers out there, but also for you. Are you among the minority who are engaged? Do you get up and go to work with a smile on your face? Do you hate Mondays, or are you excited to get back to doing great things? And if you're not engaged, why not? You might have a bad boss, or a hostile work environment, low pay or long hours, but the main reason for disengagement must be you. Stop with the excuses. Are you really doing what

---

[10] Gallup's Q12 Employee Engagement Survey

you are passionate about? First, let's look at what passion is. According to the Cambridge Dictionary, it is:

"a very powerful feeling, for example of sexual attraction, love, hate, anger, or other emotion or an extreme interest in or wish for doing something, such as a hobby, activity"

Commonly it is divided into two main fields:

1. Harmonic Passion
2. Obsessive Passion

Harmonious passion is free from pressure or obligation and is characterized above all by a positive relationship with it. We love what we do. It is a part of us without dominating our lives. It leaves room for other activities and thus does not take up all of our lives.

An obsessive passion, on the other hand, is characterized by pressure. It is still a passion. It makes us happy and gives us social recognition, but it gets out of control. Like an addiction. People with an obsessive passion often get great results, but at the expense of everything else. They are out of balance, and that leads to internal and external conflict.

If you were to say that you belong to the dedicated part of the work world, is the first statement a good description of your work? Read it again. Does your work leave enough room for your family? Or to put it another way, despite your passion for work, do you still have time with your family or friends? Is there enough time for travel, stamp collecting, fishing, or attending a demonstration? Think carefully and be critical. Does your passion control you or do you control your passion?

The usual management literature (and probably your psychologically gifted friends and family) would advise you to pursue only those areas that fall within harmonious passion. Work-life balance and mental health rules! But I tend to slightly disagree. The question, as mentioned above, is what you want to achieve. If you have a clear vision of what you want, and a realistic understanding of the trade-offs involved, then the decision is yours.

If you want to become the next Jeff Bezos or Elon Musk, you may have no choice. If you read the autobiographies of very successful people, the word "obsessive" appears in almost all of them. If you want to reach those ranks, you have to be prepared to work like a maniac and follow your passion in a way that leaves no room for anything else. You won't get that as a gift or by taking advanced online awareness training courses or just reading books. Success comes from hard work, smart decisions, and a great team around you. During the time I was writing this book, I was working full time as an associate director for a major online marketplace and later as a vice president for one of the best energy startups in the world. When I got home after a long day at work, I would take a 30-minute nap and then work for my own startup, "Terum," which was about to go live in the app stores. We were in the process of testing the app to prepare for the launch.

After I finished conference calls with the mainly US-based teams, I tried to write at least four to six pages for this book. I slept as I needed to stay more or less functional. I have a goal and am passionate about it, but that doesn't leave much room for social interaction or anything like that.

At the beginning of my working life, I was pushing my career and only that. My first marriage fell apart because of it, and I only see my daughter on the weekends. I would never recommend anyone to take me as an example, and I would never consider myself a role model as mentioned earlier. But am I happy? Yes! I need to be a little more specific here: I am happy because I see the larger puzzle of my life coming together as I had envisioned. I see all the little steps toward my vision and my big goal. I see my plans coming to fruition and becoming reality. But was it worth the high price I paid? I won't know for a few years. I consider myself lucky to be in a relationship with a partner who is more or less in the same situation as me. We support each other through ups and downs. We look out for each other and make sure our passion doesn't control all the other things we want in life. We anchor each other in harmonious passion and alert one another about potentially drifting into unhealthy states. An earlier chapter was about finding companions, so this is another good example. It doesn't have to be the love of your life; a close friend, your child or your mother might be good too. If you want to set sail on wild seas, you need to make sure you are surrounded by trustworthy people who know how to batten down the hatches.

To come back to the most successful people in the world, (not counting those who inherited their wealth), you rarely find a resume that screams: ideal world. These people also had to pay for it, and not only with money.

Will you make it in harmony? Certainly, there are examples of people who were fortunate enough to reach this stage by following only harmonious passions, always being in balance with their lives and never struggling. But I would guess that they are the rarest outliers of a sample size that is already made up of outliers compared to the rest of the successful people. So, the probability is close to zero. To look at this another way, Malcolm Gladwell, in his book "Outliers" includes a long list of high-tech billionaires, including both Steve Jobs and Bill Gates, who were all born between 1952 and 1958. If you weren't born within this window of high opportunity, you are denied entry into this elite group, because the very top of the very top need everything to fall into place perfectly, and part of that is just luck. This book is not for those 1 in a billion people with everything, including luck, going for them. It is meant to help a larger group of people advance in the workplace. Do you really think that being accepted into the outlier club in a field that is not your passion would work? I doubt it.

But there is another caveat to this topic. If you don't love your job, you should quit as soon as possible. Does that work? You need to pay your bills, you might be contractually bound, or you might not have other employment opportunities in your area.

Among the many reasons that could force you to stay in a job you don't like (I'm not talking about love), I'm sorry to say that most are just excuses. I fully understand that you may enjoy visiting your family every day, or that you like the bakery around the corner, or that you have a crush on the pretty person behind the register at the Starbucks near your office. But are these valid reasons that keep you from following your passion and being happy? No. There are tons of opportunities out there. Now get off your lazy butt and take them. And by "out there" I also mean that there are actually countries outside the US or Europe.

And if you're not qualified, get qualified. And if you don't have enough money to do it, then go to another country where studying is free (yes, there are several!) or go earn money to pay for it. Learning never ends, and even if you already have a college degree, you might refocus and study something else in another country. Of course, it's not that easy when four hours of Fortnite, three episodes of the latest Netflix series, or watching the latest hundred TikTok videos are part of your daily routine. Your choices determine what you do with your time. When I stopped drinking alcohol, weekends simultaneously became longer. Fewer parties, better sleep, more energy and mornings free of hangovers. It's crazy how much time I gained, especially on Sundays.

Again, if your life depended on it, could you do it? Could you get a better paying job at a better company if you really tried? Usually "yes" if you apply for jobs within your abilities.

If you are unhappy where you are, then make a plan in place to get where you want to be. Be as analytical and impartial as possible, and work to get to where your passion falls on fertile ground. Be ready for plan B and plan C in place when plan A fails (and don't be surprised when plans don't work out). Our social ecosystem is so incredibly complex that each plan involves risk and chance. As famed boxer Mike Tyson responded to an interview question about his opponent's (Evander Holyfield) plan, "Everybody has a plan until they get punched in the mouth." In other words, plans tend to work perfectly in the mind's eye, until they crash into reality.

Find your passion and follow it relentlessly, without shame or second thoughts. Surround yourself with the right people. Ultimately, it's up to you (and only you). Don't blame others.

"Verily, I would that their madness were called truth, or fidelity, or justice: but they have their virtue to live long, and in a miserable comfort.

I am a railing on the river: seize me who can seize me! But I am not your crutch."

Reading and Writing

"Of all that is written, I love only that which one writes with his blood. Write with blood: and you will experience that blood is spirit.
It is not easy to understand foreign blood: I hate the reading idlers.
He who knows the reader does nothing more for the reader. Another century of readers - and the spirit itself will stink.
The fact that everyone is allowed to learn to read corrupts in the long run not only writing but also thinking.
Once the spirit was God, then he became man and now he becomes even rabble.
He who writes in blood and proverbs does not want to be read, but learned by heart."

This speech contains three main points relevant to us:
- When you do something, do it as well as you can. Challenge yourself and your ideas, but make sure no one waters down your ideas by talking them down.
- We all have opportunities, but it's up to us to decide to take advantage of them.
- Your worst enemy is "the spirit of gravity" - don't let inertia drag you down.

The worst feedback I ever got was from my mother. She once said, "Son, you always start something and never finish it. You need to focus and finish the things you start. You throw yourself into crazy ideas and give up when it gets too complicated. One idea after another."

This feedback was repeated during my studies. I was ex-matriculated from my first-degree program for partying instead of studying. I lived my own interpretation of a party animal from Van Wilders (Myriad Pictures, 2002 with Ryan Reynolds and Tara Reid). I lived in one of the biggest student dorms in

Berlin and worked in a nearby pub. The dorm was an ERASMUS dorm, designed for people from other countries who wanted to experience life in Germany. Most came only to party. The door to my apartment was kept unlocked because I had lost my key, so there were always other people in my apartment. This was funny for a while, but I didn't really study there.

Wrong priorities and bad decisions resulted in failure. Nevertheless, I took my academic expulsion seriously and did a 180° turn. I dumped the booze and changed my course of study. I worked hard and completed both a bachelor's and a master's degree. I landed a great job (rather by accident) and had a decent career. I realized that if you want to be good at something, you have to focus on it and fight for it. You have to be on fire for it. I love the line from Zarathustra that said:

"He who writes in blood does not want to be read, but learned by heart."

That means so much and is so powerful. If you want to write a book, put all your strength, your feelings, and your heart into it so that it will be remembered by your readers. I've always wanted to write a book, but I've always struggled with this sentence. Is there an ear for my mouth? The same goes for what Zarathustra struggles with at the beginning of his journey. But that's the wrong question to ask. It's impossible to predict if a book will be well received, or go down in a shitstorm, or just go unnoticed. Those are all the reactions of others, but our passions are personal. Just make the damn effort and write it. Be brave and publish it and you'll find out. As I said, I welcome all feedback, challenge me and my thoughts - I look forward to the discussions.

When I think of real challenges, special people come to mind. In particular, people who volunteer to help in crisis areas around the world or extreme athletes. People who stand firm in heated political debates and bravely continue to argue. People who give emotional speeches even in the face of death. The metaphor of writing in blood is for them all. They don't just do something, they inspire us. It's a metaphor not only for writing books, but for work in general. Martin Luther King's speech about having a dream was a great piece of rhetoric, but influencing others was his profession. He was a Baptist minister, and his job was to spread the word and set an example. He decided to go far beyond his job description as an evangelical preacher. His job description was not a limiting factor, but a springboard to something he could define for himself that could be greater than what all the other pastors were trying to accomplish. He knew he was risking his life, but that didn't hold him back. Facing constant hatred, dismissal and ridicule, he pushed forward. Surrounded by companions and carried by the masses.

There are numerous examples of people who quit their jobs and strive for something great. They use their passions to turbocharge their aspirations and achieve their vision, no matter what the cost. Usually, they break with the virtues agreed upon by most in a given field.

Jagadish Vasudev or "Sadhguru" is a great example. A yogi who is also well known beyond the borders of India, especially through his book "Inner Engineering: A Yogi's Guide to Joy" (not quite as easy to understand as

"Yogananda," but definitely worth reading). As far as I know, he never faced any major negativity from any group. But he is on a mission, and you can feel it in every video. He shares his wisdom and experience in a way that I really admire. He's just great on the Joe Rogan Show. He's so passionate about what he does, and he does it in such a relaxed way that it's stunning. He has a confidence that surpasses anyone I've seen, but with an ease that is just cool.

These two fought (or fight) a different battle in very different environments, but all are examples to me of what it means to "write in blood." Almost every person in the public eye understands that they will be criticized, but for these people, it's just crazy how they can build on feedback and get better and better. So, write in blood or remain a reader - it's your choice.

That leads to the next point. Zarathustra mentions being exalted and looking down with ease. He asks for those who look up and want to be elevated as well.

"I no longer feel with you: this cloud that I see below me, this blackness and heaviness that I laugh at, - this is precisely your storm cloud.

You look up when you ask for elevation. And I look down, because I am uplifted.

Who of you can laugh and be uplifted at the same time?"

This does not mean that he is better than everyone else, but he places himself outside of categories such as above and below. The "above" exists only for people who are not elevated, who are not striving to become their better selves. There are only creators and consumers, and you have the freedom to decide what you want to be. Every consumer is a creator who has not yet explored their possibilities to create. Yet there are only a tiny number of people who understand this and have the willpower to do so. I assume that you, the reader of this book, are at least considering becoming a creator and thus evolving into that category, or possibly are already there.

The message here is that it depends only on your will to achieve the greater good. If your will is strong enough and you challenge yourself hard enough (he talks about always gathering leprechauns to challenge him), you will reach that level. And this does not mean a material level, but a spiritual level. When you reach that higher spiritual level, things like class, race, and gender no longer count. You can fully focus your energy on your goal without even wasting a tiny bit of it towards unhealthy competition or even a thought that is not directed towards your goal.

For example, when you read a book or listen to a speech of Sadhguru, he completely ignores the differences in people, he just doesn't care who is sitting in front of him, if the person has the will to improve their inner self. It is amazing to see how carefree this guru is. He doesn't have to think all day about such unimportant things as skin color or whether people love or hate him. It's so liberating not to have to worry about how much your boss likes your colleagues compared to you. You have so much more time to focus on the important things you can accomplish. On the contrary, it's incredible how much time people spend on their status. When you find your passion, you don't need to look over your shoulder to make sure that others approve. Stop focusing on others. It's not your status that matters, it's just your will to go "from peak to peak". Lion status is not the end but merely the middle of the evolution toward becoming a great leader.

What goes hand in hand with losing focus on status? You immediately stop seeing enemies and opponents everywhere, because you have nothing to gain or lose from them. In his three metamorphoses of the mind, this is the "child" stage, in which you become a natural leader. You are not consumed with ambition and fear that the next promotion won't come fast enough. Or worse, that someone else (completely unqualified, of course) will get the coveted job before you do. Don't get me wrong, Nietzsche favors real fighters with an incredibly strong will to power, but that doesn't mean physical violence and vicious behavior. If you want to grow in your company and get the promotion you want, don't focus on the people around you, focus solely on yourself and improving yourself.

Closely related to this topic is mankind's worst enemy according to Zarathustra, the spirit of gravity.

Let me share a difficult time for me at work. The company had planned to promote me, but due to economic circumstances, they had to impose a promotion freeze. I understood the company's needs, and that this was the right decision from a company perspective. Nevertheless, I ruminate over it on sleepless nights. Chaos reigned in my head, as I wondered what to do next. Should I leave the company, or apply for another internal job? Will my superiors help me or drop me? Where do I stand in the job market? I probably wouldn't get a similar salary at another job, but I was going nowhere here. I was in a vicious cycle, and the more I thought about it, the worse it got.

I suppose everyone has experienced situations like this where the outlook was very bleak, and the more your thoughts circled around it, the worse it got. That's the spirit of gravity pulling you down, sitting on your back like a heavy weight, making it hard to move. All your thoughts turn inward instead of focusing on your future goals and mission or the people around you. I'm going to assume that you know this is not helpful at all, but why do we all do this all the time? These thoughts are called intrusive thoughts. They are usually irrelevant and occur all the time in everyone. They are programmed into every body's brain. Excessively and frequent intrusive thoughts are the main cause of depression[11]. But to reiterate: These intrusive thoughts are always within us. You can't avoid them, but you can be aware of them so that they can be put in their proper perspective. intrusive thoughts play a vital role in creating anxiety that eventually leads to depression.

---

[11] Unwanted Intrusive Thought -Martin Seif, PhD, ABPP & Sally Winston, PsyD; 2018

As I lay in bed thinking about the missed promotion, I finally became aware of it and said to myself, "Enough; stop, that's the spirit of gravity, stop focusing on it, and think of the positive opportunities you have. Talk to your superior and make a plan together." Of course, my supervisor wasn't happy with the situation either. I reminded myself that I trusted him to work with me. We sat down and made a plan. There was no need to waste all those thoughts on negative outcomes. And to be fair, this is also quite a first-world problem.... Most people in the world face much more serious situations. People struggling to make ends meet, who don't know where they're going to get food tomorrow, so they don't starve. So, if you put things in perspective, that's usually a first step to getting out of the vicious cycle. But as I said, as long as you are aware that this evil spirit of gravity exists, you can stop it before it permanently harms you.

"And when I saw my devil, I found him serious, thorough, deep, solemn: it was the spirit of gravity, - through him all things fall.

It is not by anger, but by laughter that one kills. Come on, let us kill the spirit of gravity!"

The Tree on the Hill

"But it is with the human being like with the tree.
The more he wants to go up into the height and light, the stronger his roots strive earthward, downward, into darkness, depth,-into evil."

Zarathustra wanders around and meets a young man who is doing his best but can't reach his goal. Bad thoughts crawl through his mind and poison his thoughts. While trying to become enlightened, he has instead become lonely and sad. Zarathustra asks him to take a walk to explore why. Eventually they find out that the reason for the young man's sadness was that he was not patient enough.

This passage is a great analogy for so many managers I have met throughout my career. Patience is one of the most important virtues we miss today (and I don't exclude myself - I was one of the most impatient managers in the beginning). Remember the young manager who asked me after only eight months what more he could do for the next promotion? Impatience prevents us from focusing on the future. Impatience is linked to the spirit of gravity. You're not getting your promotion? Guess what, there might be a good reason. Did you really achieve all your goals? And if so, after achieving all those goals, did you step on the gas and strive for even more without being asked? What did your peers do? What is the macro environment in which your company operates? Continue to strive for more, but don't tie success to a specific position or salary. Is status really the only goal you seek? I once had a supervisor who changed the license plate on his car every time he got promoted. The license plate then read "L3" for his current employment level. After the next promotion, he changed it to "L4." How embarrassing... But some people pay more attention to status than anything else.

You always have to be aware that you only have a certain amount of energy. Just like a battery (have you ever seen the movie "Matrix"? If not, you should).

Every action, movement or thought uses energy. Every joule of that energy should be spent on achieving your goals and dreams instead of checking for approval and status.

Why is it so important for you to have "Senior" or "Director" or "Lead" in your job title? Psychologist Cameron Anderson finds that the desire for status is ingrained in everyone[12].

I would never advise you to stop trying to increase your social status or to stop climbing the career ladder. A great leader should rise as high as possible. I love people with a strong will to power. But what is the right path and channel for your energy?

Most people don't grasp what is really important along the way. They can see what virtues work best to ease their way to the top. Impatience is a roadblock, not an expressway. The result of this impatience is the downfall of your highest hopes and greatest virtues. If you believe too soon that you will not get where you want to go, you will begin to question your virtues. You might think that your virtues didn't help you get there so they must be wrong. Instead of properly recognizing the downsides of impatience, you will criticize yourself as too gentle, too kind, too calm, or too patient. Then as you try to rid yourself of these "obstructions", you become a smaller person. And sooner than you expect, you have become a big asshole with power. A bad manager who makes life hell for others. Someone

who has had their virtues poisoned by impatience from the spirit of gravity. I have seen so many of these managers. And at the beginning of my career, I may have been one too, but the good news here, you can change that again and re-learn the values that will help you to become great.

Impatience must not drive you. Our society today drives many people to expect too much too fast. The student who after finishing an MBA thinks that

---

[12] Anderson, C. 2015. "Is the desire for status a fundamental human motive? A review of the empirical literature". Psychological Bulletin, Vol 141(3)

becoming the CEO of some Dow Jones company within the next two years is no problem, can only fail. The expectations of oneself are simply too high. You stand in your own way and the spirit of heaviness pulls you down as the expected successes do not come fast enough. The vicious circle begins.

Perhaps this vicious circle has contributed to the strong increase of mental health problems in our society today.

According to studies by Prof. Dr. Matthias Sutter, a Director and Scientific Member of the Max Planck Institute for Research on Collective Goods in Germany, patience is one of the main characteristics of a great manager. In his book "The Discovery of Patience - Perseverance Beats Talent" he describes the art *"of balancing a smaller reward in the present and a greater reward in the future and choosing the reward in the future"*. Also very interesting is that his studies showed that: *"everyone considers that success depends solely on intelligence or family background. Perseverance is at least as important. Perseverance and determination in pursuing goals can make up for initial disadvantages in IQ and family backgrounds."*

So be aware of your impatience and deal with it actively so that it can't control you. We'll talk later in the book about the average time it takes for a new hire to get to a leadership position in a large company. As we complied the necessary traits earlier and came up with an average, patience should rank highly within the table. The above-mentioned quote should serve as a clear indication to all those who cannot wait to be promoted. Patience is a virtue that develops through all three phases. Only those who can be patient camels and patient lions will eventually develop into the child phase and become a great leader.

"Ah, I knew nobles who lost their highest hope. And now they slandered all high hopes.

Now they lived insolently in short pleasures, and during the day they hardly threw goals.

"Spirit is also lust," they said. Then their spirit broke its wings: now it crawls around and soils in gnawing.

Once they thought to become heroes: Lascivious are they now. A grief and a horror is the hero to them.

But by my love and hope I beseech thee: cast not away the hero in thy soul! Hold sacred your highest hope!"

The Preachers of Death

"The earth is full of superfluous, life is spoiled by the many-too-many. May they be lured away from this life with the "eternal life"!"

We have seen before that Zarathustra is no friend of the "hereafter". He wants people to stay in the "here and now" and focus their energy on a higher good for themselves and others, rather than wasting energy preparing for a great hereafter. To focus on the afterlife is to strive towards death - the only way to reach the afterlife. Not in all religions, to be fair, Sadhguru and other yogis would disagree. For them it is very much about the focus on the afterlife. Living a good life now will award you a pleasant spot in the next one. Without heaven, all of your energy can focus on the here and now. And believe me, every joule of energy counts if you want to become a great manager.

Another important point to mention here is that Zarathustra makes a distinction between "preachers" and priests or religious people in general. He summarizes all people who solely focus on something supernatural, something that cannot be explained scientifically, as preachers (this will become clearer in the chapter "The New Idol"). Some use this chapter to categorize Nietzsche as a super atheist, but I strongly disagree. It is just not that simple.

Focusing on death is a waste of energy because you lose focus on life. Death is certain, but not the desired motivation or goal. I highly doubt that the average western company could motivate their employees with references to paradise after death. I mean, I'm hoping for at least 30 years between my retirement and leaving this world. That's a pretty long time between the end of work and death, to predict the end with a reasonably good probability. How could a company motivate you with the outlook of paradise when you always work as hard as you can? Think back to what the world was like 30 years ago.

So, the gist of this speech is that anyone who advises you to spend (or save) your energy for the afterlife is a preacher of death. There is a caveat: Not every religion focuses exclusively on the afterlife at the expense of the here and now, and even within Christianity there are subdivisions like Calvinism that need to be treated separately and not all lumped together. This is not a book about religion, but it would be interesting to discuss what makes a good religious leader and whether it is different from a normal manager in a company.

If we look at churches, especially in areas where they are not fully subsidized by the state (as in many Western countries) and therefore concerned about money, the issue becomes quite interesting. These religious institutions (be it a church, a mosque, a synagogue, or the sacred bowl of the flying spaghetti monster) must be managed and thus, by definition, run by managers. Most theological degree programs don't prepare the leaders to run a financially profitable business. For example, if you do a bachelor's degree in theology in Germany, the focus of your studies is on:

- ❖ Old Testament
- ❖ New Testament
- ❖ Church History
- ❖ Systematic theology: dogmatics and ethics
- ❖ Practical theology and religious education
- ❖ Religious Studies
- ❖ Judaic Studies
- ❖ Ecumenical Theology

Nothing in these studies would qualify you to run a multi-million-dollar company, although I am convinced that ethics are required to run a multi-million-dollar company. If you look at what a church is in this day and age, you might be surprised. Take, for example, the Evangelical Lutheran Church in Hanover, Germany. Like all regional churches, it is a corporation under public law. As of December 2020, the church had nearly 2.5 million members, making it the largest regional church in Germany. It administers 48 church districts, 12 church district associations, 58 parish associations, 1,248 parishes, 111 chapel congregations and 9 institutional congregations. What a large enterprise, and that is only one of twenty Protestant churches in tiny Germany. How many companies do you know that have 2.5 million members? Let's look at a larger example from the United States and take one of the largest, the Southern Baptist Convention (SBC). According to a census released in 2020, it has 47,530 churches and 14,525,579 members. It administers 1,161 local chapters and 42 state conventions, as well as fellowships covering all fifty states and territories of the United States. Through its Cooperative Program, Southern Baptists support thousands of missionaries in the United States and around the world. The SBC Executive Committee exercises authority and control over seminaries and other institutions owned by the Southern Baptist Convention, but neither the national convention, state conventions, nor local associations have any administrative or ecclesiastical control over local churches. Nevertheless, it is a huge organization, much larger than most corporations we know today, and a lot of money is involved.

Certainly, the members of a church cannot be compared to the employees of a business. They might be close to premium customers or something like that, but churches live off the donations of their members and therefore must have a pretty good sales plan. So, you would assume that these companies are run by well-educated MBA rockstar managers, right? That's not entirely true. Most church business leaders are theologians. In the Western world, there seems to be a lack of theological emphasis in current MBA programs, and this may inhibit graduates from applying for the manager positions in churches. This is an interesting milestone in the book.

The central pillars of my philosophy of work so far include:
- 1. Challenge drives Innovation
- 2. Don't speak to the Death
- 3. Explanations not Excuses
- 4. Be happy where you are
- 5. If you write, write in blood

These are not the main headings for the courses in an average MBA program. So, what do students learn in these courses to prepare them for leadership? The answer is simple, the technical tools. Nothing more. So, if you are an MBA student or graduate (as I am), from time to time recall the famous quote from Ygritte, while being led in chains by John Snow in Game of Thrones: "You know nothing John Snow". Theory alone does not prepare us for reality with its billions of complex ramifications. You don't come out of a degree program prepared to be the perfect manager, and anyone who thinks that is an idiot.

I have listed only five principles above, and the number may change over time. Don't worry, we won't even get close to the 300+ entries of Ray Dalio's - Principles, although his book definitely influenced my work philosophy. To learn from one of the most successful managers of all time is incredibly good for building your own work philosophy. But his principles came from what he learned through mistakes and experience.

The comparison between the managers of religious bodies and the average manager in large corporations seems quite different at first glance. But if you look more closely, success goes all back to principles that are not rooted in the economic realm of today's studies. It is not about your study or education in general, it is about what you learn on that journey. The religious institutions serve as an example that it does not matter how well you paid attention in school but that you are passionate about your task. You can run a huge organization without a degree from a leading business school and you can have the best degree and still be useless.

Grades in school cannot predict a natural leader. What is important is the feedback of the people who work under your influence. Understanding this is among the first steps that leaders must take. Don't get me wrong, I'm not saying that no religious leader has any sense of business, they most likely do (and some have attended fancy MBA programs). But their main focus on becoming these leaders was not triggered by economic studies, but by ethical or clerical ones. And yet they run much larger companies than the average manager in the corporate world. One could also argue about how successfully most churches are run today, considering that membership continues to shrink and huge scandals rock many, especially Catholic churches, but it's the same in our corporate world. But the corporate world just spins faster, and we see the effects of poor management directly as the focus is solely on making money. The green god is not so quick to forgive.

Summarizing the above points, I come to the clear conclusion that you can't learn to be a good manager in school. Focus on your people in the "here and now", have a clear work philosophy and stand to it. A clear call to recruiters worldwide to stop focusing only on educational background! Or as Elon Musk so beautifully put it: *"I hate when people confuse education with intelligence, you can have a bachelor's degree and still be an idiot."*

War and Warriors

"We do not want to be spared by our best enemies, nor by those whom we love from the bottom of our hearts. So let me tell you the truth![...]
You shall be such to me, whose eye is always looking for an enemy - for your enemy. And with some of you there is a hatred at first sight.
Your enemy you shall seek, your war you shall wage, and for your thoughts! And if your thought is defeated, your honesty shall still shout triumph over it!"

This is one of the most controversial chapters of his book. It is said to be one of the ideological roots for the militarized mindset of the Nazis in Germany or other cruel regimes. That the Nazis may have taken it up may be true and I don't want to challenge that. The Nazis misappropriated Darwin too, but that does not negate Darwin's insights. Parts of Nietzsche's text could be shouted by warriors marching into a hopeless battle in a dramatic Hollywood movie. However, all the analyses I found are superficial in equating "war" and "warrior" with the "warmonger" behind Nietzsche. Zarathustra is mentioning that warriors are there to follow. They can't by definition be super humans as they are not creators but followers. They are lions and cannot (yet) develop into the child stage.

"To a good man of war, "thou shalt" sounds more pleasant than "I will". And everything that is dear to you, you shall first be ordered to do."

As already mentioned in the book, the spirit of the lion is the fight against the golden dragon, on which is written "you shall" and this lion roars loudly "I will". Consequently, the warrior cannot be the ultimate goal, just as war is not the goal. Of course, it is different if you look at it from the warrior's perspective. War is the highest joy. And furthermore, it is not about winning, but about fighting. But Nietzsche is in no way promoting war or claiming that we should all become warriors. Quite the opposite - if you want to evolve toward being a superman, you can't be a warrior in war. Moreover, Nietzsche fundamentally rejects collectivist societies. So, all of society that blindly and bluntly follows a great leader are per se to be rejected in his world because they put individuals in the background and the masses in the foreground. I can't help but think of our society today, which subordinates the needs and rights of individual talents and initiative, to equalize success for all. In many schools in America, there can be no 100 m dash, because such an athletic race leads to winners and losers, and "as everybody knows, we are ALL winners." Perhaps if we proclaim this lie loudly and often, the dream will come true (but it won't).

What I would take away from this chapter is that if you are still in the "lion phase" of your mind, you most likely relate to the warrior. And if so, fight! Fight for everything you must carry before you can turn into a child. Fight for the education you need, fight for the job you want that will help you learn and build the skills of the future; fight for your fair share of everything you need. And don't be ashamed of fighting, be happy and proud of every experience you gain along the way. And be even more proud of the challenges that exist along the way. Overcoming enemies will give you the experience and joy that will inspire you on your way to even greater successes. Don't give up, find new ways and tricks to achieve your goals. Don't be afraid to deal with difficult people and situations, because it will enable your growth. But never forget, if you want to become truly great, you must transcend this stage.

I once had a phone conversation with my brother who was actively unhappy with his job. His supervisor, the CEO of a mid-sized real estate company, was an incredibly bad manager who was a year away from retirement and no longer cared about his employees. On the days he showed up at all, he hid in his office all day. He delegated all tasks, even if they were impossible for the employees. My brother wanted to leave the company. I listened to him for a long time, and when he finally stopped complaining, he asked me for advice.

I thought for a moment and then told him that this was a great thing, and I couldn't imagine a better environment for him to be in. He was a little irritated and asked me what the heck I meant. He was in no mood for jokes. But I was serious. His plan was to become CEO soon after the old boss retired. So, he was learning (the hard way) all the things to avoid when it was his turn. He learned that he needed to set clear goals, that he needed to have a vision. While he complained about his boss's lack of vision, he developed his own. He spoke with passion and evaluated why this idiot boss couldn't pull it off. Any employee who had experienced this disaster would have immediately followed my brother's inspiring call for change. He learned how to engage with his colleagues and control his temper during these difficult times. His time under this "enemy" helped him develop his personal and professional experience and demeanor faster and deeper than any management book or study ever could. The soon-arriving moment when my brother would get his turn, he could start with a fully committed, hungry team that already trusted him.

There's a saying that people don't leave the company, they leave the manager. And that's true, but most don't realize that bad managers are great teachers for the observant. It's also pretty easy to blame every mistake on a bad boss, or a bad environment. Take a critical look and ask yourself if it's really all your boss's fault. Society is changing to a "meaning-driven" society, where the meaning of things is more important than money. And if meaning is more important, you probably don't want to spend your time struggling in an environment you don't like. But that's where you learn the most.

Paraphrasing Churchill's famous quote, becoming a leader takes *"blood, toil, tears and sweat"* and is the result of *"many, many months or years of struggle and suffering."* I know I have twisted the quote to fit my argument, but he said these words within days of becoming British Prime Minister and forming an alliance of all parties to wage an existential war in defense of his country. He became this great leader through war, and he was right, it was through blood and pain. But it doesn't necessarily take a war to become a great leader. Gandhi, Martin Luther King, and many others are proof that you can become a great leader without violence. But the great achievements of Gandhi's "Satyagraha" - which means "active, non-violent pursuit of truth" - required intense tears and pain.

There is the famous quote, *"Hard times create strong men, strong men create good times, good times create weak men, and weak men create hard times"* from "Those Who Remain," a post-apocalyptic novel by G. Michael Hopf. Even though this phrase is not quite applicable in real world history and should be expanded to include women leaders, it is quite an interesting analogy for our first pillar - Challenge drives Innovation. In the example above, I know that my brother came out of these challenging situations stronger than ever. I remember countless managers I have seen in my professional career who went through very difficult situations, major and minor. And all of them who persevered, came out of them better and more professional than before.

Like the child above, who wants to rescue the cat in the tree and tinkers together a flying machine, we need to accept challenges as they might inspire us to really innovate ideas as pieces of our own philosophy of work. Once you get past the lion stage and are ready to evolve into a child, you need to leave the battlefield. You need to use what you learned in the early years of combat to create an environment that will be better. And that doesn't mean it's easy, but not every challenge needs to end in tears. The people who work for you need to recognize you for creating a challenging environment where they can run into the wall (safely). An engaging environment where you are all there to climb over the wall. A place where they feel free to ask for help. Where you have a keen sense of when that help is needed and how far you can push without becoming cruel. I know from personal experience that bad bosses really suck. And there are lines that no one should cross. Sexual harassment, bullying in any form, unfair treatment or violating laws especially labor laws are some. If a boss crosses those lines, you need to stop fighting and leave, because hopeless perseverance can cause psychological problems and do serious damage to your well-being.

I once had a manager who was really funny. We managed a really challenging project together but unfortunately, it didn't go as planned. Due to various errors, we were simply unable to achieve the overly high planned targets as an operational team. Instead of closing the gap as far as possible, he was busy expending all his energy looking for culprits and making up the best excuses for us. Of course, the higher management were more interested in results than excuses and increased the pressure. At some point, it became too much for him and he withdrew from work and left us hanging. A vicious downward spiral turned faster and faster. Unfortunately, he dragged down the management team below him - that is, my colleagues and me - and our reputation in the network suffered enormously. The worse it got, the more he vented his frustration on us during the few days he was there. This went so far that he plunged a great colleague into a deep crisis. She would only see her family on weekends, especially during our project. However, as the situation at work deteriorated, she had to spend more and more weekends at work as well. After a while this became a problem for her husband, who eventually gave her an ultimatum: come home the next weekend, or he would separate from her. She told our boss that she could not be here that weekend, and I agreed to cover for her. Even though things were under control, our boss ordered her back to work, out of spite. This was one of the low points I've had to witness in my career. The boss was fired a little later when additional similar cases became known. That was a year of pure pain at work and a torment for all colleagues. The question remains, how much shit are you willing to accept, and what will it cost you?

Challenge yourself about where that line is and don't give up too quickly. And if you are the one setting the challenges for your teams, make sure they know they can fail and safely learn from mistakes. They need to be happy where they are. Of course, in this context, that only works if you see challenges as something good that can make you happy. For us, it is first important to understand that the concept of challenge is fundamental for someone who wants to become a great leader. You have to challenge yourself and also your colleagues and employees to see them and rise above them.

"I spare you not, I love you from my very heart, my brother in war!"

The new Idol

"State? What is it? Come on! Now open your ears, for now I tell you my word of the death of nations.
The state is called the coldest of all cold monsters. Cold it also lies; and this lie creeps out of its mouth: "I, the state, am the people."
Lie it is! It was the creators who created the peoples and hung a faith and a love over them: thus they served life."

I find the phrase, "Too many cooks spoil the soup" to be very true, especially in the working world. Many companies advertise flat hierarchies and fast promotion opportunities. But these are just empty phrases that may only apply to small startups in the early stages or the lowest levels of more advanced companies, advancing from "Grunt" to "Senior grunt". Career progression that is too fast is almost always completely unhealthy and ultimately only shows that the company is unhealthily understaffed. It indicates that other mistakes have been made in management, or that employees have been hired at the wrong level.

In the phase in which one of my employers expanded our business vertically, many managers were needed for all the new and sometimes very small locations. Because of our high requirements for hiring, not all positions could be filled in time, so the company assigned stretch roles and promoted managers who had four to six months of company affiliation. Some of them were still in their probationary period, and it was not even clear whether they would be retained, because their performance had not yet been fully evaluated. The ability to relocate was the only criterion used for promotion decisions. Thus, management teams in the small locations were extremely young and inexperienced. In large locations we used "old hands" and experienced colleagues could still cover. These new managers were now left to their own devices, and they failed by the dozen. Disappointed, they left the company of their own accord or were dismissed. This, of course, fueled the hiring problem even further. High turnover in management reduces the commitment of the workforce, and we know what that produces. This is an example of a flat hierarchy.

Flat hierarchies are only okay if you have a very clear and specific vision, coupled with clearly outlined goals that all people understand and are committed to. Vague visions and overlapping or even competing goals (which is clearly the case in most established companies) cause flat hierarchies to fail. The times when companies succeed in this are exceedingly rare. Turning a great idea into a profitable business requires extremely smart, empathetic, and knowledgeable leaders who can motivate employees to the maximum and lead teams to success.

When Zarathustra talks about (or complains about) "the state" as the coldest monster, he does not mean the country or the political system itself, but the society that underlies it. Systems are built by the people who build them and currently govern them. Just like in a company.

In an average democratic state today, there are usually a few different parties representing the entire political spectrum from far right to far left and some specialties. The backbone of the system usually includes three powers, the legislative (lawmaking), the judicial (evaluating the laws), and the executive (executing the laws). Like many others, I would add a fourth power, the media (opinion forming). In combination, the parties and the powers represent (or at least should represent) the vast majority of people in a state. If they don't, the next election will remove them from power (through the electorate or internal systems). This system, that is, the representation of the masses, is the bone of contention of Zarathustra.

Returning to the Gaussian curve mentioned earlier, rule by the masses is not ideal because most people are clustered at the center of the distribution, and the center is not the place for the most intellectual or creative minds. (Think of a

Harvard educated leader on the campaign trail, talking about what he intends to do for "workin' folk" as if they have to dumb down their language to be relatable). Experts are the rare exception, and millions of people simply cannot be at the very top of any particular field.

The idea of a democratic system is that a smaller group represents the majority and finds the best possible way for the majority of people through active debate and compromise. But unfortunately, these representatives are usually chosen not for their skills, knowledge, empathy, or experience, but through the majority of voters' affiliation with a particular party. The opportunities for voters to vote for a particular candidate based on their qualifications are very rare and usually found only in the lower hierarchies of power. The likelihood that the brightest, most insightful, and most enthusiastic leaders will occupy positions of power within a government is quite low - although some shining stars do emerge from time to time. Similarly, in many companies, moving up the ladder is tied to belonging to a certain circle or falling favorably into a quota. They are not always officially elected, but many similar mechanisms play a role that we see today in Western democracies or democracy-like countries.

Democracy as we see it today is mostly not ideal democracy. The rule of the people - which is the definition of democracy - is mostly just lip service with voter turnouts below 50% or party bans, or generally democracies like the U.S., where the two parties now find themselves concerned only with the defeat of the other party and not the well-being of their constituents. While this worked very well for the last 225 years, with the increasing verbal radicalization on both sides, there are only two sides that are pushing each other up and no balancing center. Money is often more important than what the mass of people really want. And the third main power in states, the media is under heavy pressure by new technologies and instead of doing their work conscientiously and to report in a differentiated way. Likes and clicks have to be generated, and for that, unfortunately, every piece of trash is only welcome.

So should we make our companies more democratic? Flatten hierarchies and distribute authority and include more representative terms in the allocation of jobs? Let's check pure economic data, which should be the baseline for business decisions.

How many of the top 10 democratic countries (according to the Democracy Index published by the German Julius Maximilians University in Würzburg) are among the 10 best performing countries[13]?

I make a paragraph on purpose so that you have more time to think about it. The question is how many of the economically strongest countries are really democratic so that we can possibly deduce whether a "democratization" of our companies might be a good idea or whether Zarathustra's passionate rejection might make us think about it.

There is only one country - Germany - which managed to be among the Top10 most successful economies in the world and also be in the Top10 of the democratic index. Six of the countries are close but no full democracies.

---

[13] according to the GDP published by Statista in 2022

Rank	Country	GDP in Billion €	Democracy Rank
1	USA	19.443,70	36
2	China	14.994,60	172
3	Japan	4.174,70	25
4	Germany	3.570,70	5
5	Great Britain	2.694,60	17
6	India	2.683,20	85
7	France	2.483,70	19
8	Italy	1.775,50	22
9	Canada	1.683,20	24
10	South Korea	1.520,70	20
11	Russia	1.501,50	144
12	Brasil	1.360,40	75
13	Australia	1.304,40	13
14	Spain	1.205,10	11
15	Mexico	1.093,30	90

There are many such very interesting facts and if you really love data, I recommend the great book: Factfulness by Hans and Ola Rosling or the Freakonomics books by Steven D. Levitt and Stephen J. Dubner. These books will certainly change your view of the world around you.

So, democracy or more significantly, the power of the masses, is not tightly correlated with economic success.

Now, of course, the legitimate question arises whether economic strength should be the highest goal for us humans or our society at all. If we do the same analysis as above and use the value for happiness instead of GDP, the results are quite amazing. Apparently, the happiest people actually live in social democracies like Denmark or Sweden. But even this should not lead to statements like that of former German Chancellor Angela Merkel, who called democracy a system "without any alternative - that can't be questioned." She, as a scientist, should know that one should never state that something must be a certain way, without any possible exceptions. It may be that we have not yet found anything better than democracy, but it certainly does not guarantee economic success.

This book is not meant to get lost in the pros and cons of social systems, but the example is well suited to illustrate the two points made above. First, that corporations are not and should not be democracies, regardless of the opinions of those who would like to see it. And secondly, there is nothing that we as creators of new values should not question.

I'm pretty sure we can develop better versions of our systems. For example, as technologies like the blockchain mature, we no longer need a set of "electors" to vote for us, such as in the U.S. electoral college, or systems where people vote for a party, and the winning party elects a prime minister. The block chain technology is already at a development stage where we could use it to conduct a completely secret and absolutely secure election/ voting without the huge organizational effort of polling booths and Sunday as election day. We can simply use an online tool and cast our vote. By means of an app, important issues can easily be put to the vote. Direct democracy is currently considered unfeasible in large countries because of the high organizational effort and the associated costs. However, once you get to grips with the new technology available, you will know that this no longer has to be the case. We can manage a direct democracy like Switzerland even on a large scale like the US or the EU. Today's technology can open the gates to new forms of society, and it will do so no matter how hard some will try to keep those gates shut. In today's public discussion there is either democracy or dictatorship. Everything that is not democratic is automatically evil. The countries that scream the loudest are usually not in the top places on the democracy index. We must discuss together which options are available and desirable for our future society. Otherwise, they will come on their own and with an unplanned big bang sooner than we would like.

We need to be careful not to shut down discussion of this by arguing that something has no alternative. We need to constantly improve our society and never stop questioning our environment. And I wish more great leaders would stop spending their time on the capitalist treadmill and instead work together on how to create a better future for everyone on this planet. But unfortunately, many rather go into the corporate world as social engagement doesn't pay so well (for now).

Back to leadership. Our current democracy does not produce the best economic outcome, so I doubt that this is the leadership structure to strive for in business. But the extremely flat hierarchies I mentioned are just that - trying to bring democracy into a business. The idea of giving as many people as possible the opportunity to participate in decision making does not work for successful businesses.

According to Zarathustra, equally distributed decision-making makes no sense at all. The doers, or let's call them builders in this context, are usually a very small number of people. They are the natural leaders who should be running the company. These people are usually extremely intelligent and know how to build the best teams to succeed. They are insightful enough to understand the tradeoffs between difficult business decisions and employee engagement. They can do the right thing at the right time, balancing profits with the needs of their employees.

Can you list many leaders in your company who have mastered this balancing act? Probably not, because they are very rare. Unfortunately, I can't name a company where the highest ranks are filled exclusively with people who fit this description. I'm sure there are some, and I've met many great executives in the past. Especially in small start-ups where the quality of the managers has not yet been diluted by numbers. You cannot fit one or two managers into a normal distribution, but one of two could be brilliant. Eventually, as a company grows, the leaders will follow a normal distribution, with a few great leaders, a few horrible leaders, and a mass of average leaders. It is important to admit, free of any false democratic ideals, that there are only a few great managers and that these few should also fill the few top positions in the company. Unlike we are told at school, not everybody is a winner, and you can't "do anything…"

The only concern should be how to become one of them or support them as best as possible. How can you develop to the point where you would be considered for such a role? Keep in mind that the likelihood of being one of those 2% is …2%. If you want to be CEO of a large company three years after graduation, then start a startup, but don't expect to grow into such an important role in an established company that quickly. A company is not and should not be a democracy and therefore they need to earn their way up the ladder through performance, not getting there through good relationships or the use of media. A democracy is the game of winning the goodwill of the majority. That's what makes corporate democratization so dangerous. Managers will start to manage the perception of themselves by their colleagues rather than focusing their energy on doing the important tasks. This mechanism is best seen in election campaigns, where politicians and their parties make incredible promises every time and then fail to deliver on any of them. It's all smoke and mirrors.

Another controversial topic in this environment is quotas for leadership positions. Support equal opportunity but oppose mandatory quotas. And it doesn't matter which quotas. To me, they are all an attempt to turn a natural distribution into something that would rarely happen naturally. It's about the number of candidates in the pipeline and the time it takes for them to develop. For example, imagine a company with 100 potential candidates for CEO.

Assume that qualifications have nothing at all to do with race or gender. Now of these 100 candidates, 90 are white men, 9 are women, and one is a minority male. With talent following a normal distribution, the probability that the best candidate in terms of skills, intelligence or creativity would satisfy a gender or racial-based quota are 9% and 1%, respectively. Thus, quotas are based on values that place diversity over merit, and it is likely that there are benefits to advancing historically marginalized people into positions of power that go beyond traditional metrics. We need more than the impassioned visions of social activists to measure these metrics. Every person on this planet should have an equal opportunity to become what they want.

Forced quotas lead to an unnatural distribution that will lead to an unattractive environment because it is perceived as unfair.

I once attended a large conference at my former employer's corporate headquarters. The purpose of the conference was to summarize the strongest quarter in terms of sales and to draw lessons to prepare for the next peak season. The entire leadership team from all operational business units sat in this conference room and discussed key strategic issues. Among these sixty plus people, there was one woman present. I remember writing to our HR manager, who was attending the same session, via the internal chat tool that we had a really big problem. The two of us seemed to be the only ones who had noticed this outrageous lack of diversity.

A few years later, the same company, after actively pushing women into leadership positions, had significantly improved this ratio. But at what cost? There are many studies that show that quotas for women significantly increase the representation of women. But without any consideration of what is good for society, is it objectively good for a company? The colleagues I still talk to (equally male and female) agree. They are disappointed in the company and reject this policy outright.

There is an interesting article written by Angela Dorrough, Christa Nater & Monika Leszczyńska and published in 2019 in The Inquisitive Mind Blog in which they asked the question: *"What are the positive and negative side effects of gender quotas?"* While they too find that quotas for women increase general interest, they also hurt companies and teams, and especially women according to the research. Anybody pushed prematurely into a leadership position will suffer from internal self-doubt and external jealous hostility. Really meaningful specific analyses on the effect of quotas on companies are unfortunately unfinished or forbidden and the few that have been completed are supported by little data and a lot of anecdotes. That may change in the future, at which point I'll be willing to revise my opinion.

I recently read the book: "What men are never asked: I'll ask anyway" by Fränzi Kühne (currently not available in English) in which she advocates for women's quotas. As an entrepreneur, she recognizes the encroachment on her entrepreneurial freedom that quotas create, so she suggests that the quota system should be limited in time. This would certainly fulfill our principle of "Challenge Drives Innovation," and perhaps we could make it work. The problem is that it still requires people to prematurely advance people based solely on gender. Quotas have sparked passionate discussion and forced people to rethink. Again, time will tell if it was for the better and the positive effects make up for the opportunity cost of feeling unfairly treated or even create a significant economic advantage. I am curious about statistical evaluations in this regard.

The underrepresentation of women is a real problem for almost all companies. I personally know so many great women in management positions and many young talents who can absolutely compete with their male counterparts. Unfortunately, there are not enough of them in the business fields I work in, such as logistics, construction and energy. The most dominant reason is that these fields are simply not attracting enough women at the ground floor for them to move up the ladder. Shouldn't we work on making them more attractive to women rather than forcing companies to create an environment that is perceived as unfair? In the company mentioned above, a flight of top people has begun. Although there were other factors at play, this quota (which was never communicated internally or externally) has contributed to an ever-worsening work atmosphere with a perception of unfairness spreading like poison. Unmerited promotion decisions drive this feeling further and further.

In another study[14] from 2019, Edwin Ip, Andreas Leibbrandt, and Joseph Vecci examine the question of whether quotas improve or damage relationships between managers and their subordinates. They conclude: *"that both opinions about gender quotas and workplace behavior crucially depend on the workplace environment. In our survey, we observe that approval for gender quotas is low if women are not disadvantaged in the manager-selection process, regardless of whether there are gender differences in performance. Complementing this evidence, we observe in our experiments that quotas lead to lower effort levels and lower wages in such environments. By contrast, in environments in which women are disadvantaged in the selection process, we observe a higher approval of quotas as well as higher effort levels and higher wages."*

In other words, if the system is seen as fair to all from the beginning, quotas are seen as unnecessary, but if the system is seen as rigged against women, then quotas are seen as needed. So, the obvious answer is to ensure that the system is fair for all. Advancing women into leadership roles based only on their gender will not solve the problem, but firing the idiots who still favor men regardless of their merit will. Eliminate the rotten fruit on leadership teams and fill the positions with natural leaders who have a great mindset - that's the solution.

---

[14] Edwin Ip, Andreas Leibbrandt, Joseph Vecci (2019) How Do Gender Quotas Affect Workplace Relationships? Complementary Evidence from a Representative Survey and Labor Market Experiments. Management Science 66(2):805-822. https://doi.org/10.1287/mnsc.2018.3234

Quotas are the try to adjust a system to a defect. Instead of fixing the root cause and thus eliminating the defect (in that case the bad managers), we create another unfair environment (and thus again bad managers).

If your company is to the point where its managers provide a true, unbiased equal opportunity to all applicants who apply for a job, you don't need quotas for gender, race, or any other characteristic. What you need are programs that increase your company's diversity pipeline. I've attended over a thousand hiring interviews and debriefings, and I can only recall three or four instances where I heard biased feedback towards an applicant from another interviewer, and that was mainly based on age. I have sat on panels full of white men who comb through applicant resumes searching in earnest for diversity candidates. I have never witnessed systematic unfair treatment of applicants based on race or gender. I also haven't experienced any down leveling or something similar. And if you take the results of the study from Ip et. al., that means that companies are harming themselves with quotas.

We need more research to put these arguments on a more solid base. But for now, data suggests that quotas shift our companies from one dead end into another and diminish morale and initiative.

There are companies where bias reigns, and there are cultures where sexism and racism are an inherent part of culture and history. But in the countries, I have worked, unfair treatment always stems from bad managers sitting in positions of power that should not be theirs. These bad managers treat everyone badly.

In the companies I have worked for, there have been pay grades, and all applicants were placed in those grades based on their experience, education, and management style. All the statistics (and we are talking about quite large companies here, some of the largest employers in the world) clearly show that there are no systemic unfair pay differentials in these companies. Already in 2015 when I was working at Amazon, a gender pay gap study was conducted by an external labor economist who found that: *"[the] review of compensation including both base pay and stock compensation found that women earned 99.9 cents for every dollar that men earned in the same jobs. The survey covered Amazon workers at various levels of the company's organization in the United States."*

You can see similar statements in the other big companies like Google. All are working on it and as a manager hiring for Amazon for years and being part of the bar raiser program - a program for especially trained interviewers - I can only echo it. There might be other problems e.g., the so-called leveling, where employees are hired in lower job levels as they should be according to their experience, but further analysis needs to be done here.

I would attribute the positive change that has already happened primarily to the fact that a new generation is slowly taking over the running of the companies and making them fairer. I am confident that unfair treatment will soon be increasingly rejected. But quotas are antithetical to fairness and codifying them as a business practice will reinforce the unfair treatment we sought to abolish.

This book is also a call to fight unfair treatment by training our leaders and removing those idiots who still hire and promote with bias. Let's create an environment where everyone has an equal chance to apply for a job and the best candidate gets it. Stop hiring based on what is currently being proclaimed as "in" in the mass media. Only average-quality decisions will ever come out of average people. Strive to have the best possible candidates for the most important positions. We have learned that economic success and democracy do not correlate. So, stop trying to make decisions with the maximum participation of your employees. Never adjust your decisions so that they don't cause resistance because they please as many people as possible. If you're fully convinced it's the right decision, you've vetted it with your colleagues and backed it up with data, and you still know it's going to cause a shitstorm, then stand the hell by it! It's not those who shout the loudest who are right, but those who have the better arguments and data. And just because they are more doesn't mean they are right. We've already learned that intelligence is generally normally distributed, so the probability of the masses making smarter decisions is pretty low.

"They all want to go to the throne: it is their madness, - as if happiness would sit on the throne! Often the mud sits on the throne and often also the throne on the mud.

They are all madmen to me and climbing monkeys and overheaters. Their idol, the cold beast, smells bad to me: they smell bad to me all together, these idolaters.

My brothers, will you suffocate in the darkness of their mouths and desires! Rather break the windows and jump into the open air!"

The Flies in The Marketplace

"In the world, the best things are still good for nothing without one who first performs them: the people call these performers great men.
Little do the people understand the great, that is: the creative. But it makes sense for all performers and actors of great things.
The world revolves around the inventors of new values: invisibly it revolves. But the people and the fame revolve around the actors: that is the course of the world.
The actor has spirit, but little conscience of spirit. He always believes in that with which he makes believe most strongly, - makes believe in himself!"

How is it that so many bad managers so often get high positions in companies? The answer is quite simple. Because they don't have to put their energy into creating great things - like innovative products, processes or ideas. Instead, they can put all their energy into creating a fairy tale of themselves. This, of course, gives these people an incredibly competitive advantage over other employees who, in addition to working hard on people, the product or process, also have to work on selling their successes internally within the company.

Very often, management can't tell the difference between these two types of people, or it would take a lot of effort to really get to the bottom of their individual stories, and the people who promote them are "too busy" to investigate. Hiring or promotion decisions are often made by committees that include several people who don't know the person very well. Often, they haven't spent more than five minutes with the person. It takes incredibly good people skills to be able to discern in such brief conversations whether a person has earned the successes they portray or whether they are selling the hard work of others as their own. It's hard, but it can be done, and I recommend that every manager look for courses on how to conduct conversations properly. How do you distinguish between people I like to call "bubble-talkers" because they just produce big bubbles under a very thin layer, and the real creators who will be your top performers in the future?

But that is not the main topic of the chapter. A few questions that throw people off and create the first cracks in the facade are usually a good start. For example, if someone talks a lot about KPIs and throws numbers around, do a short statistical test with that candidate. Use for example the Monty Hall Problem or another statistical problem and give it to your candidate. It is not about knowing the answers, but actively working with you to find it. There are very entertaining tests available on the internet. They usually fit into five to ten minutes of the conversation. Also, during the interview, ask only one or two questions and then keep expanding on the topic and keep questioning the answers. One of the questions should be about how the person helped a colleague or a co-worker after finding that the person was disengaged or had difficulty getting back on track. From this, you can learn a lot about that person. But enough about interviews.

This chapter hones in on the chapter before. It goes from the overall view of a country to the much smaller view of a city (or more specifically, its marketplace).

On a larger scale, there is no difference between people's behaviors. Creators create value and users simply participate and benefit from what has been created. They consume. What is becoming clearer on a smaller scale, however, is that there is no longer a diffuse mass of people making life as difficult as possible for the creators of new value. Problems can be narrowed down to one or two people, they are no longer hidden behind statistics. The opinion of the mass is led by some who, driven by envy, lack of creativity or sheer stupidity, prefer to steal the achievements of others or try to look good through cheap imitations rather than working to achieve great results themselves. These people can also be smart and certainly consider themselves highly intelligent. They achieve great results for themselves with a very small expenditure of energy. But their skills are based on gaming the system for personal gain. They study people on how to manipulate them into thinking they are great, rather than focusing on **being** great. They get to the top much more easily than people who really put blood, sweat and tears into their work.

But here's the problem for them. These people eventually get into a role where real leadership is critical. They can no longer fake it, and since they cheated their way to the top, all they can do now is blame others for their inevitable failure. To be a natural leader, you have to have gone through the three metamorphoses of the mind and you can't skip levels! There are no cheats or hacks here to tunnel through the camel or lion stages in God Mode. Anyone who tries to cheat here is doomed to fail, because the staff has a pretty good sense of who has passed the natural leader test and who hasn't.

Let me give two more examples. We had a general manager in a fulfillment center leave his position for a new assignment. Since no successor had been hired, another manager stepped into his leadership role. The new interim manager created a huge upswing in engagement at all work levels and work culture and the facility became one of the best performing parts of the network. After a few months, it was clear to all of us that he was a great natural leader who had proven himself on the job.

But when it came time to announce the new leader, a woman with a mediocre track record was promoted from another site. Engagement immediately dropped, and no one understood the decision to replace a great manager with a poor one. As a result, the former interim manager left the company dissatisfied and the company lost one of its best natural leaders. A few years later, the same position was advertised again, and this time two managers, one female and one male, entered the race to become the new site manager. Both applied for the position through a normal application process. He passed it successfully, but she did not. One would naturally think he would get the job, but not in this case. Another external panel was quickly organized just for her, which she eventually passed, and as a result she was promoted to site manager.

What are the consequences of such actions? What does it say about fairness and equal treatment? How likely is it that this company will continue to attract the best talent? Of course, this became public through gossip and the damage to both candidates was obvious. The reputation of the new female site manager dropped to zero. If managers know that you were given your position unfairly, you will never be able to succeed. You will never be able to engage your team because they will never fully trust you. The company has put her in the worst position imaginable and is ensuring that she will fail regardless of her talent.

And that's true also the other way around and for all other quotas, not only for females. I have now also seen male colleagues promoted instead of women into departments with a high female share. I have seen underrepresented minorities were rejected as the team was already "full" and the hiring manager argued that also representatives of the white group need to be in the team.

A position of power comes with a lot of pressure. If you haven't learned everything you need to withstand that pressure along the way, if you haven't learned how to use the pressure relief valve, the kettle will explode.

It must be your true goal to fill your role as best you can. People's livelihoods, and even their whole well-being depends on you! And I mean that literally. When you lead people directly, their engagement depends on you as a leader. Their level of engagement affects their mood and therefore their personal life. If you make someone's job a living hell, you need to be aware that you are also destroying their personal life. Your behavior directly affects their well-being and mental health, their families, their children, and even the people around them.

But even if you don't directly supervise people, but, for example, "just" develop source code alone in a dark room, your work can have the same impact because the product or service depends on it, and so does the success of the company.

The success of the company directly affects the mood of the leadership and shareholders, and the cycle starts all over again. Every little cog in the gearbox counts and collectively, has a huge impact on people. Be aware that every action results in a reaction. Managers who's only skills are self-promotion are a serious threat to any company. As a great manager, you need to identify them quickly and make sure they can't do any further damage. You must get rid of the parasites. They suck out the energy of your teams and the money of your company. And more importantly, if you find that YOU don't fit in, get yourself out of the way. Your job is to remove obstacles for your teams, even if you are the obstacle. A great leader must always consider the possibility that they could be wrong, and if you are wrong, don't double down to make it worse. I know this is a difficult thing to do because we usually don't realize when we are the problem. If you don't create a trusting environment, employees won't dare give you constructive feedback, and so you can't know that you're not doing well. Do you think any of Putin's advisors ever tell him the truth?

In many companies, there is no systematic appraisal process for employees, so they can't be calibrated and compared to their peers. In my experience, the leadership virtue I find most lacking in the managers I've met is self-reflection. They can't accept feedback and don't critically reflect on themselves. This prevents them from recognizing that they are causing harm to those around them, or at least preventing them from progressing. They will never get beyond the camel or lion stage, because the heaviest burden one can take on is awareness of one's own weaknesses. This takes time, but it's up to you, and the sooner you start, the better. And self-reflection should never stop.

After determining who is adding value and who is not, you must act. Marginalize the people who are not adding value and minimize the damage they can do.

What if you determine that **you** are the problem? You may have taken on a task that is just too big. Perhaps the team you assembled is not performing. It may be that your company is going through a realignment and then you're just not in the right place. This is always possible and says nothing about your intelligence or positive abilities.

If you have made it this far in this book, you are intelligent enough to perform a variety of jobs offered in your country. Your interest in leadership suggests that you are already in or on the verge of assuming a leadership role. Therefore, it is also very likely that you have experienced parasitic bosses, and personal failures. There are enough jobs for you around the world, there is absolutely no reason to stay in a role where you are not adding value. You are smart enough to find something that suits you better. Don't become an obstacle, and if you do become one, remove yourself. Care for a quick example?

As I write this, I find myself in a similar situation. The company I work for was thriving during the Covid pandemic. They had bright forecasts and a great outlook. We were hiring to handle the growing business and build the launch pad for future scaling. I was in the process of successfully building and ramping up a line of business in a newly developed country and was close to completing the task. I had already hired my successor and began to train him. But then the pandemic ended and another macroeconomic shock hit - the war between Russia and Ukraine. Customer demand plummeted, and to save the company we had to lay off employees and impose a hiring freeze. The exciting new projects I was aiming for were postponed or canceled, and I was asked to stay in my role. And there we were, my successor and I.... redundant and not sure what to do.

He's a great manager, and there wasn't a single moment when I thought about letting him go. When I looked closely at the requirements of the job and the needs of the company, I realized that I would become an obstacle once my successor was trained. With no development opportunities in sight, my only logical decision was to quit my job and seek a new opportunity outside the company. Of course, I could have stayed and fired my successor instead, but what would that say about me? Could I still be happy in the position if I stayed? I changed my status on one of the major job networks to "Open for offers" and it only took a few days before I had some interesting offers in my inbox. I didn't hesitate for long and chose the one that sounded the most interesting. The rest is history.

At least at this time, there is plenty of work for people who want it and are flexible. So if you find that you are becoming an obstacle, get yourself out of that situation. And that doesn't necessarily mean quitting your job or leaving the company. It's usually easy to find a new internal position where you can contribute if you're smart and the company values you for it.

Good managers know how to handle these situations, and the company certainly doesn't want to lose great talent.

Parting with people often sounds tough, but parting with people doesn't mean firing them. Very few people come into a workplace to intentionally harm the company they work for, and when they do, it's usually because of a long history of mutual failure and poor management. You need to understand the superpowers that lie dormant in everyone, regardless of their intellect, age or other characteristics. There is an area of destiny for everyone, it is your job to find it and unleash its power. It sounds like a tired cliché, I know… but it is a pure and simple return-on-investment calculation. Remembering that time equals money, you must ensure that the time you invest in a person is worth the expected outcome. And if that investment is not worth it, you should support them in finding a job that is a better fit for that person.

I know this is challenging, but again, challenges drive innovation. In this case, the innovation involves your personal experience of managing people. If you can't part ways with someone, you are not a leader because this is an essential part of the business.

Managing bad employees is tough, but also something you can feel good about as it strengthens your skills (unless you are usually responsible for hiring them, in which case you should take another critical look at yourself.) Firing somebody is usually difficult for both parties. A good manager is empathetic, and when they have to let someone go, they fully understand the consequences to that human being and their entire family. I have rarely seen people enjoy this task. I have seen many people handle these difficult decisions with grace and skill. They were empathetic when talking to people and went out of their way to make the experience as easy and flawless as possible.

I had a manager whose performance fluctuated wildly. Some days he delivered the best results of his peer group while other days he didn't meet the minimum goals. I had several conversations with him to find the cause. We discovered that the cause was private and had nothing to do with work. Work was the most stable and important thing in his life. He had come from the United States and stayed as an expat, with no close friends or family here to support him. As he realized how important his work was to him, he became afraid of losing the job. Even though he knew that his performance was sporadic, this anxiety fed a vicious cycle that was hurting him and would get worse in the future.

He needed to come clean with himself, and that's not something I could help him with. Although I have a lot of experience with these issues, I'm not a psychologist. I knew that I couldn't fix something this complex without formal training. Real damage can be done by taking a layman's perspective where a professional is needed (I wouldn't remove his appendix either). To go back to the ROI point of view: This would not have been something I could have resolved within a reasonable time frame, and so we had to find a solution to end our professional relationship. However, I knew that as a foreigner, he would likely lose his visa to stay in the country, with disastrous consequences for him. In our next conversation, I spoke openly and honestly with him about this and asked him to work with me to develop a plan. He told me that he could get permanent residency in a few months and that helping him with this would relieve his fear of, which would at least reduce his greatest anxiety. At the next interview, I offered him an agreement between us that would cover the time it would take him to obtain his residency status, and in return, we developed a work plan for the meantime.

I asked him what his biggest dreams were, and he named a few. He wanted to see the Northern Lights for example. We agreed that he would have to accomplish several of them in the next six months and that I would give him the time to do so. Since he needed to come clean with himself, we agreed that he needed to accomplish two of them and then he would walk the Camino de Santiago: A 547-mile (880 km) pilgrimage route that you can take from different starting points to reach the supposed tomb of the Apostle James in Santiago de Compostela in Galicia (Spain). This time alone would help him to find his inner self.

He was amazed by all the time I took and the work I invested in him. He agreed and we had a deal. I kept my promise and followed up with him to see if he was achieving his goals. We kept in touch, and when the time finally came for him to begin the pilgrimage, I knew it would be one of the most difficult challenges of his life, and I wasn't sure he would make it. But I was sure that if he could do it, his life would change. He kept sending me videos of the course, and at times, I had tears in my eyes watching him celebrate his successes along the way, screaming and crying about the pain he was feeling. I saw and felt the energy building inside him with each extra mile. When he reached the finish line, he told me he felt like he could accomplish anything in his life now. We parted ways and he went on to find a new job with renewed energy.

You might ask why I put so much time into an employee I wanted to part with anyway. I knew that breaking up with him was the best thing for him to do to get his personal life in order and make him successful for the rest of his life. I wasn't forced to do it but it's our responsibility to invest in the people who work for us, especially if the relationship ends in a breakup.

Now while we have been talking about people who are worth investing time in, we must talk about a special group of people as well, bringing us full circle to Zarathustra's speech. Let's call them bootlickers. People who buzz around you like flies in the marketplace, telling you day in and day out how great you are. People whose greatest contribution is to bask in your light and highlight your contributions and successes. For some reason, many senior managers develop a need for these people around them. You see this everywhere in society, not just at work.

There's a wise saying that goes, *"Those who flatter you have either cheated you or hope to."* Keep them at arm's length. Be attentive and attentive again. If these people start buzzing around you, it's a clear sign that you're doing something wrong. They may sense that you reward flattery.

If people feel they can't give you honest feedback, two things will happen. First, the good people will leave you and the gap will be filled by the lower performers. As a result, engagement will drop, and so will productivity and quality. Then the remaining sycophants will adapt and praise your every move, leaving reality behind. This can be observed for example in autocratically run countries. The population is starving and/ or there is corruption and mismanagement, but the leaders don't see it. This is because they are surrounded by low performers who constantly tell them how great they are and how well they run their country.

Niccolò Machiavelli once said, *"There is no other means of protecting ourselves from flatterers than to show that no one insults us by telling us the truth."*

If you build and maintain a trusting environment, people will feel comfortable telling you even painful truths. Then you are on the right track. Once you are aware of a painful truth, you must make a serious effort to resolve it. So again, if you are surrounded by sycophants, you are in a big mess, and this mess is your fault. You must correct this flaw as soon as possible. Don't get me wrong, positive feedback is fine, as long as it is honest, and you don't demand it or reward it. But as soon as the feedback is no longer about WHAT and HOW, but only about WHO, you need to draw a line and have a serious discussion with yourself.

"What we recognize in a person, we also ignite in him. So beware of the little ones!

Before you they feel small, and their lowliness glows and glows against you in invisible revenge.

Did you not notice how often they became mute when you came to them, and how their strength went from them like the smoke from a dying fire?

Yes, my friend, you are the evil conscience of your neighbors: for they are unworthy of you. So they hate you and would like to suck your blood.

Your neighbors will always be poisonous flies; that which is great in you - that itself must make them more poisonous and ever more fly-like.

Flee, my friend, to thy solitude and where a rough, strong air blows. It is not your lot to be a fly's wing."

Chastity

"And look at these men: their eyes say it-they know nothing better on earth than to lie with a woman.

Mud is on the bottom of their soul; and woe, if their mud even has spirit!

That you would at least be perfect as animals! But innocence belongs to the animal.

Do I advise you to kill your senses? I advise you of the innocence of the senses.

Do I advise you to chastity? Chastity is a virtue for some, but almost a vice for many."

Although chastity is not really part of what we are examining in this book, there are nevertheless two very important points in this speech. First, lust - as the opposite of chastity - is just a synonym for virtues that are demonized by society and thus declared bad. Second, one cannot simply acquire values that are not inherent in one's nature and live them out.

Zarathustra takes up the first point and advises not to blindly embrace or reject the virtues imposed upon us by the current environment, or society in general. This applies to both current trends about socially "correct" views and to virtues that have evolved over a longtime. For example, in many cultures, the mother is the one who stays home with the children once they are born, and the father goes off and earns the money. A stay-at-home father is unusual, and many people would disrespect this man, even more so 20 years ago than today. But anomalies of the past can become the norms of the future. Chastity is another good example. Back in Nietzsche's days, chastity was a defining virtue. Today, talking about chastity seems quaint, and out of touch with society. The point is that it doesn't matter which virtue you look at, at some point in the past or in the future, society's view of it was or will be the complete opposite. So, you are free to challenge it and question the status quo. Maybe your view and challenge build the future. Of course, your view could be absolutely wrong, and the risks you take in fighting consensus should be linked to the confidence that you have that you are right. If you know you are right, fight like hell. But be prepared to suffer if you are wrong. Before you go down in flames for your beliefs, make sure you are not just a fool who is wrong.

Another good example is punctuality. Why is this so important? In my opinion (and yes, I'm German, I can't help myself) it shows that you respect the time of your colleagues and stakeholders, but it's even more important for your employees. If you don't value their time, you clearly show them your contempt for them or at least that their time is less valuable than your time. That can destroy any good working relationship. However, in some environments, punctuality is not so important. For example, if you are invited to a party that starts "sometime around 7-ish", showing up exactly at 7 could even be perceived as rude, especially in some cultures.

This comes back to the mantra: Challenge drives innovation! Question everything! Challenge virtues that are considered true by everyone around you. You might think that there are fundamental and eternal truths. For example, perhaps you think that division by 0 is not possible, and it will be forever. Well, I have to disappoint you. Someone came up with the wheel-theory and poof, division by 0 is possible after all.

Fortunately, someone heard that this problem was unsolvable and had the courage to take on the challenge. Without this kind of challenge, our society would slowly perish. Stagnation is death. This is how science works. Unlike what most people think, science is not primarily about "facts". Science deals with challenging hypotheses. Tested explanations of observations develop into theories, but theories never become facts. Even the theory of gravity remains a theory. Any scientist who could disprove Darwin's theory of evolution through natural selection would skyrocket to fame and prominence, become the founder of a new paradigm, and the target of new challenges.

The topic of challenging the status quo becomes especially important when it comes to hiring decisions. Over my career, I have always invested time in underperforming managers, but only to a point. Having a clear Performance Improvement Plan (PIP) for someone who is underperforming is important to maintain the right balance in terms of return on your time investment. Under pressure from a continuing spiral of labor shortages, especially in leadership positions, more and more companies are relaxing their standards because they are desperate. And I'm not talking here about companies that hire and promote unqualified friends or relatives. Those are just pathetic. I am talking about good companies that make questionable promotion and hiring decisions based on short-term needs that won't help companies in the long run.

It seems to be generally accepted that everyone has value and can be used properly if managed properly. There are no bad employees, you just have to develop them well enough. In other words, it's not the subordinate's fault, it's the managers. From my point of view, this is wrong. Let's face it, some people are stupid, and others are lazy, or dishonest. People have clear limitations in terms of IQ and EQ that prevent them from being successful. The company I work for should have a clear goal to be as successful as possible, and therefore needs the best employees to work together to strive to achieve the highest possible goals. If I spend most of my time on underperforming managers, I can't support the great innovators from doing what they should be doing: investing every minute at work in creative ideas, challenging the status quo, and inventing products that customers need. Time is fixed, so that time given to one person cannot be given to another. Wasting time harms the company or - if you take this idea further and apply it to a medical technology company, for example - I'm endangering the health of many people. It is therefore urgently necessary to manage bad employees within clear limits so that it quickly becomes clear whether the employee has a chance or not. This process should always be well documented so that it is clear for both sides what is happening.

Assigning an underperforming person to a PIP with:
- a clear timeframe (usually till the next review cycle but not more than six months)
- well defined goals and deliverables that the person can commit to
- in a clearly defined work environment
- and most important: with the clear message that failing the deliverables of this plan will result in this person losing the assignment to the project / task / job.

Companies go to great lengths to hire the brightest minds and the best talent to ensure that the IQ and sometimes already EQ of their leaders is on the right side of the bell curve. However, hiring great people is not enough. You also need to make sure that your leadership population stays there, or better yet, develops even more toward the bright side of the curve. If your company is small, it is quite possible to hire 3 brilliant managers to run it. But in a large company with 1000 managers, you will have a normal distribution of talent among them, with some on the wrong side of the bell curve, and most of them close to the average. You need to develop a strategy to develop, promote and retain the good managers and find other roles for the underperformers or remove them from the company. The bell curve is not the only possible distribution. What you want is a distribution of talents that is skewed to the right, with a short-left tail, and a long right one.

Everyone has something they are good at, but not always in the value chain of a profitable business. This was common sense a few years ago, but seems to be quite controversial today, in a society that claims that we are all winners (at everything). Regardless of the current fads in pop psychology, I would rather work according to what I know, than follow an agenda-driven approach where the agenda is set by people with no experience in business, with no skin in the game. For the most part, the architects of a social utopia have never had to make hard business decisions and sit through them to avoid greater impact on even more people. So, if your values are different from the current mainstream in terms of hiring decisions, that's good. It's up to you to build your team according to your vision.

The second issue, the adoption of values that are not one's own, can also have a huge impact on us. People who have to contort themselves to meet the demands of their jobs are pre-programmed to fail from two directions. First, you will fall into a behavior of hiding something and pretending you are not, destroying yourself from the inside out. Your mental health will suffer and so will your physical health. Secondly, the people around you usually know your behavior and will always feel that there is something wrong with you. They will never trust you completely. And since we know how important trust is, there is nothing to discuss here. Don't take on values that you can't represent. If the company you work for has values you can't represent, try to change them, and if that doesn't work, leave the company. If your company has not defined any values according to which it works, well, maybe you should discuss this with your reporting line and come up with a great white paper on why this is important and suggest some.

"You have too cruel eyes for me and look lustfully at sufferers. Has not only your lust disguised itself and called itself compassion?

And also this parable I give you: not a few, who wanted to cast out their devil, thereby drove themselves into the swine.

If chastity is difficult for you, you should be advised against it, so that it does not become the way to hell, which is mud and heat for the soul."

Let us discuss chastity again as a synonym for any virtue that is not inherent in one by nature. A sort of way to deny yourself something you really want. Nietzsche takes aim at chastity at the Catholic society of his time. In the Old Catholic Church (in Switzerland Christ Catholic Church, in the Netherlands Oud-Katholieke Kerk, refers to the community of independent Catholic churches, some of which are united in the Union of Utrecht) for example, clergy have generally been exempt from celibacy since 1878. The Church has made the life of chastity basically optional, and a large proportion of its clergy have openly stated that they will, of course, continue to live in chastity. I'm pretty sure Nietzsche added this chapter as a kind of reaction to their grandiose proclamations. He tells them pretty clearly what he thinks of the cocky announcements of the clergy. Celibacy is a self-imposed burden that he assumes the very fewest clergymen will ever keep. It is simply lip service. However, the late 19th century was also a difficult time for the "managers" of the Church at the time (as it is today). An eternally solid corporate value changes and all of a sudden, the managers are free to stick to it or not. There is no clear direction and employees are left hanging in the air. How are they supposed to make the right decisions? A blatant conflict of loyalty arises and many clergy are certainly torn apart inside. They are supposed to be role models for their members, and of course, despite the voluntary nature of their work, they are supposed to think very carefully about whether they want to violate celibacy or not. Terrible situation and Nietzsche's criticism is understandable.

When I think about it and adapt this internal conflict to today, it still holds true. There are companies that put their employees in situations that are extremely difficult to resolve. For example, the company requires that all managers comply with the law. What company does not require this? But if there are, for example, specifications for working hours, then the company already expects that you work significantly more than legally permitted. If a leader does not adhere to these requirements, the employees will not adhere to them either.

I once had a colleague who managed a location in North America. He took almost no vacation a year and spent at least twelve hours a day at work, six days a week. If he doesn't have a problem with that, you would think, then let him do it. However, an evaluation of the working hours in his location showed that his subordinates and their employees also worked significantly longer hours than the average and also took significantly less vacation. The sickness rate in this location was also significantly higher and the turnover of employees far above the normal average.

I have had conversations with managers who have told me that they just can't handle some of their responsibilities in working with people. Firing someone or having difficult conversations, making tough business decisions or just witnessing tragic stories is not for everyone. I have been in so many situations, big and small, where I've had to stop for a moment to digest what just happened and consider if this pain is worth the money I'm getting for the job. The most difficult situation I have had so far took place on March 22, 2016. I was on a business trip from Berlin to Birmingham via Brussels. I was frequently traveling for my company at the time. The airport in Brussels is built like a big "U", and when transferring between flights, I usually had to go from one side to the other. As I walked to my gate, a sudden bang interrupted my thoughts. Part of a storefront had fallen to the floor, and I assumed a gas cylinder had exploded inside. Most likely an accident I thought. But a few seconds later a sound like a machine gun rang out.

As I write these words, years later, I can still feel the adrenaline of this moment.

Suddenly, another explosion, people started screaming and running. I saw them trip over a baby carriage, toppling the mother and baby to the ground. It was crazy! I just stood there and watched and thought about what I should do. I tried to remember the armed assailant training at work, a training that you usually just click through because you never think something like this could happen to you. I tried to stay calm and not panic, helping people who had fallen or couldn't move. After a few minutes, everything calmed down. No one knew what had happened. I decided to proceed to my terminal. Then a special forces commando came running and yelled at me to drop my bag and run to an evacuation point. Apparently, things were really serious, and I did what they told me. I found myself on the tarmac under the wings of an Israeli plane with people sitting inside looking at what was happening outside. You could see the fear in their eyes. The cellular connection was unstable, so I couldn't check the Internet to see what had happened. There was no communication anywhere. The whole situation was surreal.

We were then evacuated to a maintenance hangar and eventually went to the assembly points outside the airport. I looked at the airport entrance and didn't know what to say. The glass front had been totally destroyed. Snipers had taken up posts on the roof and the military was everywhere. It was the Brussels airport bombings, and I was in the middle of it.

After finding out that this had been a terrorist bombing, I tried to figure out what to do next. Fortunately, my partner at the time had relatives in the small village near the airport, and her cousin came to pick me up. I was going to drive to the center of Brussels and get a rental car, since it was clear that there would be no flights leaving Brussels that day. But there were more bombings in the city center as well and everything was closed. Thanks to my partner's cousin who drove me to another nearby city, I got one of the last available rental cars. I drove the car to my company's European headquarters in Luxembourg, and on the way there I turned on the radio and listened to the latest news. After I had been driving from Belgium to Luxembourg for a while, a column of armored vehicles passed by on the other side of the road and headed toward Brussels. I can proudly say that I stayed cool, even at the airport, but the sight of those tank-like trucks driving at high speed to where I had just been flipped a switch. I got goosebumps all over my body, and I had to stop the car, get out, and take a deep breath.

These were suicide bombings. Two terrorists blew themselves up around 8 a.m., 10 to 15 seconds apart at the entrance to the airport and another in the center of Brussels at the Maalbeek metro station. The glass front of the hall shattered, and parts of the hall ceiling collapsed. An AK-47 assault rifle and a third bomb that had not detonated were later found at the explosion site. This third bomb was defused. According to official figures, 32 people from 22 countries were killed, including three of the attackers. More than 300 people were injured.

Enduring terrorist attacks was not in my job description. And since then, I try to avoid traveling, at least for professional reasons. But if you're applying for a job that requires a lot of job-related travel, that's a risk you're exposing yourself to. Although terrorist attacks are still unusual, travel is always statistically riskier than remaining exclusively on-site. If you can't handle that, you shouldn't choose a job with those kinds of demands. I know this is a very rare extreme, but when I think back over the last 10 years working with people, I can't even count the occasions I've had to deal with serious situations like suicides, natural deaths in a building, work-related deaths, and fatal accidents on the way to work, just to name the most serious. I have had to work with police, co-workers and supervisors, and the media or outside parties (such as families on occasion). You may not be prepared for this when you start a job. Few people are until such an event occurs for the first time. If you know you can't handle human drama, you shouldn't apply for a job where the main job is managing people. To get through such things, it is important that you can dedicate yourself to work for the company that puts you through this kind of strain. That it lives and demands the same values from its managers and employees that you would demand for yourself. Only then can you carry these heavy responsibilities.

The company I was working for at the time had a global security operations center (GSOC) and not 15 minutes after the first bomb went off I got a call. They were inquiring about the situation on the ground and how they could best help me. I was taken care of all the way through, even as I arrived at the headquarters without my suitcase. They provided me with a new work laptop, and I was allowed to completely change my clothes. My management team took the time to take me out to dinner and organized a hotel and the flight back to my family. I felt so cared for and valued by the company as they demonstrated that they stood by their values. I am still impressed today. Although the story ended smoothly for me, it became a touchstone for whether I wanted to stay in this job. I was highly engaged and knew I had to take care of this company as much as they had taken care of me. I loved working for this company. You always have to ask yourself, "Do I love what I do? Am I happy where I am?"

If you don't like children, don't become a kindergarten teacher! Even if this is the only job you can get, it will do serious damage to your mental health. You won't be engaged, and the children who depend on you will be harmed.

Rather, spend as much time as possible finding your destiny area where the work environment suits you and where you feel comfortable with your responsibilities. I love the extremely challenging environments found in startups or struggling companies where you can achieve great things by working with people. The key to success for new or struggling companies is usually to focus on the people first. You have to build and develop a great team and get them to either create something great or rebuild something that's broken. In both cases, you have to keep people focused even in very difficult times and work with them to develop a great mindset that goes along with the vision of the company - that's my superpower. But it's extremely time-consuming and demanding. It's an environment that a lot of people don't want to be in, and that's fine. It's very important to define for yourself where you want to be and how committed you are. When you are in your destiny area, everything seems to come naturally and easily. The virtues are in harmony, and you don't have to bend like Zarathustra accuses the priests of doing.

"Truly, there are chaste people from the bottom of their hearts: they are milder of heart, they laugh more gladly and more abundantly than you.
They also laugh at chastity and ask: "What is chastity?

Is not chastity foolishness? But this thoroughness came to us and not we to it. We offered this guest shelter and heart: now he lives with us,-may he stay as long as he wants!"

The Friend

"Our faith in Andre betrays what we would like to believe in ourselves. Our longing for a friend is our betrayer.

And often one only wants to leap over envy with love. And often one attacks and makes an enemy in order to hide the fact that one is vulnerable.

"Be at least my enemy!"-so speaks the true reverence that dare not ask for friendship.

If one wants to have a friend, one must also want to wage war for him: and to wage war, one must be able to be an enemy.

One should still honor the enemy in his friend. Can you get close to your friend without going over to him?"

The concept of a friend is essential for Zarathustra. People should support each other. From earlier speeches we know that he is an enemy of collectivism and therefore does not think that support will ever come from the masses. The support you need comes from individuals. You may get applause from the masses, but not the support you need on the rocky path to great leadership. You need one or a few real friends.

In front of a friend, you can be free. You can be yourself, without hiding anything, no matter what society might think of you. A true friend is a concept outside of the moral construct that today's society prefers. You don't have to be politically guarded, and you can discuss and test ideas that a wider or anonymous audience would completely tear apart before adjusting them based on the discussions.

The friend(s) should be recruited from a very close circle and from a group that you can provide mutual benefits. The friend(s) should be able to challenge you intellectually and emotionally, and more importantly, this person should be a sparring partner who is able and willing to push you hard. This definition already excludes work-related relationships. I strongly recommend not looking for friends (as defined above) at work for two main reasons:

First, there is often a disciplinary relationship at work that makes friendship impossible. If you are dependent on someone higher up in the hierarchy, or someone who is dependent on you because you are higher up, there will always be a block (perhaps only subconscious) that prevents you from "being fully yourself." And don't forget that with colleagues there is always the possibility that one will be promoted and become the superior of the other. Let's say you have some kind of addiction, alcohol or drugs. Would you discuss this with someone who could become your supervisor next year? Someone who would eventually have to write your evaluation and make important decisions about your growth potential? This person would be biased toward your potential promotion, keeping in mind that your addiction could negatively impact your performance. When Zarathustra talks about friends, he means someone with whom you can share everything without hesitation. I'm not saying that if you have an addiction, for example, you should keep it a secret. On the contrary, you should get help as soon as possible from discrete sources outside of work. Hopefully you also have a real friend who can help you. Even if it is just to relieve you from some pain by "just" talking.

Secondly, you need to make sure that you can take time off from work for some time during the day. You need to recharge your battery so that you can be at full capacity when you get back to work. When Albert Einstein once mentioned that you only need four hours of sleep per day, he might have been right. But you still need time off work - even if it is only some hours where you can relax. If all your friends are at work, you won't be able to do that, because even if you and your work friend kick back and relax at the pub after work, your small talk, your gossip will always come back to work. Inevitably, if you spend your time at work as well as your free time together, what the heck would you talk about but work? You need a safe space where you can talk about the bad things at work and be sure that they are not shared with other colleagues on secret channels. You would also like to voice your thoughts about leaving the workplace or department and get an unbiased response, which you most likely won't get if the person you are talking to has some sort of agenda of their own for their work environment.

The "friend" described by Zarathustra is a person who would most likely not fit our current description of a friend. Social media gives us the idea of a kind of mass fraternization. Every follower is a friend. We add people to our virtual networks, and they all become friends. At work, we are all friends and one happy family. The inflationary use of the word "friend" dilutes the real meaning and gradually makes the concept disappear into meaninglessness. The British anthropologist Robin Dunbar found in a study[15] a correlation between primate brain size and average social group size. He concluded that human beings are able to maintain about 150 connections at once, which includes a group of around five close friends, followed by circles of more casual friends.

Today's working world demands a high degree of flexibility from its managers, especially in terms of local relocatability. Moving from one place or country to another over a period of years leaves little time for real friends. And friendship takes time, dedication and some expectation of permanence.

Friendship also says a lot about you. As Zarathustra mentions in his speech:

"Art thou a slave? Then thou canst not be a friend. Art thou a tyrant? Then thou canst not have friends."

---

[15] R.I.M. Dunbar, Neocortex size as a constraint on group size in primates, Journal of Human Evolution, Volume 22, Issue 6, 1992,

I love this quote because it really says a lot about a person. Life as a bully is lonely, that's for sure. If no one wants to be your friend and the only people around you are sycophants, it's usually because you can't accept honest feedback, nor are you willing to invest time or listen. As mentioned earlier in the book, when the sycophants start buzzing around you it's definitely time to make a change.

Many people make friends at work because work is such an important area of life. It's easy to declare that the people around you all day at work are friends too. But there is a difference between being friendly at work, and having true friends that you can be honest with, and count on. Zarathustra complicates things by adding that there can be no opposite-sex friendship. Oscar Wilde agrees when he says, *"No friendship is possible between men and women. There is passion, enmity, adoration, love, but no friendship."*

In reality, neither are exactly right. Friendship is possible between a woman and a man, but not between a man and a woman (although here we are talking only about heterosexuals, and even here there are exceptions). A 2012 study by April Bleske-Rechek of the University of Wisconsin-Eau Claire and others published in the Journal of Social and Personal Relationships found that there are large gender differences in how men and women experience opposite-sex friendships. Men were much more attracted to their female friends than vice versa. Men were also more likely than women to believe that their opposite-sex friends were attracted to them. Men assumed that any romantic attraction they felt was mutual and were blind to the actual level of romantic interest of their female friends. Women were also blind to the mindset of their opposite-sex friends, as they were generally not attracted to their male friends and assumed that this lack of attraction was mutual.

From all my experiences, I can only agree with this and give this as a little hint when looking for a good friend. I fully agree with Zarathustra that one needs at least one friend and can only advise to choose this person wisely. You might imagine that times have changed and that we are no longer ruled by outdated traditional values. But even if you think that I am wrong about this, look around you and assess your own history, and the experiences of others around you; you are safer selecting close friends from your own sex.

The next point would have also fit well in the previous chapter, but I think it is better placed here. I have seen so many managers stumble over this point that I have lost count. For me, a sexual relationship in the workplace is an absolute no-go. The points about friendship apply equally strongly to love. I've seen many managers have to leave the company because of this very issue. And rightly so. You can never really anticipate and then rule out the conflicts of interest that arise from romantic relationships in the workplace. Don't get involved, don't try it out, don't f*ck at work!

If you find the love of your life at work, one of you must leave the work environment so that there is not the slightest possibility that your relationship can affect your decision making or how you are perceived by your colleagues.

One final thought on this text. Sometimes Nietzsche's proclamation that men and women cannot be friends is taken as evidence that is a fanatic. I can't see that, because from my point of view, he puts men and women in the same position here with the statement:

"Women are not yet capable of friendship. But tell me, men, which of you is capable of friendship?

Oh about your poverty, you men, and your stinginess of soul! As much as you give to your friend, I will give to my enemy, and I will not become poorer with it."

For me, another proof that he is not misogynistic, but sees human beings - regardless of gender - as imperfect (to put it politely). It doesn't matter if you are a man or a woman, you should all strive to become a greater human being - the superman. Nowhere in the text are women excluded from achieving this goal as well.

No matter how strong you are, if you don't have someone with whom you can openly talk about your weaknesses without fear, you are at a significant disadvantage. You need someone who will challenge you and make sure you get better and better. Someone who can be a role model for you and whom you like to listen to. Someone who can also simply bring you to other thoughts. And now it comes, if this is also your partner, then you have almost won.

Your friend should be someone with whom you can go to war and love.

There is comradeship: may there be friendship!

The Thousand and One Goals

"Verily, the people gave themselves all their good and evil. Verily, they did not take it, they did not find it, it did not fall to them as a voice from heaven.

Only the man put value into the things, to preserve himself, - he created only the sense to the things, a human sense! That is why he calls himself "man," that is: the appreciator.

To estimate is to create: hear it, you creators! Appreciation itself is the treasure and jewel of all valued things.

Only through estimation there is value: and without estimation the nut of existence would be hollow. Hear it, you creators!"

If you want to find out how satisfied the people who work for you are, you typically conduct an employee engagement survey, one-on-one interviews, or focus groups, just to name a few tools you can use to hear the voice of your employees. There are many important questions you can ask different audiences, but there is one that I think is the most important:

Do you feel valued?

This chapter is about value and appreciation.

Let's start with you! You should periodically ask yourself this question, too. Do you feel valued for the effort and passion you put into this work? Go deep within yourself, take some time, and look for the answer. Most people answer "No" or "Partially" to this question. A resounding "Yes!" is rare, but why is that?

According to Zarathustra, if something is to be valued, it must first have value. Value is "given" by people, not earned, taken, or found. People give value to things or to other people. For example, the value of a loaf of bread depends on the individual's point of view. It is worth much more to you when you are hungry than after a good meal.

A value is always an agreement between two parties based on their needs. The same is true with money. I have met so many people who did not understand where money actually got its value. How much is a dollar worth? Exactly as much as someone is willing to give you for it in kind in exchange. No more and no less. That can be one roll or ten. It always depends on supply and demand. But the same is true for your employees and also for yourself. How much are you worth to your company?

You get your salary, let's say you get $50,000 a year - your value now is $50,000. But what are you giving back to the company? Is it worth $50,000? Are you developing a product that sells and generates revenue that would cover all the costs associated with you, plus a little bit more to make a profit as well? Have you done projects that save the company $50,000 or more per year in costs? Your value is created by you and determines your feeling of worth.

Let's say you did a great cost savings project and helped the company save $100 million. At some point, you'll start to wonder if your value to the company is really "just" the $50,000 they're paying you, right? Then it's time to kick down the door to your boss and ask for a hefty raise, right? The answer to that is not so simple. After all, if they made 100 million in savings, surely you should get at least 50 million of that. Fifty-fifty, that would be fair.

However, if your job was to save 200 million, then the deal you made with your company was that they would give you 50k for saving them 200 million. However, you actually "only" delivered 100 million, which technically reduces your value to 25k. The tricky thing is that you could have also said from the beginning that this deal is not fair, and you want at least 100k. The value is a given. The company puts a value on the job you are doing and so do you. At a certain point you agree, and the contract is sealed. It is an agreement between two parties and your value to them depends on how well you perform the agreed upon tasks set out in the contract. The answer to the initial question of why so many people feel unappreciated at work is, in no small part, right here.

First, job descriptions are usually quite vague and do not define exactly what is expected of you in terms of value. Following an unclear job description, many employees also don't receive clear goals and deliverables from their managers with a clearly assigned value, and they also lack ongoing feedback on where they stand in achieving those goals. So how should you determine the value your company or supervisor expects from you? You can't. In addition, employees tend to overestimate the value they deliver. The vast majority of managers I have met over the course of my career do not clearly define or communicate their value to their company and/or supervisors.

We are talking about a mutual failure here. One of the main causes of the great demotivation among today's workers is the unclear expectations and the different valuation of the contribution. The company gives you value and values you accordingly, and you give the company value and value it according to what the company gives back to you. As you can already imagine, this is a huge field for human error and misunderstanding. Especially if what is expected of you was never explicitly defined. This is a minefield where every step of your engagement can blow you up. How do you navigate through it?

It is your responsibility as a manager to ensure that every person in your organization understands the expectations you have for them. Clear definitions of what they need to deliver, coupled with the value they need to bring to the company.

You don't hire someone because you like having them around so you're not alone half the day. And if you can't put a clear price tag on a job, you don't need it. When someone asks you if they can hire someone, have them tell you how much value that person will bring to the company. Give them time if they need it to go back and crunch the numbers. If the inquirer can't give a clear answer to that, the company most likely doesn't need the job. Probability, unpredictable events and random fluctuations play a role in many financial calculations, but even these uncertainties can and should be part of the value estimates. We're all not psychics or fortune tellers, so educated estimates are absolutely fine - if they make sense.

Let's say you want a fancy barista in your office, thinking that this will make everybody happier and more productive. How the heck do you put a price tag on such a position? Conduct a survey and ask your employees if they would appreciate a good coffee in the morning. Based on the result, estimate a potential increase in engagement scores and compare it to the potential productivity increases we see statistically with more engaged employees. A one percent increase in engagement score from your new coffee god or goddess could increase your sales team's productivity by one percent, leading to higher sales. This allows you to calculate a return on investment and justify (or not) the barista position. Of course, you'll need to constantly monitor whether the assumed one percent increase in productivity is actually happening.

From my perspective, an investment in engagement is almost always worth it because we're not just talking about productivity gains, but also all the other positive side effects. Decreasing employee turnover, for example.

Now let's look at the problem from the employee's perspective. As described earlier, people tend to overestimate their contributions. If you are interested in the psychological background and research, you can read about the phenomenon known as the overachievement effect, superiority bias, hindsight bias, sense of relative superiority, Lake-Wobegon effect, or (very interestingly) the Dunning-Kruger effect, a form of illusory superiority that people exhibit on a task where their skills are low.

You have to be amazingly self-reflective to appreciate the real value you have to your company. The fact that you are there and they are paying you a lot of money is not a justification for yourself! Write down the services you provided per quarter and put numbers to them. I know this can take some time and be painful at times, as many companies (even the most developed) are unable to define performance metrics for a variety of tasks performed in different places.

Do it yourself, you're smart - that's why they hired you in the first place. Show them your value - that will set you apart from all the managers who tend to just manage their impression instead of adding real value. The point is that people who understand their value usually get to the top much faster. If you think about it, it's easy to understand. If one manager invests all their energy into the perception that they are great (without substance), while another manager invests in actual performance, there is a clear imbalance in value between the poser and the doer. Invest in real accomplishments, summarize what you've accomplished, put a price tag on it, and set the bar of what a manager in your peer group needs to achieve. The others need to do the same and those "impression managers" won't be able to do that. A great impression without results usually only works if you are a politician.

To summarize for both views: there must be a goal! A clear goal that the company wants to achieve, and that's why they hired you, to work toward it. And value does not necessarily equate to money! Our society and economy is largely based on these assumptions, but it's not true. The best example is a family. Parents expect something from their children - for example, some cultures expect that children will take care of elderly parents. Children also expect something from their parents, for example, protection, guidance, food, shelter, or love. There is an agreement between them based on values, but they are not monetary.

So what is your goal, and does it match that of your employer/employees? If it does, then you can feel valued. If you know how much value you are expected to create, and if you also know how much value you have created, then the fundamentals are together. Now, if you have a great leader who recognizes that, then you feel valued. If you are that great leader, make sure you have that conversation with your employees on a regular basis.

There is almost no other as important question than whether you feel valued. Our employees are the oil in the gears and the gold in the scales, the most valuable thing we have.

"A thousand goals existed until now, because a thousand peoples existed. Only the shackle of the thousand necks is still missing, the One Goal is missing. Mankind does not yet have a goal.

But tell me, my brothers: if mankind still lacks the goal, isn't it also missing itself?"

Neighbor-Love

"You crowd around your neighbor and have beautiful words for it. But I tell you: your love for your neighbor is your bad love for yourselves.
You flee to the neighbor from yourselves and want to make a virtue out of it: but I see through your "selflessness". [...]
You invite a witness when you want to speak well of yourselves; and when you have seduced him to think well of you, you think well of yourselves."

You know that famous quote by motivational speaker Jim Rohn: "You are the average of the five people you spend the most time with."?

I first came across Jim Rohn on TikTok and the video made a pretty disturbing impression. It was of poor quality and looked like it was from the 1930s. But the content was amazing. What he said just sounded so convincing that I had to research it. I came across so much good content about him, his work, and his inspiring life story. A person who comes from nothing and becomes successful by working really hard. He shared his knowledge and accepted feedback throughout his life and also changed his mind when he received suggestions that made sense to him. The quote about being the average of the five people around you got me thinking about who the people around me are, and their influence on me.

I came across a 2018 article by David Burkus in which he states, "You are NOT the average of the five people you surround yourself with." He mentions quite interesting studies done in 2007 and 2008 by Nicholas Christakis and James Fowler, who took the results of the "Framingham Heart Study[1]" and looked at the impact of the people around you on yourself. Amazingly, what they found is that it's not just five people around us that influence us, it's much more. The 2007 study[16] cited obesity and smoking as examples and they added happiness

---

[16] https://www.framinghamheartstudy.org/; Christakis, Nicholas A. and Fowler, James H.; The Spread of Obesity in a Large Social Network over 32 Years;

in their 2008 study[17]. Looking at the spread of happiness their results are as follows:

"People who are surrounded by many happy people and those who are central in the network are more likely to become happy in the future. Longitudinal statistical models suggest that clusters of happiness result from the spread of happiness and not just a tendency for people to associate with similar individuals. A friend who lives within a mile (about 1.6 km) and who becomes happy increases the probability that a person is happy by 25% (95% confidence interval 1% to 57%). Similar effects are seen in coresident spouses (8%, 0.2% to 16%), siblings who live within a mile (14%, 1% to 28%), and next door neighbours (34%, 7% to 70%). Effects are not seen between coworkers."

This is already impressive and even more the impact of second and even third row friends. As Burkus is writing in his article:

"[...] But if your friend of a friend of a friend is happy with their life, then you have a 6 percent greater likelihood of being happy yourself. Now six percent might not seem like much, but consider that other studies suggest that if I gave you a $10,000 raise, that would only trigger about a 2 percent increase in your happiness."

As shown earlier, the influence of happiness, especially in the workplace, is essential for a healthy life and a productive work environment, which in turn is one of the foundations for success. So, taking both studies into consideration, it becomes clear that the people around you have a tremendous influence on you, and again, you should choose wisely who you include in your inner circle, as their friends also influence you, and even the friends of their friends.

New England Journal of Medicine; 357; 4; 2007 https://www.nejm.org/doi/full/10.1056/NEJMsa066082
[17] Fowler J H, Christakis N A. Dynamic spread of happiness in a large social network: longitudinal analysis over 20 years in the Framingham Heart Study BMJ 2008; 337 :a2338 doi:10.1136/bmj.a2338

The question that was on my mind now was: how likely is it that the people around you are already as successful as you want to be? How likely is it that the people around you are as intelligent as you want to be? The probability is pretty low - especially if you set your sights very high. The values that make for very successful people are spread very thin, which leads to a simple indirect correlation. The bigger your social network gets, the less likely it is that it will help you achieve your goals. And the larger the sample size, the more likely it is to tend toward the mean. If you are surrounded by the mean, the probability of ending up or staying at the mean increases.

Management literature likes to claim that the "brutal truth" about successful people is that they are lonely or alone. I disagree, they are not lonely because they are successful. No, they are successful because they are lonely. It's because successful people set a very high standard for themselves and the people around them, and there simply aren't many to choose from.

They choose their friends wisely and don't waste their energy on parties, alcohol, drugs, watching the latest Netflix blockbuster series or the like. Instead, they spend their time focused on their goal, surrounding themselves with people who share their values and help them grow.

Pretty bad news for the social networkers among you, right? But it doesn't have to be. It is important that you are aware of social mechanisms and act accordingly. You don't have to stop socializing or ignore your friends from now on and become a hermit. What you do with your time, and who you spend your time with must become a conscious choice. You can, of course, have a beer on a Friday night, or even do stupid things once in a while if you are aware of how far they set you back in the race. If you understand the costs and benefits of your behavior, you can make up for them. Maybe you don't go to an after-work party every other day, but only once a week? How much does it cost you, and what do you gain from your behavior?

"I love not your festivals either: too many actors were there, and even the spectators often behaved like actors."

Anyway, you make the decision - now you are aware of it.

It can all sound pretty selfish and anti-social. And that's exactly the point Zarathustra is trying to make. If you are a value-creating person, that's what you need to focus on. That's what creates the most value for the world and for society. His point is that you should not care about the people around you as much as you care about yourself. In the context of his criticism of religion, this also makes sense because most religious communities have charity as one of their pillars. In his view, charity suppresses innovation and especially innovators who might become problematic for the religious framework. Zarathustra says that the times are marked by disputes between science and the church, and following faith over facts is a major obstacle for someone who wants to turn the world upside down. His argument against "charity" here is twofold. First, the anti-clerical view, and second, the philosophical view that a "creator" is one among thousands and therefore should not be distracted by the thousands. The creator should be surrounded by creators and people who appreciate the creator's efforts. People who push each other and struggle to become better.

So again, it's up to you. The common thread that runs through this philosophy. Only you are responsible for your success, no one else. You chose the people around you, no one else. And if your favorite thing in life is spending time with friends and family, that's perfectly fine and you should focus on those things. But don't complain afterwards that you don't have enough time for your career or making money or whatever success means to you. If success instead means having the biggest Facebook friends list or more followers on LinkedIn or Instagram than others, that's fine too, and in some cases can lead to financial success. But again, the odds are pretty low, and when you compare the people, you look to as role models in terms of success and the career goal you want to achieve, try to figure out how social they were in building their empire and what their main motivations were. Again, it's not about not having friends or a social life. Yes, you desperately need friends, but if you confuse the words follower and friend, sooner or later you'll learn that friends don't follow you, they lead you.

"Let the future and the distant be to you the cause of your today: in your friend you shall love the superman as your cause.

My brothers, I do not advise you to love your neighbor: I advise you to love the farthest."

The Way of the Creating One

"But you want to go the way of your tribulation, which is the way to yourself? So show me your right and your power to do so!
Are you a new power and a new right? A first movement? A wheel rolling out of itself? Can you also force stars to turn around you?"

This speech is the continuation of the one before. After accepting the fact that the way to become a great leader is a tough and rocky road that on top needs to be mastered by yourself with very little help. This also means that you have to be pretty lonely most of the time. What does that mean to you? This speech can be read as a kind of motivational speech by Zarathustra to re-engage himself and the people who have chosen the same way. I highly recommend re-reading it from time to time.

Brian Tracy, a Canadian-American motivational speaker states there are three main enemies of success:

1. The comfort zone → the tremendous resistance to change
2. Learned Helplessness → using excuses to justify that you can't do whatever is necessary
3. The path of least resistance → looking for the easiest way to achieve results.

These can be combined. There is really only one great enemy of success: avoiding pain. Normal people are not ready for challenges because they usually come with pain, in the form of mistakes, losses, stress, conflicts, or physical pain. And who could blame them? What do we call someone who actively seeks out cruelties? Crazy, at the very least. That's why, for example, tattooed people are treated with suspicion, even to this day. A 2017 study[18] called

---

[18] Kristin A Broussard & Helen C Harton (2018) Tattoo or taboo? Tattoo stigma and negative attitudes toward tattooed individuals, The Journal of Social Psychology, 158:5, 521-540, DOI: 10.1080/00224545.2017.1373622

"Tattoo or taboo? Tattoo stigma and negative attitudes toward tattooed individuals." by Kristin A Broussard and Helen C Harton published in The Journal of Social Psychology comes to the conclusion that: *"Tattooed targets [people], especially women, were rated as stronger and more independent, but were rated more negatively on other character attributes than the same target images with the tattoos removed. The stigma associated with tattoos appears to still exist, despite the prevalence of tattoos in modern culture."*

These people actively expose themselves to pain to achieve their goals, such as being more attractive, shocking their parents, or whatever a tattoo means to them. That these goals could be considered superficial by many only adds to our suspicions.

This is also why there are so few truly successful athletes. Becoming great at any sport is psychologically and physiologically extremely demanding and therefore painful. It goes through hell and back and requires extraordinary courage and willpower. And more importantly, it's inevitably a pretty lonely road, as you can see above.

"He who seeks is easily lost himself. All loneliness is to blame": so speaks the flock. And you belonged to the herd for a long time.

The voice of the flock will still sound in you. And when you say "I no longer have a conscience with you", it will be a lament and a pain."

The pain you suffer on your way up is twofold: inevitable and necessary. Suffer pain to accomplish superior results. But the goal is the superior result. The pain, in itself, is not the virtue we seek.

Do not be afraid and accept the pain as a gauge of your development. It is an active choice, you can choose to live comfortably, earn an average income and be happy, or you can strive for the extraordinary, but that will be more expensive. "Good enough" might keep you employed, and that may be enough, but working to the absolute best of your abilities, pursuing the hard way if that is the best way will involve pain. Both choices can lead to real happiness and a fulfilling life, and I would never say that you should choose one or the other. If you'd like, we can do a visioning workshop where we figure out what your real dream is and then deduce which path is right for you. There are tons of offers from great and also quite questionable people to help you find your way. There are countless books on the subject.

The vast majority of people don't have a grand plan in life. They have goals in life like finding a good partner, having one or more children, living in a comfortable house, and earning a good income that allows them to pay their bills and go on vacation twice a year.

55% of the world's population has personal wealth of less than $10,000[19]. Calling that "wealth" seems pretty cynical, but okay. In 2020, approx. 580,000[20] people in America were counted as homeless. According to a Feantsa report, about 700,000 people were homeless in Europe in the same year. For them, the goals are even very different, such as getting enough to eat, having shelter at all without calling it a comfortable home. So they can't afford to dream "big."

The average American, with an income of $63,214 (or median income of $44,225) can already dream and achieve some of their dreams.

But what if your dreams are bigger than that? Or even much bigger? You could play the lottery.... Or set yourself up for a lot of pain and suffering.

My long-term dream is to start a foundation to manage the money I earned. I'll give the foundation a great name that makes it clear that our goal is to save the world - for ourselves and our children. The foundation will have subgroups that focus on specific areas. For example, one will focus on promoting science, another on animals, another on nature, and so on. Every month, enthusiastic scientists, dedicated associations or passionate individuals can submit their project ideas for the areas and a jury will select the best ideas. Winners then receive a certain amount of money, say $1,000,000, and that's how we

---

[19] Statista 2022
[20] HUD 2020

encourage creative minds to create new value. I am not looking for a financial stake, I just want to help. I would be happy to mentor these creative people and help them develop their ideas if that's what they want. Especially for crazy ideas that normal investors would reject because they might not be profitable. A quick rough calculation: one million times twelve months times four fields make 48 million per year. With an average life expectancy of around 80 years, that means I have a good 40 years ahead of me. I want to run this foundation for at least 30 years. That means I need $1.44 billion to fulfill my dream. I know, I know, when you factor in interest and blah blah blah, the math looks a tiny bit different, but that's why I said a short and rough calculation.

Since I didn't count on the money falling out of the sky or some rich patron coming around the corner and giving it to me, I have to come up with it myself. That's been my goal since graduation and everything I do professionally is supposed to pave the way for me to get there. I am confident.

And I am aware that this means a lot, but above all one thing: a lot of pain. I'm willing to put up with that and fight as hard as I can to get there as realistic or unrealistic as this plan might be.

So what is your plan?

On the way to my plan, I've had to overcome so many painful obstacles and fight my way through so many difficult situations that I can't even count them. What my stories all have in common is that they have shaped the person I am today. I learned and grew through them, and I will continue to do so in the decades to come. Even though they were painful, I am grateful for them, and all involved. That specifically includes any bad bosses I've had along the way (thankfully they've been few and far between), or the people I've fallen out with, had to cut out of my life, or lost because of my mistakes or misjudgments. Again, stop complaining about problems or looking for excuses - instead, see them as challenges and climb the damn wall! The only person who could have stopped me in this way was myself. So, to pick up on Brian Tracy's worst enemies of success, they could also be summed up as follows: The worst enemy of success is YOU. But the good news here: The YOU is obviously in your own hands and can be transformed by you to reach your highest capabilities!

"But the worst enemy you can meet will always be yourself; you yourself lie in wait in caves and forests.

Lonely one, you go the way to yourself! And your way goes past yourself and past your seven devils!

Heretic you will be to yourself and witch and soothsayer and fool and doubter and unholy and evil one.

You must want to burn yourself in your own flame: how would you become new if you have not first become ashes!

Lonely one, you go the way of the creator: you want to create a god out of your seven devils!

Lonelier, you walk the way of the lover: you love yourself and therefore you despise yourself, as only lovers despise."

Old and Young Women

""Why do you creep so shyly through the twilight, Zarathustra? And what do you carefully hide under your cloak?
Is it a treasure given to thee? Or a child that was born to you? Or dost thou now thyself walk in the ways of thieves, thou friend of the wicked?"-
Verily, my brother! said Zarathustra, it is a treasure that was given to me: a little truth it is that I carry.
But it is unruly like a young child; and if I do not hold my tongue, it cries aloud."

This chapter is the main reason why Nietzsche is considered by some to be misogynistic. You might say that this topic has nothing to do with this book and that it is far too emotionally charged to be discussed objectively. And that is probably the case, but we have learned that challenges should be faced.... So, let's dive deep into the dark soul of Nietzsche and see if there isn't something to learn from it for your professional life.

Let's start with the famous quote that is considered THE proof:

"Thou goest to women? Do not forget thy whip!"

No one knows what was going through Nietzsche's mind when he wrote that, and it could be that he was an angry old white man who hated women. I have the impression that all the angry critics stopped reading at this point and banned or burned the book out of fear, as is common in societies that have forgotten how to argue and discuss and that use "solving by banning" or, as it is called today, the "cancel culture" as a tried-and-true means.

I am convinced that this chapter is, among other things, a trick of Nietzsche to annoy politically correct readers. Yes, they existed back then, and it seems to me that the great philosopher foresaw today's society and is still turning in his grave laughing at the accusations.

Quite apart from the fact that he does not present the relationship between man and woman as if the woman is subordinate to the man, but on the contrary, that there is an eternal struggle between the two, in which both support each other unconditionally and the happiness and success of one depends on the other, at the end of the book he solves the mystery of the whip itself. Attention SPOILERS! In the chapter "The Second Dance Song," he uses the whip when he tries to bring order to the chaos called life, only to find that it doesn't work, and the whip is useless.

Furthermore, the chapter states that both men and women are special and have their respective advantages (there is no mention of disadvantages at all). For Nietzsche, it is clear that there are two sexes, both of which have certain functions (e.g., the woman has the function of "having children" because only she is biologically capable of doing so).

But I am not a philosopher and I'd be happy to be proven wrong. I am also aware that it sounds harsh on first reading, but throughout the book Nietzsche uses harsh words to make his point - one of his favorite stylistic devices.

So much for my assessment of the text, and I want to use the chapter to talk about social conformity in this context.

I'll be brief, since I wrote about conformity earlier in the book. An environment that tries to remove all barriers for everyone makes a big mistake. Figuratively speaking, following every whim of what some unelected group of "reformers" put out abolishes the walls over which successful climbers build ladders to get over. It forgets that these ladders we build are precisely what constitute our personal development. Effective ladders are built in a process of personal development that involves overcoming mistakes and learning from them. If you can no longer make mistakes, and even worse, if there is no environment in which you can safely make mistakes, you can no longer learn. You and your company will end up in decline. The only way to learn in an environment without challenges is to trust the current teachers and teachings. New deviant teachings are not wanted. This is the start of autocratic systems, and I am afraid that today in the society we call the freest ever, we are on the path to a new autocracy.

You have to be able to make any thesis, then listen to the counterarguments, and finally improve your thesis. Nothing can be taken as "fact," and every established paradigm is a target for destruction. This is the way science, and therefore the progress of our various societies, works. Constant questioning. Never let anything or anyone stop you from thinking differently or punish you for disrupting. Question everything and everyone if you feel you must. Ride out the storm that comes with it, and you will find that you are better off than you were before.

We all know those stories of people who have a crazy vision or idea, and everyone tells them it won't work. But they believe it and stick with it, work hard and fight through it - and in the end they're often right. As much as I love these stories, they point out two important things. First, our world could already be so much more progressive if it weren't for the majority of people pushing back a small minority of creative people by discouraging them, not supporting them, or worse, actively preventing them from achieving their goals. "We do things this way because that is the way we have always done them" is what crushes innovation. And second, it raises the question of how many creative people never became creative because they felt intimidated by social conformity and never really walked the rocky road.

We must all weigh the risks and benefits of overturning standard accepted paradigms, but each person falls into a certain place on a spectrum between conforming to the norm and rejecting it. Those who only confirm and perhaps slightly modify what is already known live safe lives but never amount to anything. Those who overturn accepted norms are constantly fighting but will eventually be recognized as innovative creators. This tradeoff between conformity and revolution is obvious in science, but it applies to business as well. Managers who would have to fire someone for economic reasons but keep the person because they are afraid of bad press. Or the worst example of all (and I firmly believe it's the one with the biggest impact on society): Teachers who have stopped challenging children to avoid conflict with parents who blame every failure of their "highly gifted children" on the teachers. In conversations with teachers, I heard some say they stopped giving bad grades because they didn't want to have any more trouble with parents. I can't imagine a worse start to life-long learning for children. If you teach children that they only have to shout loud enough to get what they want, then guess what these specialists will mainly do later in life.

If you really think your kids are the next Marilyn vos Savant or Stephen Hawking, send them for an IQ test. The Mensa Society offers them almost everywhere, and they're pretty reliable. Use data instead of guessing, and let teachers educate your kids to the best of their ability. And if you're still not convinced, there are plenty of special schools that care about kids and really support them to develop their best talents outside of the regular school system. I had to write this in the book for a loved one who is a teacher and really struggles with parents and the politically influenced system they establish in schools. She loves her job and working with the kids, but it's getting harder and harder for her - not because of the kids, but because of the parents and the new social paradigm that states that every kid is a winner. To me, she exemplifies a whole army of disillusioned teachers in the Western world.

I want to work in an environment where I can confidently represent even controversial points of view and where I can reach many people in an open dialogue who can share their feedback openly with me. This is one goal of this book. I am stating my point of view, my philosophy of work. I don't claim that it is the only one, and there are almost certainly other approaches that work better under certain circumstances. Share them with me and help me improve my management style so that my managers can benefit from your views as well.

As P. D. James, the famous English novelist once said: *"I believe that political correctness can be a form of linguistic fascism, and it sends shivers down the spine of my generation who went to war against fascism."*

The Bite of the Adder

"One day Zarathustra had fallen asleep under a fig tree, because it was hot, and had put his arms over his face. Then an adder came and bit him in the neck, so that Zarathustra cried out in pain. When he had taken the arm from the face, he looked at the snake: there it recognized the eyes of Zarathustra, wriggled awkwardly and wanted to get away. "Not yet, " said Zarathustra; still you did not accept my thanks! You woke me up in time, my way is still long." "Your way is still short, said the adder sadly; my poison kills." Zarathustra smiled. "When did a dragon ever die from the poison of a serpent?-he said. But take back your poison! You are not rich enough to give it to me." Then the adder fell around his neck anew and licked his wound."

This story gives us several meaningful clues to our path. Zarathustra uses the rest of the chapter to explain to his community the meaning of the story and what is to be learned from it.

The whole story takes a seemingly odd turn. Both for the adder and for Zarathustra. Although he was shockingly awakened, he did not lapse into bad behavior, yelling and attacking the adder as any other person would have. Instead, he takes a step back and analyzes the situation. He was late and needed to wake up, and if he could convince the adder to take back its venom, he would not be harmed. He could even befriend the adder for helping him. He loves his animals anyway and they love him, so there should be no problem at all. And when the snake realized who it had bitten, it became remorseful and apologized, and of course took back its venom. Moreover, the conversation is completely free of offensive words, disrespect, or even hatred. This story is a great metaphor for so many small struggles at work. We'll look at examples of this in this chapter, but first another question comes to mind when I read this metaphor.

Why did the adder bite Zarathustra in the first place?

She was not attacked by Zarathustra, nor was she in danger, so her animalistic protective reflex had not been triggered. It could not eat the great man. So, there is no obvious reason, is there? Maybe she's just mean and bites everyone and everything? Normally, snakes don't bite for that reason. A snake would never bite without a reason. And when it bites a human, the reason is usually - both human and snake feel threatened. Answering why the snake bit is a very good way to understand the metaphor and also Zarathustra's explanation. We usually don't have the full picture of the situation. And so, it is with Zarathustra. Can he be sure that he did not roll around in his sleep and force the snake to bite him?

When he wakes up in pain and sees the snake, Zarathustra basically realizes that the snake would never have harmed him out of hatred. So instead of defending himself or attacking, he spoke calmly and kindly to her. He even thanked her for the good in the situation: that she woke him up at the right time. His reaction was completely unexpected. The snake - having realized that she had bitten Zarathustra - was in an extremely uncomfortable situation. It "wriggled awkwardly" and tried to escape. Expecting something bad to happen after she made an obvious mistake, Zarathustra reaches out to her and creates a situation free of guilt and anger. Although he has every reason to freak out, he does just the opposite. Out of gratitude for this way out of the unpleasant situation, the snake gives it all and heals him.

The whole conversation between the adder and Zarathustra can be summed up in one word: Humility. If we search for the definition of the word humility, we find the following in the Cambridge Dictionary: *"the feeling or attitude that one has no special importance that makes one better than others; lack of pride"* or *"the quality of not being proud because one is aware of one's bad qualities"*. It is the opposite of pride or better arrogance, and that is the important point here.

Let's imagine a similar situation in our world today. A homeless person is sleeping on the sidewalk. An executive is hurrying down the street with a smartphone to his ear, obviously in an important conversation, and does not see the homeless person. It comes as it must, the executive kicks the homeless person and falls. The smartphone also falls to the ground and the display shatters. Due to the fall, the homeless person is slightly injured and in pain. We all know there will probably be a huge argument and noise. Why the hell are you lying there? Can't you watch where you're going? Do you know how expensive that phone was? Do you know how much that hurts? And so on and so forth.

But there is another way. Sorry if I didn't see you, is everything okay? Sorry for being in your way.

Every bump doesn't have to end in anger. It depends on the people involved and how they think. Of course, the same is true at work. People generally do what they do for some reason, and that reason is rarely just to hurt you.

I once saw a Ted Talk by Adam Grant. He's an American author and professor at the Wharton School of the University of Pennsylvania. He was talking about the habits of very successful people. It wasn't about getting up at 5 in the morning, doing an hour of yoga and meditating for another hour, but he stated that one key to success (among others) is humility.

What we need in leaders is not confidence, but confident humility."

A study[21] published in Administrative Science Quarterly in 2014 looking at the topic, backs up as what Grant suggests.

---

[21] Ou, A. Y., Tsui, A. S., Kinicki, A. J., Waldman, D. A., Xiao, Z., & Song, L. J. (2014). Humble Chief Executive Officers' Connections to Top Management

"We find CEO humility to be positively associated with empowering leadership behaviors, which in turn correlates with TMT[22] integration. TMT integration then positively relates to middle managers' perception of having an empowering organizational climate, which is then associated with their work engagement, affective commitment, and job performance."

Humility is often not seen as an advantage but as a disadvantage. A value of the weak and in the Christian context, humility refers to the creature's attitude toward the creator. But we need to be clear that we are not talking about sycophancy in the sense of humiliating oneself to others. There is true and false humility. False humility is when one intentionally devalues oneself or contributions in an attempt to appear humble. When Zarathustra in the rest of the chapter explains to his fellows the moral of the story, he is exactly referring to this point. Accept your weaknesses *"A small revenge is humaner than no revenge at all."* and be humble *("Nobler is it to own oneself in the wrong than to establish one's right, especially if one be in the right. Only, one must be rich enough to do so.")*.

True humility is what Grant calls self-conscious humility, and what comes with reaching the childlike stage of Nietzsche's three metamorphoses of the spirit.

Back to Zarathustra and the adder. Neither of them is angry or rude, they respect each other and try to solve the problem. Zarathustra knows the nature of the adder and could assume that he himself was most likely the cause of the accident. He does not assume a bad intention, despite his pain and impending death.

Let's apply this metaphor to a concrete example from the world of work. I once had a cheerful, articulate and dedicated supervisor. But when it came to hitting his KPIs, he couldn't take a joke. He became angry with his subordinates when

---

Team Integration and Middle Managers' Responses. *Administrative Science Quarterly*, *59*(1), 34–72. https://doi.org/10.1177/0001839213520131

[22] Top Management Team

they made mistakes, posing a potential risk to his shift's performance. He would yell at people and belittle them. Once I learned about this, I went to the area he was working in to meet with him. I became an eyewitness to the situation and asked him to follow me. We went to another meeting room, and I asked him point blank what was going on. He complained that he had told these people a thousand times what to do and they still screwed up. He talked and talked about how bad this was and how it would hurt his reputation and that of the team. I let him talk, and when he was done, I asked him what he thought our company was doing. He looked confused and slowly began to answer that we were shipping items to customers. I agreed and asked him if that was important. He wasn't sure what I meant. I tried a different approach and said, "We don't save lives here. If a pediatric surgeon has a small child on his table who dies because the care team forgot to prepare the equipment they needed, that would be cause for anger that I could relate to. I fully understand the surgeon who starts screaming at the sight of the dead little body on the operating table because of such a stupid mistake.

But when a customer receives their milk frother a day later than expected? Is it necessary to destroy someone's confidence, pride or dignity over this?

And why do employees screw up? On purpose? Surely not. Most people come to work, not to hurt the company, but to do a good job for the money they get. Could he have done a better job of explaining the day's goals to all employees at the start of the shift? Could he have planned the shift better? Could he have better assessed the strengths and weaknesses of the team to better staff the various production lines? What is the probability that his employees' failure to meet the daily target is a result of his failure to build the team? Certainly not zero. Yes, the surgeon can be upset over tragic deaths. But shouldn't the surgeon have checked the equipment before starting the job? Was the team well selected before starting? What is the surgeon's responsibility for the child's death? He is at least partially responsible. So be humble, because there is always a chance that the mess in front of you was a consequence of your behavior.

"But if you have an enemy, do not repay him evil with good, for that would put him to shame. But prove that he has done you good.
And rather be angry than ashamed. And if you are cursed, I do not like that you then want to bless. Rather curse a little bit!"

Child and Marriage

"I have a question for you alone, my brother: like a plumb line I throw this question into your soul, that I may know how deep it is.
You are young and wish for a child and marriage. But I ask you: are you a man who may desire a child?
Are you the victorious one, the self-conqueror, the master of senses, the master of your virtues? So I ask you."

In the chapter "Charity" we talked about being the average of the people around you, and we saw that this is extremely important and crucial. This chapter is now about the greatest thing you could ever accomplish and the most important person to help you do it. Zarathustra is talking here about your child as the greatest thing you can achieve, and the partner with whom you have that child.

But you can also see the child as a metaphor for the achievement of the North Star in life - no matter what it is. For many people, it is indeed a child, and Jordan Peterson, for example, has said that you can't grow up or call yourself an adult unless you've taken responsibility for a child. No matter what it is, a child or the TOP1 goal in your life, I can only recommend finding a trusted friend or partner to help you achieve it.

Referring to Zarathustra's speech and the chapter before it, there is an often-over-read issue here that to me is the real heart of all this. It is the question you must answer before you begin all this. *"Like a sounding-lead, cast I this question into thy soul, that I may know its depth."*

Are you worth it? Are you deserving of a great partner - a true ally? Are you worth your North Star goal? Will you be a good role model for your child? Will you make the team proud as a leader? Are you so great that a bunch of smartasses will follow you? How do you know that these things are obviously true?

We've talked about the values of great leaders, and being a great leader is the same as being a great parent. Being a great project manager, being a great salesperson, being a great doctor, or being a great bus driver. There's a lot of room between being a good person and great. You don't necessarily need this book, or others to be great. You may achieve true greatness by finding completely different values, but what will always remain true is that you have to be worth it first. True greatness is not a facade. It can't be faked.

So, are you worth it? Are you a *"victorious one, the self-conqueror, the ruler of thy passions, the master of thy virtues"*?

Maybe not yet? Then get off your butt and become one. Nothing stops you, because it all starts in your head. What Zarathustra is alluding to here is the mastery of inner temptation. It's not about being the extroverted great orator who confidently stands before thousands of people and convinces them to go to war tomorrow. It's about calmly mastering inner temptations. Aligning yourself with your values, being clear about what drives you, and then rigorously living and working by them. And once again, your values don't have to match the values of the herd, but those that you are convinced will lead you to success.

It's about putting yourself out there and coming to terms with your inner values. If you can withstand this challenge, you are worth it. And lastly, you alone decide whether you are worth it, and no one else.

I want to expand on some of my past mistakes even though it's painful. I wasted a large part of my youth into my college years drinking and partying. I almost lost control of these habits. When I decided to stop drinking alcohol, I took the first step to control my inner temptation. From that moment on, my life changed drastically. I suddenly had time to spare, with long weekends. Given all this time, I started reading again - one of my favorite pastimes when I was younger. This sparked the development of my own philosophy of life and later work. I realigned my values and reclaimed parts of myself. Even at this moment, as I write this sentence, it's all running through my head like a movie, and I get goosebumps. I was never part of the mainstream, I was always a kind of rebel, which almost cost me everything, but I dealt with my inner self and critically questioned my passions. That's the only way I could find my north star. Don't get me wrong, I had a lot of fun, with few regrets (although I'm really glad that there were no smartphones with video functions at that time). All this experience made me appreciate how precious time is. They showed me how not to waste it and made me appreciate my current life so much more.

I'm not here to convince you to stop drinking alcohol (although many billions per year are spent on alcohol-related health consequences in my country... Costs that I pay for). Eliminating alcohol was just my way to master one of my inner temptations. There are several others that I had to master, and I am still trying to do so. For example, I really don't know where people get their energy to exercise in the morning... Don't listen to all the books that tell you exactly how you should be and exactly what to do. Many will tell you that if you just follow this principle or that principle, you will be successful. This attitude may sell books, but it does not help people become independent leaders. Greatness has to come from within yourself first and foremost and it certainly doesn't have to be the way everyone else thinks.

One of the most encouraging messages that I hope to convey in almost every chapter, is that the main protagonist - Zarathustra - does not fit into the mainstream of his time. And that's a good message. Just because you don't fit the ideal today doesn't mean you can't achieve greatness. Quite the opposite. If you don't conform to the mean, you are much more likely to be great than the other way around. Who actually represents the so-called mainstream? If following the mainstream is the recipe for success, then the most successful people must also be the most famous, right?

I remember speaking with my daughter about being rich. She was eleven years old and said that she wanted to be rich like her idols at the time. These idols were some moderately interesting YouTube streamers and TikTok celebrities. I asked her if she thought they were really rich, and she replied that they must be since they were so famous. I suggested a little challenge: I would read the names of the richest people in our country, and she should tell me who they were and what they did for a living. After the top 15 names she didn't recognize any of them. She was a bit disappointed, and I asked her why. She said that she thought that you have to be beautiful and famous and that the most beautiful and famous should also be the most successful. In other words, it was clear that success directly correlates to one's ideal in terms of beauty, fashion and fame. The most successful people (from a financial point of view) are entrepreneurs and heads of large companies. And I'm sorry to crush so many dreams, but none of them got rich by posting YouTube or TikTok videos or half-naked pictures on Instagram (at least not during the time they were successful) or trying to be influencers on any other social network. Rather, they built the social networks that others eventually used to digitally paint their dreams. They were all exceptionally hard-working people and invested their entire lives in their success. If you read their biographies, they were a lot of things, but not mainstream. The same is true when we expand the list to the TOP100. If you were to do a street survey and put out the list of the top 10 most successful people (from an economic standpoint) and now stop random passersby and ask them what the list represents and who the people on the list are, I would bet my ass that the overwhelming majority have ever heard those names with few exceptions. Have you ever heard the name Bernard Arnault, for example? Yes, I know you have heard of Steve Jobs, Bill Gates and Warren Buffet, but these are the rare exceptions where extraordinary wealth and creativity have translated into fame. Even for them, their deeds preceded their fame. For most successful mortals, fame and fortune are uncorrelated.

If you really want to become a great leader and rise above, you have to do it from within yourself. The seed for your career must be planted within you and allowed to grow there first. The sprouting seed must not be eaten up by your inner temptations before it has grown to full maturity. You must protect it, nurture it. And then - when the seed has matured - it's time for the harvest.

Remember that for the garden of your dreams often a single gardener is not enough. As mentioned earlier, every great leader needs other people as support. You can also act as a role model to those who support you. Support can mean pulling someone up to the next level. Also, there will always be people who are better than you in many ways. Let them help you. Don't proudly roar like a lion that you can do it all by yourself.

As in my example, I always try to help broaden my daughter's horizons. But how often my daughter has been a help to me, sometimes just by her presence, I can't count. The same goes for my partner and my family and of course for the good friends I have.

Everything results in a symbiosis. Your goals and your relationships. See that you can bring both in harmony. Your relationships (also with yourself and your inner world) must support your goals. Your goals should not be contrary to your relationships. If you bring this scale into the right balance, then nothing can stop you.

"Beyond yourselves you shall love once! So learn to love first! And therefore you had to drink the bitter cup of your love.

Bitterness is in the cup also of the best love: so it makes longing to the superhuman, so it makes thirst to you, the creator!

Thirst for the creator, arrow and longing for the superman: say, my brother, is this your will for marriage?

Such a will and such a marriage is holy to me."

Voluntary Death

"Many die too late, and some die too early. Still strange sounds the teaching: "die in due time!" [...]
Of course, who never lives in due time, how should he ever die in due time? Would that he were never born! So I advise the superfluous.
But even the superfluous still do important with their dying, and even the most hollow nut still wants to be cracked."

I remember a speech our vice president gave at an internal company conference in Luxembourg. He said that you should never be in your role for more than two years. If you do, you become blind to the processes and ignore small mistakes that have always been there. You become too proud of what you've accomplished and too close to the team. Your enthusiasm, and therefore engagement, diminishes, and all KPIs related to engagement go down. I agree with this important sentiment. I have rarely stayed in the same position for more than two to three years and I have never found my work to be boring. I can't imagine working in the same role for a long time and always doing the same tasks with the same responsibilities and the same people. That doesn't mean you should leave companies; it just means your role within the company. Keep your learning curve steep and continually challenge yourself.

A great company is a constantly changing variety of projects, improvements, and tasks. A wheel that never stops turning keeps reinventing itself. As Zarathustra would say: a wheel that rolls out of itself. That is, there are always new possibilities and opportunities. Natural attrition deals the cards over and over again. If there is no such movement in your company, what are you waiting for? Be part of the movement yourself, think about how to improve things, contribute ideas, organize meetings and workshops, write white papers and contribute new ideas, or support colleagues who have great ideas. Out of all of this could come great things that you are passionate about that will change your scope of work and responsibilities and present you with new challenges. Again, challenges drive innovation and the only way to go from camel to lion to child is through experience. The broader the experience you gain, the better your personal development.

I often hear the complaint that a company is not that innovative, and ideas are not heard. Or that the boss only takes ideas from the inner circle. These are all just excuses. If your company is bad, change companies. If your company doesn't value your contribution, either they are not good, or the company is just bad. You should not be working in such an environment.

This chapter is about knowing when to quit. Zarathustra says it rather harshly, but as a written picture it illustrates quite well what is really hidden here. For everyone, even the greatest, at some point it is time to set out for new shores and leave their previous environment. Just because you're good at something doesn't mean you always have to do it, because maybe there's something else you're not only good at, but great at.

Before I went to college, I decided to do an apprenticeship, learn a trade, and earn money laying concrete. If college failed and I realized I wasn't good enough to work with my mind, at least I could come back and do something with my hands to earn a living. I became a Reinforced concrete worker, and I was also trained in the art of carpentry, roofing and masonry. I was pretty good at it and even participated in a district championship in my craft. I won second prize and was able to shorten my apprenticeship. Perhaps I would have become one of the best craftsmen in my trade. But when I was standing on a fresh reinforced concrete slab one cold winter morning just above freezing in the sleet and wind, all I could think was: *What a mess.* I had forgotten my gloves and my hands were constantly wet and cold. I swore to myself that I didn't want to freeze in the gray sleet or bake in the sun to build concrete slabs anymore. Although I loved my job, that morning I decided I would never freeze at work again. I decided that just because I was good at something didn't mean I couldn't be great at something else. I went to college and never looked back.

Dr. Georg Kraus, a German management consultant who studied the average age and tenure of CEOs of Germany's leading TOP30 companies in 2010, writes the following on his blog:

"The average age of the CEOs of the Dax 30 companies is around 53. And they have been in office for an average of five years. So they were appointed CEO at just under 48. And to get there, they had to go through an average of six career steps. With an entry age after graduation of just under 26, this means: A CEO needs around 22 years to get to the top. This means that they have just under 3.7 years per career stage."

That hasn't changed a lot since 2010. Even today is the average age 54[23] and the term of office decreased only slightly to 4.3 years. The rest hasn't really changed. It's not the two years that my former vice president mentioned, but three to four years is still not too long and remember that these are averages. There are many arguments for longer or shorter deployments, and I would like to highlight the most important ones.

Let's start with the main argument for longer assignments. Continuity is essential, especially in the highest positions. Employees want to trust their managers, and frequent changes prevent them from developing any loyalty or interest in a boss they know will be gone soon. Imagine where Apple would be now if Steve Jobs had left (again) shortly after he had returned to save the company from financial ruin in 1996. Continuity is important to building trust, and trust is one of the most important sources of engagement. According to our Metamorphosis of the spirit framework, early in your career you should focus on faster-paced changes to learn as much and as diversely as possible, and as you mature and move up the career ladder, you should spend more time on the

---

[23] According to the "DAX report 2021" by the Management Consultancy Odger Berndtson

roles you hold. The more responsibility a role brings, the longer the time you need to learn the ropes and fully master your position. Large teams or even entire business units want to see people with character and a relatable working philosophy as their leaders. But establishing a philosophy that both works for the company, and fits your personality takes time. You can't just go ahead and demand that everyone adapts immediately. So, if it takes 18 months to settle into maximum efficiency in your position, and then you leave 6 months later, you will find yourself learning the ropes of a new position (keeping your learning curve steep), but operating at less than 100% efficiency most of the time.

The most important argument for shorter assignments is career development. But not your career development, but the career development of your team. You have to realize that staying longer in one role also means you are blocking someone else's career path. There's the adage that you should always hire people who are better than you (which is part of surrounding yourself with great people). Usually, you do this to build a great team and achieve the challenging goals you set for yourself, but also because you want to quickly find a successor. When I talk to my managers about their teams, I usually make sure they have someone in mind who could take over their job. I can't promote you if you can't be replaced. Doing so would hurt me and the company. The only way to replace you would be to hire a replacement externally. This is linked to higher cost and efforts and a high uncertainty.

So, if you stay in your position, you're denying opportunities to great talent. Of course, if there's no chance for your own promotion, you could leave the department or even the whole company, even when the move is horizontal. There's nothing worse than getting the stamp of approval that your department is a dead-end street for people who still want to make a career. These bad outlooks or rumors close the door to the good ones and act like a magnet for the employees who don't want to or can't move much anyway.

So don't become the roadblock that you seek to avoid. Look critically at the time you spend in your roles and don't push into new roles and areas till you master the old one. You are the master of your career development, and it is in your hands to develop it at a certain pace. Be open and honest with your manager but also with your subordinates about the times you have set aside for the role and ask for feedback on what others expect from the role in terms of continuity. There is a high chance of you losing the loyalty of your team after telling them you will leave next year anyways. But if the job is intended to be a three-year assignment, let the people around you know so that successors can be put in place in time and people don't disconnect too early or too late.

Make a plan. As seen above, the average CEO takes 22 years to arrive at this position. How much time are you planning for? How many career steps would it be for you? So how many years do you have per career step? A little math example. In a big online retailer, I once worked in, the manager entry level was level 5. The CEO was level 12. Levels 9 and 11 did not exist. So, for me, theoretically, that resulted in six promotions to become CEO. That's not that much. But if I now distribute that over the average 22 years, then I would have a relaxed 4.5 years per job level. Now you apply the logic from above and say that you should be promoted faster at the beginning and slower towards the end and you have a great schedule to realistically estimate how hard you should push in which level. I hope that this view helps many managers, especially young ones, understand that you should not expect to be promoted every year. This is unhealthy and absolutely contrary to any logic and statistics.

"Some also become too old for their truths and victories; a toothless mouth no longer has the right to every truth.

And everyone who wants to have fame must say goodbye to honor at times and practice the difficult art of leaving at the right time."

The Bestowing Virtue

"Tell me, how did gold get its highest value? Because it is immense and useless and shining and mild in glamor; it always gives itself.
Only as an image of the highest virtue gold came to the highest value. Gold-like shines the view of the giver. Gold's shine closes the peace between moon and sun.
The highest virtue is uncommon and useless, it is luminous and mild in shine: a giving virtue is the highest virtue."

Zarathustra, who spoke a lot about values and virtues, now finished his speeches and left his community to return to the solitude of his hermitage. When he left the city, his followers made him a gift of a new hiking staff, so that he could lean on it during his long wanderings. The staff was beautiful, with golden handles and beautiful inlays.

However, the gift was made without the expectation of anything in return. Sure, Zarathustra had already given them much in the way of wisdom in his speeches, but they did not ask him for anything in return. They didn't ask him to stay either. Just the opposite. The staff is, after all, the sign for wandering, that is, for leaving. Zarathustra was stunned and thereupon gave his last speech about the most important virtue from his point of view. It is not so obvious from the beginning. He said that the highest virtue is giving. You might now think he is referring to altruism. Altruists are happy to give their time for others with no expectation of return. That would pretty much fit the followers who just gave Zarathustra his baton. So, is altruism the highest virtue?

The opposite of altruism is selfishness or egotism. If we follow the logic above, we expect Zarathustra to call selfishness a bad thing. Although he does, he adds an essential caveat. For Zarathustra, there are two kinds of selfishness. A distinction is critical for us today as well, because it will help you over the course of your career. There will be times when you must be selfish here and there - but in the right way. So, let's dive deeper into this topic.

If someone wants to give something to someone, they must possess it first. And this is true even for intangible things like love or time. If you want to give a lot, you have to have a lot. And to have a lot, you have to create a lot. Both materially and immaterially. Zarathustra sees precisely this upstream process as the key to success. Work hard to have what you can then give back. And in no way be ashamed of these tangible or intangible possessions.

Pay no attention to the envious people who attack you along the way, who instead of seeing your growth as preparation for much greater giving back, accuse you of greed or lack of compassion. They are simply blind to the greater plan behind it. It is your philosophy and goal that is important.

If the goal, as in my example, is to build up some wealth to promote as many people as possible doing good in the world, there can be nothing wrong with that. Again, we need a plan, and a long-term one at that.

For me, though, giving doesn't start when I realize my dream of (as in my example) my foundation, but also with this book, for example. One can give both tangible and intangible wealth. I am firmly convinced that this book can help readers make better decisions in difficult situations and thus do a lot of good.

But it started earlier, when I decided to implement the basis of this book, my own leadership style based on engagement, creating an environment where as many people as possible work in a place where they are happy. It started with the birth and care of my daughter, who I hope will also be a giver. It continues with being there for my partner or family and friends when they are in need. You can have big plans that take years to bear fruit, but along the way, you can elevate others at every step.

Almost everyone is a giver in some areas - try to extend this to even more areas, especially at work.

The book by the aforementioned Adam Grant, "Give and Take: A Revolutionary Approach to Success," addresses the same issue. The highest-performing people Grant finds in his analysis are people who give; he obviously calls them the "givers."

Perhaps the points described in this book will trigger readers to become successful and along the way, encourage them to share their experiences, bringing others up. I hope that this book will trigger discussions that inspire other people to give something away as well. If you will, a giving away virtue machine.

Nietzsche and all his fellow philosophers, both before and after him, have set this process in motion by writing down their thoughts. They helped to bring an ever better and changing philosophy of ultimately everything into the world. They have given the world something that is invaluable.

So, what can you give? And just as important, how can you give? Find your own way. It doesn't depend on the value; it can be as simple as a kind word to a person. You don't need millions to give.

Or as Zarathustra would say: *"It is your thirst to become sacrifices and gifts yourselves: and therefore have ye the thirst to accumulate all riches in your soul.*

Insatiably striveth your soul for treasures and jewels, because your virtue is insatiable in desiring to bestow."

But be aware that not all giving is gift giving. The main intention behind it must be that you don't expect anything in return. Giving can also be a wise investment or a sinister bribe. Gift giving must be economically nonsensical. People will otherwise always associate it as transactional, and the gift gets a negative touch. And this is the main distinction Zarathustra makes between egoism and selfishness. You could say there is a healthy selfishness and an unhealthy one.

Some readers may have spotted a bit of hypocrisy. If this book is a gift, I wouldn't charge money for it, would I? You got me there, I'm guilty. However, the proceeds from this book (if any...) will go towards my higher goal of someday helping as many creative people as I can. So, I would call this healthy selfishness, as mentioned above. Nothing to be ashamed of. This book is one piece of the puzzle that I have created.

In contrast, there are people who do not want to give, but only take. Everything they give is attached to expectations of something in return. We all know that one person takes all the credit for a successful project, even though it was the team or even someone else who was responsible. There are lazy people who have no shame in taking credit from others. These people are poison to any team. Grant refers to them as "takers".

The egoist thinks of themselves as more important than other people, or simply superior. So egoists take every advantage for themselves. In their view, why shouldn't they? Along with their exaggerated opinions of themselves, egoists also display a lack of empathy for others. This is the part about unhealthy egoism. We all have egos and cannot function without some confidence in ourselves. Once again, personality traits follow a distribution curve. At the far end of the distribution are sociopaths and psychopaths, who would throw a baby into a woodchipper for a nickel if they thought they wouldn't get caught. At some point, ego takes over and becomes unhealthy.

Spoiled children are always the center of attention. When the center shifts starting in kindergarten or at the latest in school, their inner image and reality collide and create cognitive dissonance. Their brain begins to adjust every situation by taking them back to their inner superior image, and any means will do. If the teacher doesn't praise them like the parents do, the teacher must be incompetent. They feel the need to be the center of attention, and so they need adulation.

I don't want to get too deep into this topic, as I am not a professional psychologist. There is a great book by Stefanie Stahl called "The Child in You" that everyone should read. It gives you a lot of food for thought about yourself on the one hand, but also helps you better understand other people and why they act the way they do. It's incredibly valuable for getting a better feel for your team and how you work with the individuals on it.

In The Soul of Man under Socialism, Oscare Wilde says, *"Selfishness is not living the way you want to live, but asking others to live the way you want to live."* Taking this to the extreme, one could say they are not only takers, but also givers. They try to give others their worldview. They give them a work environment that fits the takers' beliefs and force everyone to follow that framework. That's not necessarily bad, as long as they think the work environment is good - that would be healthy selfishness. If you're absolutely certain that the environment you've created is great, based on data like peer, employee and stakeholder feedback, you should push for it. The main problem with this is that selfish people would not adapt if it turned out their view was wrong. They can't because this clashes with their inner image of themselves that their parents built. And then the trouble starts. They make life very difficult for everyone else. There is a hidden danger here: the selfish taker is not self-aware. They believe they are superior and deserving. Since there is a little "selfish taker" in each of us, we must constantly adjust our egos to reality.

So why can't we all be altruists? I mean, Grant's research tells us that the most successful people are the ones who give and don't take. Who wants to actively be a selfish person? Sadly, lots of people. Although widely considered immoral or undesirable, some philosophers and scientists promote the value of selfishness. So, the boundaries between selfishness and altruism, which are considered virtues, are not so clear. People usually do not distinguish between positive and negative egoism. For them, an egoist is an egoist, done. We have already learned to distinguish between good and bad selfishness, but what about altruism? Is altruism now the ultimate?

You can evaluate the virtues and liabilities of both selfishness and altruism. Most people would say altruism is good. But not Zarathustra, the giving virtue should not be equated with altruism, that's the point. Pure altruism excludes healthy egoism.

Ayn Rand's famous books "The Fountainhead" and "Atlas Shrugged" revolve around this theme. She even goes so far as to say that pure selflessness and pure altruism are symbionts of pure evil - *"incompatible with freedom, with capitalism, and with individual rights."* She argues that the core of authoritarian regimes is to do things *"even if they are detrimental to oneself."* A ruthless person with power will subsequently exploit this altruistic "weakness" in people to gain control, or at least an advantage. Give your all to the Fatherland! This brings us back full circle to Zarathustra. For him, creators with the ambition to do good for the world should lead it. He is aware that there are always people with an enormous lust for power. Unfortunately, most of them are unhealthily selfish, and the world suffers from sociopaths in power. He wants people with a strong will to power, but with great virtues, such as a giving virtue. This would exclude all unhealthy egoists.

Zarathustra calls this unhealthy egoism "degeneracy," a rather negative word, especially in Germany, where the Nazis used it to describe behavior or characteristics that did not fit their ideology. It's not all history, as we see this same interpretation of "degeneracy" in Iran, Afghanistan, and Russia today. It seems to be a common vulnerability among us that can be exploited. However, Zarathustra's point is that those who are not willing to sacrifice themselves for a higher goal are not worthy of that higher goal. The question is, what is this higher goal? For Zarathustra, we don't find out until much later in the book, but for us, it's about how to become a great leader or manager. That means creating a good working environment for the people in that environment, allowing them to create something good.

Zarathustra lays the foundation that Grant and so many others have confirmed. Great leaders are giving leaders. They cannot be altruistic; they must be selfish. In an interview 25 years after the publication of "The Fountainhead", Ayn Rand recounts that the original version had a quote from Nietzsche as its introduction. However, she deleted it for fear that it would scare off readers.

Jim Collins' book, From Good to Great, is another example of valuable research that supports the idea that great leaders are givers. His Level 5 - Leader is *"someone who demonstrates a combination of strong personal humility and professional will."*, just as Nietzsche would have described it. One of the key insights from Collins and his team was the point of humility. We've covered this before, and it underscores the power of Nietzsche's book. Although it is phrased in sometimes very drastic terms, leading authors and their research teams have said the same thing time and time again.

Another study from 2020 by Scott Barry Kaufman and Emanuel Jauk called "Healthy Selfishness and Pathological Altruism: Measuring Two Paradoxical Forms of Selfishness"[24] looked and the statement that *"not all selfishness is necessarily bad, and not all altruism is necessarily good"*. They divided the topic into healthy selfishness and pathological altruism and found that healthy selfishness *"...was related to higher levels of psychological well-being and adaptive psychological functioning as well as a genuine prosocial orientation. Pathological altruism was associated with maladaptive psychological outcomes, vulnerable narcissism, and selfish motivations for helping others."*

---

[24] Kaufman SB and Jauk E (2020) Healthy Selfishness and Pathological Altruism: Measuring Two Paradoxical Forms of Selfishness. *Front. Psychol.* 11:1006. doi: 10.3389/fpsyg.2020.01006

I am certain that to become a great leader, you need to be selfish, in a healthy way. As you won't be able to determine if your selfishness is healthy or not by yourself, you can only validate that by the feedback from others.

Get constant feedback about your leadership style and the things that you are doing to make sure you are still on the right path. Otherwise, your leadership style will 'degenerate' into something that is doing harm to your company and the people around you. Be self-critical to always stay in touch with your line of action and keep questioning if you are on the healthy or unhealthy path. Zarathustra is calling it to stay grounded to the earth.

"Remain faithful to me, my brothers, with the power of your virtue! Your giving love and your knowledge serve the purpose of the earth! So I ask and implore you.

Do not let them fly away from the earthly and beat their wings against eternal walls! Oh, there was always so much virtue that flew away!"

We come here to the end of the first part of the book. We have learned from Zarathustra how to become an ideal role model. Friedrich Nietzsche's teaching resonated with me and is reflected in my gained experience. That these same ideas have been expressed and supported by the quoted studies and various bestsellers in management literature convince me that Nietzsche is still relevant.

In the summary of Part I, we learned that a great leader must always, without exception or abbreviation, pass through all three stages of the metamorphosis of the spirit. One starts as a camel and loads up on all the knowledge and experiences that one is given in kindergarten, school, university and the first years of work. Then you become a lion and realize that the learned knowledge can be transformed into something good. That you are good at certain things and that you can be successful. You become proud and loud and show the world how great you are. This is where most people get stuck, intoxicated with the positive feeling and self-satisfaction. But a great leader takes the next step.

The transformation to a child. The final step of becoming a natural leader, someone who no longer needs to shout loudly and spread fear, but who walks through the world with ease and playfulness. Someone who knows that everything can be achieved.

Basically, someone who wants to be a creator cannot obsess over today's values but must create the values of tomorrow. This ultimately means that conformity to social norms, or the constant search for affirming admiration is fundamentally wrong, because it recommends allegiance to today's values and scrupulously avoids deviating from them. But how can you move boundary fences if you don't outline them first?

Great leaders don't talk their way out of uncomfortable situations but take responsibility and act accordingly. They own up to their mistakes and learn from them. This is extremely difficult and challenges us physically and mentally to the maximum. That is why it is important to be mentally and physically fit. "*Mens sana in corpore sano*," as the Latin saying goes. This by no means excludes people with mental or physical disabilities; on the contrary, they can even benefit from their disabilities to their advantage, both in terms of personal growth, and as inspiration for others.

Your values must be fed by your deepest passions, otherwise they cannot form a truly solid framework for your work philosophy. You must be on fire for what you do, and that must come from within and not be talked into you by anyone.

Your work philosophy must be based on engagement at its core. The people who work with you and for you must be happy where they are. That doesn't mean you have to pamper them all day, quite the opposite. Challenge them as often as possible and as creatively as possible. Never mean or humiliating, positive challenges will make you and your team grow.

Your work philosophy must be written in blood. That means you must be fully committed to it. No ifs, ands, or buts. Don't get distracted and off course. Never forget that it's always you that gets you off course, not the others (remember the topic of excuses?).

Be patient. If you do a good job, it will pay off, always, but always at the right time. It's not about who's watching. If doing a great job is part of who you are, you can be sure that when they are watching, you will be noticed. And a promotion after six months is simply not healthy, it's just a sign that a mistake was made in the hiring process and you're in the wrong place or the wrong company.

Education does not equate to intelligence. Personally, I have never seen the important qualities of a great leader taught in a university curriculum. A great leader cannot be fresh out of university, and anyone who expects that simply has not understood how knowledge acquisition works.

"Be a monster and then learn to control it." This phrase by Jordan Peterson is important for the path you want to take. Many people will put stones in your path, some for fear that you will run too far, others for fear that you will get too close or even overtake them. Take them seriously, but don't let them stop you. If you think your direction is the right one and you can back it up with enough data, then follow through.

It's been proven that democracy is not the ideal foundation for business success, and if your company is focused on business success, it shouldn't be a democracy. Ultra-flat hierarchies and title spamming are counterproductive and will only work for a very few companies in specific environments. Quota systems are in most cases blind actionism and absolutely unnecessary.

Avoid bubble talkers in your environment. People who accomplish a lot and people who talk a lot can make the same superficial impression, or worse, those who accomplish a lot make a worse impression because they spend less time on self-promotion and more on getting the job done. Train your people skills to recognize this difference, because finding the right talent will be one of the most difficult tasks of the future. You are never too busy to know the people under you or thoroughly look into your hires. If you're surrounded by ass-kissers, you're not a great leader. You're an idiot.

Invest in your best people in the form of continuing education, training, seminars or whatever is available. Pay critical attention to the time you invest in "saving" your underperforming employees, because it's often not worth it. Every hour you invest in them has to pay off in the end. If the math doesn't add up, ditch it and draw a clear line.

Be clear that you have a hard road ahead. Prepare for it and don't cry if you weren't well prepared because it was your own fault. This includes discussing the impact on your personal life with the important people around you and communicating what it means to have a career and, most importantly, what it will cost you and your loved ones. After all, if friends and family leave you because you didn't invest the time they need, the likelihood that you will be successful drops. Above all, realize what appreciation means to you and include this idea in your employment contract so that it is clear from the start what you and also your employer or co-workers think is the value of their work.

Surround yourself with people who are better than you (yes, they always exist) and learn from them.

Avoiding pain is the biggest enemy of success. My parents used to say that medicine has to taste awful, or it won't help. That's what the law says!

Confident humility is another pillar on which the philosophy of work should be built.

Find your best partner, your comrade-in-arms, without whom it will be difficult. Keep moving and constantly challenge yourself. A lifetime in the same position makes the brain sluggish as long as you are not properly challenged outside of work.

Finally, develop a healthy egoism, which is the foundation for the giving personality you need to become a great leader.

"Verily, I advise you: go away from me and defend yourselves against Zarathustra! And better still: be ashamed of him! Perhaps he deceived you.

The man of knowledge must be able to love not only his enemies, but also to hate his friends.

One repays a teacher badly if one always remains only the pupil. And why don't you want to pluck my wreath? [...]

Now I call you to lose me and to find you; and only when you have all denied me, I will return to you."

After summarizing everything that could lead to becoming a great leader, after all the speeches and data delivered, after all the partially emotional stories, Zarathustra reflects on everything he has taught before, and his next words (part 3 of the chapter on bestowing virtues) are the most amazing. He basically tells them to stop repeating what he has told them and rather look for the errors and gaps in what he has said. He even goes so far as to say that they should be ashamed of him.

To me, this is the best way to end a chapter on the fundamentals of a great leader. You can't make a better reference back to the introduction. All that I wrote above, and all the quotes and studies and books mentioned, that is all the work of others and their interpretation of that work. It is not you or your view. Don't just adopt my view or thoughts or anyone else's. Steal the best parts and create your own philosophy of the work. Put it out there to be challenged and discuss, argue. Argue and learn and come back to the drawing board and recreate, argue again and argue and learn some more. Keep this cycle going. Make an appointment to talk and let me hear your thoughts so I can challenge them to help you improve them and you to improve mine. To blindly follow the advice of others means that not only will the copy be inferior to the original, it will also not fit who you are.

Stop reading books with the expectation that they will give you the one single truth about what it means to be a great leader. You seek to learn with the recognition that you wish to grow, but your teachers are imperfect. There are thousands of books about leadership, all with great hints and tips and stories, written (I assume) for the reader's best interests.

I'm under no illusion that some of the points I've made, even controversial ones, will generate both legitimate and unwarranted criticism, and that's okay. Just do me a favor and share it with me so that I too can improve. If you accept that this book and all the others are just steps on your ladder of success, you have understood the meaning of Nietzsche's book. Your goal should never be to be like someone else, but to be better than them.

With all our knowledge, expertise and advancement, the world is still in disarray. Things have surely improved from our ignorant, barbaric past but we are still fighting wars wasting our planet and its resources and tolerating the death of millions of people from things we could solve if we wanted to. Things like starvation and diarrheal diseases.

It would be nice to be as rich as Musk or Bezos, or as popular as Dwayne Johnson or Scarlett Johansson, but that shouldn't be your goal. You need to target a different goal, your energy needs to be focused on becoming your own better self, not on copying someone else, especially since they have failed to solve some of the most fundamental problems of our society (although I must admit I am impressed by how hard and creatively so many people are working to solve them). They have achieved their goals or are still working hard to achieve them - take inspiration from them, but no more.

Zarathustra's statement, that his followers should depart from him, challenge his ideas to an extent where they can even forget them is as powerful as it is humbling. Don't focus on the people society has elevated to god-like personages. Or even on the gods themselves. They won't solve your problems; only you can do that. It is up to you to solve your problems and achieve your goal. Perhaps your religious framework will lead to the results you hope for, but it is not done by God, only by you.

Zarathustra's *"Dead are all the gods"* should also be understood in this way. If you want to be great and achieve the unattainable, you must fight for it and not rely on someone else to do it for you or speed you along the way.

Let go of hoping that someone else will give you the solution to the most important question in your life. We can explore the answers to your questions together, but you must find the treasure yourself.

"Then the perishing man will bless himself that he is a passing man; and the sun of his knowledge will be in his midst.

"All the gods are dead: now we want the superman to live. Let this be our last will and testament at the great noon!"

Part II

The Child with the Mirror

"One morning, however, he woke up before dawn, pondered for a long time on his bed and finally spoke to his heart:
Why was I so frightened in my dream that I woke up? Did not a child come to me carrying a mirror?
"O Zarathustra-the child said to me-look at yourself in the mirror!"
But when I looked into the mirror, I cried out, and my heart was shaken: for I did not see myself in it, but a devil's grimace and mocking laughter.
Truly, I understand the dream's sign and warning all too well: my teaching is in danger, weeds will be called wheat!"

Part I of this book is my subjective interpretation of Nietzsche's Zarathustra. Interpretation is, by nature, influenced by the mind, the emotions and the personal goals of the interpreter. For context, I read other interpretations. Most of them, whether they see Nietzsche as great and brilliant or as pure evil, sound reasonable to me and make sense in the context of the author.

Anthony Ludovici, a British philosopher, interprets the whole Part II of Zarathustra as Nietzsche's reaction to the feedback he received from readers. Nietzsche was shocked at how many people misunderstood and misinterpreted the first part of Zarathustra. He published the first part of "Thus Spoke Zarathustra" as a stand-alone work in 1883 and the other three parts in the following years. Parts two and three in 1884 and part four in 1885, so he was only getting feedback on the first part.

Ludovici says that, in general, you have to have read almost all of Nietzsche's books to really understand Zarathustra. But my book does not aim to understand Zarathustra. It is a kind of spin-off, if you will. I take the text and formulate an idea that came to me while reading it, and ultimately develop from it a mechanism that has helped me become a better leader and may work for others. This may be a far cry from what Nietzsche was trying to say or not, but that's okay.

While the first part of the book was about the most important virtues and values to have in order to build a proper work philosophy. The next part of Zarathustra's journey will be about how to use these virtues properly in different situations.

After a dream in which Zarathustra looks into the child's mirror and sees the devil's grimace, he realizes that everything he has taught is in danger. The devil indicated to him that people don't see him when listening to his followers and them preaching his wisdom. When people speak about Zarathustra, they associate him with evil. As such, his former community was not able to develop his wisdom into something even better that would evolve on its own and iterate into a better philosophy, but rather was in danger of being destroyed by its enemies.

After putting all his energy into something that doesn't blossom, you might expect him to be filled with self-doubt, frustration and depression. Remember how he sat alone in a cave for a decade building his philosophy, and then was laughed at when he made it public. Then after a lot of hard work and gaining some followers, it's all falling apart again.

And what is his mood after hearing this? Dejection? Anger? No, it's the same as when the adder bit him - he's just happy to get out of his cave, talk to people and start over. So, let's start over again and see how he deals with this set back and what he develops out of it. And more importantly, what we can learn from it.

"With these words Zarathustra jumped up, but not like a frightened man searching for air, but rather like a seer and singer whom the spirit attacks. His eagle and his serpent looked at him in amazement: for like the dawn, a coming happiness was on his face. [...]

Wounded am I by my happiness: all sufferers shall be physicians unto me!
To my friends can I again go down, and also to mine enemies! Zarathustra can again speak and bestow, and show his best love to his loved ones!"

No anger, no frustration, just genuine joy and enthusiasm. And above all, no blaming anyone. No blaming his former followers for not making it.

Quite the opposite. When he sat back in his cave with his animals, he developed and improved his philosophy so that it would fall on much more fertile ground and convince even more people.

Take this as a kind of motivational boost. Failure is not the end, but the beginning of something even better. Failure teaches us what does not work or that we need to try harder. You may have heard of the quote from American inventor Thomas Edison when he was asked by an interviewer about all his failures. He said, *"I have not failed 10,000 times - I have successfully found 10,000 ways that will not work."*

He was a person who embodied the attitude of failure better than most. One of the main reasons for his success. Edison was 36 when the first part of Zarathustra was published, and was already running his research facility in Menlo Park, New Jersey. I know there is a lot of discussion about whether it was actually Edison who invented these great things, or whether he just took advantage of the great things that people like Tesla or Ford, who worked for him. It's just about attitude, which is important for this chapter. Zarathustra is basically happy to take up the challenge again, and so should you. If you see things failing but are still convinced it would work (supported by data), don't hesitate to try it from a different angle, consider the feedback and reinvent it, regroup the team and approach it differently. But most importantly, be excited about the opportunity. The results could end up being even better. Let me share another personal example with you.

The idea for Terum, a startup I launched with friends, had been floating around in my head for years. We launched the social app successfully in 2022 as an

MVP and gained several thousand users in quite a short time. Fueled by the early success, we were looking to see if we can get an investor for the idea. But this is not where the story actually started.

Fifteen years earlier, I had tried to launch it in a completely different way. The original idea was to enable communication without having someone's number, but some other unique identifier. I founded a company with a friend, wrote a business plan and registered a company. We hired a development company and began development with full vigor and commitment. After a few months, we found that the development company stopped working on our product because they got a more lucrative job, and we were just a side project to them. I was distraught because I had invested a lot of money, not only mine but also my family's. But there was nothing to do, after two unsuccessful and very emotional years we had to give up the business and take a break. But I never stopped believing in the cause. I spun the idea to different managers I had met over my career and finally found one who was interested. So, I revamped the business plan, picked up on the latest developments in technology, and came up with a revised plan. We gathered a small team around us to help us hone the idea and figure out what might work and what might not. It was a lot of fun and we were a great team. The meetings were constructive, and we decided to start a new business, building the first real green social network as a baseline for the first green metaverse. We were ready to try it, so that's what we did. The company was registered, and we started working. We hired a development company and did a lot of research. After a few weeks, the same pattern showed up as the first time. The development company failed us, and it became clear that our idea would fail. The company was dissolved again - another setback.

We lost money again too. But I still believed in the idea, and we decided to give it a new twist and try again in a different way. We focused on a very specific niche, becoming much smaller and therefore more flexible. We basically reinvented a completely new product out of it. Starting over again, we founded a new legal entity with the remaining team and completely rebuilt it. This time we hired our own developers and Julia, our CEO, decided to fully commit and give 100% of her time. We also recruited some volunteers to help us, and a lot of students who were attracted to the idea. And off we went. The app is available to all app stores, and we gain thousands of new users every week, especially in countries where sustainability is still just a lofty idea. We see so many people inspiring others with funny, sad, interesting or even shocking stories and changing our view of the world for the better. After going through so many low points, we finally see that our efforts are bearing fruit and we are making a difference in this world. We are creating something positive through our work, suffering and efforts. This is one of the best feelings I have ever had. This is the feeling I wish for every person who is willing to walk this rocky road and fight through all the shit to find the famous pot of gold at the end of the rainbow. Our pot of gold was not money, but a metaphor for happiness. For true happiness - nothing and no one should stop you from realizing your dreams, because that's where you will find yourself.

If I had to guess where a normal person would have stopped working on the idea, I would guess after it failed the first time. Some would have tried a second time, but the few enthusiasts would keep going. I find it hard to imagine anyone mustering the energy to try more times. You always have to learn from failure and invest time, money and effort to try again. We learned the old saying, "If you want it done right, do it yourself." The point is, we learned from our mistakes.

To quote Thomas Edison the "Wizard of Menlo Park" here again, *"Many of life's failures are people who did not realize how close they were to success when they gave up."*

He talks about perseverance and about having the strong will to overcome obstacles and never letting them get in your way. But the inner attitude towards it is even more important. Like Zarathustra, you can't let anything demotivate you. Your whole idea is going down the tubes? Your business is going under? Your job sucks? Your relationship is falling apart? Your project isn't going in the right direction? Okay, accept the fact and then try to find the root cause, starting with yourself first. What was your contribution to this? What could you have done better? Never blame others first, because it is rarely the case that a problem is caused solely by someone else. We could have blamed our subcontractors, but it was our fault for expecting them to bring the same passion to our project as we had and have.

And when you find the root cause, solve it. If you can't do it alone, if you are in a partnership, get your partner's help. Get the help of your colleagues, openly ask for help. There's nothing wrong with that. And then go full throttle and build something new and great.

It's your motivation that makes the difference. If you're whining all day about how bad your colleagues are or how hard your job is or something like that, you have the wrong attitude about it. Your struggles can be real, but you need to stop complaining and change your attitude. Take Zarathustra as an example. Instead of whining about all the idiots who can't see that his philosophy is great, he just keeps trying. He sharpens his arguments, and with each setback he becomes more committed to delivering. He could have quit on his first try when he was booed off the stage in the marketplace. He could have followed the recommendation of the other hermit who laughs and cries and mumbles alone in the forest writing and singing hymns. The hermit in the forest is the embodiment of the sentence: don't worry, be happy! But Zarathustra is not ready to take the easy way out, and neither am I, and neither should you. You should worry, and you should be happy about those worries, and you should use those worries to charge yourself with energy and then put it into the things you want to accomplish. The secret is to find a way to get energy out of those situations instead of allowing them to drain all your energy. That's exactly what Zarathustra is doing here (and Nietzsche too according to Ludovici). Or as

Simon Sinek, the famous American motivational speaker and author, once wrote on Twitter, *"Don't quit. Never give up building the world you can see, even if others can't. Listen to your drum and only your drum. It is the one that has the sweetest sound."*

So Zarathustra begins his second part of the book with a motivational speech for himself, and what a speech it is! He concludes that his philosophy has gotten even better, and perhaps was not good enough for it to have endured, and so his wisdom seeks new fertile ground to plant the seeds for a newer and even better formulated philosophy. While the kernel remained, the way it was implemented was refined and he tried again. And so should you.

"My wild wisdom became pregnant on lonely mountains; on rough stones she gave birth to her young and youngest.

Now she runs foolishly through the hard desert and searches and searches for gentle turf-my old wild wisdom!

On your heart's soft grass, my friends, on your love she wants to lay her dearest!"

In the Happy Isles

"God is a measure of courage; but I do not want your measure of courage to reach further than your creative will.
Could you create a god? Then keep silent to me about all gods! But you could create the superman.
Not perhaps you yourselves, my brothers! But to fathers and ancestors you could re-create the superman: and this will be your best creation!"
God is a conception: but I want your conception to be limited in conceivability.
Could you think of a God?-but this means to you the will to truth, that everything is transformed into what is humanly conceivable, humanly visible, humanly perceptible! You shall think your own senses to the end!"

The quote I chose for kicking off this chapter could easily be misinterpreted. When reading it, you could come to the conclusion that Zarathustra is complaining about people who believe in god(s). But the truth lies deeper and hidden for me.

Under Frederick the Great of Prussia in 1740 and later also massively driven by the French Revolution (1789), atheism began to spread in Europe along with the renunciation of the omnipotence of the church at that time. Frederick the Great became famous with his sentence: *"Everyone shall be blessed according to his own way"*, according to which he simply did not care what people wanted to believe in, or at least under his reign no one would die at the stake or otherwise be prosecuted for calling themselves atheists.

In the same year as the French Revolution in 1789, the American Bill of Rights was passed by the U.S. Congress on September 25, which directly states in the First Amendment that there is no state religion.

So, the power of the church was diminishing, but not everyone rejoiced. Many people felt lost and depressed. As written in the first part of the book, many people tend to blame their problems "on otherworldly entities". The question that came up was, of course, if there is no God, then who is responsible for all the suffering and bad things? The answer is of course simple, the people themselves. But for a culture so used to not having to take responsibility, it was incredibly difficult to accept this shaking of their conviction. This pessimism became widespread, and a lot of philosophers tried to deal with it, as Nietzsche did.

Nietzsche now writes against this pessimism because he sees it as almost ideal that now mankind can and have to be the architects of their own happiness. He asks: *"what would there be to create if there were Gods"?*

As in the previous chapter, it stutters with optimism and zest for action. According to Zarathustra, we have to focus on things that we can actually achieve and not on things that can only be done through miracles. His philosophy on reaching the superhuman does exactly this, it is focused on something that is achievable by humanity itself. It will take a while and may not be achieved by this generation, but maybe the next or another after.

For me this gives a great hint on building our philosophy of work. We and our teams need to focus on goals that are achievable under our own power. This of course means we need to be aware of our abilities and limitations.

One of my dreams is to travel to Mars or at least the moon. I want to be part of creating something that is absolutely necessary for humanity to develop, and I think that it needs to be done someday. Travel to other planets holds so many interesting new opportunities. But should I invest money and effort into it now? No.

I like to cross reference here to Jim Collins book "From good to great" where he and his team came up with what they call the hedgehog concept, which was part of all the really great companies he was involved with. They suggest that every company and person should focus on three main circles: what are you (1) deeply passionate about, (2) what can you be the best in the world at and (3) what can be your commercial engine.

I am deeply passionate about flying to the moon, but my current physical condition with a spinal disk error would make me a poor candidate for a trip and it would be exorbitantly expensive and mean financial ruin. A clear and data driven result. I will not fly to any extraterrestrial planet or satellite in the foreseeable future and thus will not spend anything else than a dream on it. Dreams are fine for fun. They can even guide your priorities. But plans are how we succeed.

But what about writing a book? I've always wanted to share all these things I've witnessed during my career, the positives and the learnings from the negative. All my ideas about management philosophy. Is it a dream or part of a plan?

Am I deeply passionate about it? For sure. Could I become great at it? There is at least a chance that the ideas might resonate with people, and it could become a great engine for a lot of people, so yes. And could it lead to commercial success? If the book sells even moderately well, it might pay for the time I put into it. And even if it doesn't, a published book could boost my consulting credentials. So, the decision should be clear, put time and effort in and do it.

I was once sitting with the son of a friend, and we talked about jobs. He told me that his dream job was to become a Twitch or YouTube Streamer. He loved playing Fortnite at this time and was absolutely passionate about it. We basically ran the same analysis about his job dream.

He was extremely passionate about the game and loved watching his favorite streamers while playing. I asked him how successful he is and there was the first barrier. He was not bad at playing, but also not amazingly good. In a normal battle royal, which includes 100 random players, he would usually make it to the top 30 or 40 players. So not world class. Not even top quartile. And inferring from that, what would be the chances of people wanting to watch his streams if he is not the best? What could they learn from a slightly above average player? So the potential commercial success was low at best, and probably impossible. Unless he has the time and resources to dedicate himself to becoming #1, every time, he should not go for it.

I also tried another analogy to make my point a bit clearer. If you take 100,000 people who study medicine and 100,000 people who want to become gaming streamers and compare the potential for success, you get a quite clear picture. The success quote for medicine students is around 95%. So nearly everyone who arrives at studying medicine will become a doctor in the end. Only 5,000 people out of our initial 100,000 would stop. Doctors in the US would arrive at an average annual salary of around $313,000 according to the Medscape International Physician Compensation Report from 2019. So pretty good outlook I would say. With Doctors, the "filter" is at the beginning: getting into medical school is hard, but once you are admitted, you have made it. And if you don't get into med school, you still have a biology or chemistry degree to use for something else.

How is that now for Streamers? The average salary of the streaming stars in our region is between $150,000 and $750,000. That would be quite comparable to doctors. But the crux lies in the success quota. According to "The Verge", only around 10% of the streamers on Twitch (which is today the most successful streaming platform) make more than $100,000 a year. To reach the mentioned $313,000 a doctor makes, according to a rough calculation, you would need around 2,000 viewers on average per month. According to Twitchtracker.com this is achieved by the top 1,300 streamers out of seven million! So the success rate here is at 0.0002%. Here, there is no filter at the beginning. Anybody can try, but only a very few succeed. And what do you have if you fail? A nice room in your parent's basement until you can finally afford an apartment of your own at 35.

So I unfortunately had to tell the young one that becoming a streaming hot shot is possible, but the likelihood of getting rich with it is close to zero. To become a doctor if you are passionate and hard working is way more likely than becoming a famous streamer. Becoming a doctor is under your control and not dependent on so many different circumstances.

This wasn't the happiest day for him, but it is better to face the reality here than to waste your energy or hope for something happening. You could still discuss the idea of becoming a streamer after you became a doctor and combine it and stream your work, that might be even better. The pre-med student has backup opportunities too.

You should also ask yourself about the things that you do at the moment and be honest with yourself. What can you achieve on your own initiative? What can your team achieve? Don't wait for someone or something to tell you what to do. Take it into your own hands and don't shy away from the hard stuff.

For Zarathustra, creation is the surest way to a better life. Doing or achieving something of one's own accord is the best way to find happiness. This applies to both mental and manual work.

But the harder the challenge, the higher the personal gain. Studying medicine is definitely both difficult and necessary for becoming a doctor.

So be clear about your goals, find a mechanism to help you understand what they are and then work relentlessly to achieve them. The solution will not fall from the sky. That only worked with Newton and his apple.

"But my fervent will to create always drives me anew to man; thus the hammer is driven to the stone.

Oh, you humans, in the stone sleeps an image for me, the image of my images! Alas, that it must sleep in the hardest, ugliest stone!

Now my hammer rages cruelly against its prison. Pieces fall from the stone: what do I care?"

The Pitiful

"May my fate always lead me over the way without suffering, like you, and such with whom hope and meal and honey may be common to me!
Truly, I have done this and that for the suffering, but I always seemed to do better when I learned to rejoice better.
Ever since there have been men, man has rejoiced too little: that alone, my brethren, is our original sin!
And if we learn to rejoice better, we can best unlearn to hurt others and to think of harm."

You know those people who constantly complain about literally everything? So many people are unhappy at work. Most of them simply bear it and carry it through the day, suffering in silence. But there are the others who let everyone know how bad everything is and - even worse - that they are the ones who suffer the most. Not everyone else, but them.

The entire world and all the gods conspired to make their lives especially miserable.

What good is our compassion to them? Will it help? And more importantly, how does it help us? Does it bring us forward if we spend our energy to console them in their suffering?

It is almost impossible to help these people without really working with them professionally. So, if you are a psychiatrist or psychologist, you are most likely qualified to help these people. If you are not, you should move on with your work.

The ever-growing ranks of hobby psychologists in the workplace are certainly doing more harm than good. And I don't mean the times where someone needs help to get better, or someone asks you to help them move. I'm talking about people who thrive on misery. They don't want your help but your pity.

If you want to become a great leader, then you need to be able to tell the difference between which of your employees need help, and which only want your pity, even though they could achieve their goals themselves.

I once asked a colleague a simple question and he sent me back a link. It was from the tool: letmegooglethat.com. After you click on the link you get redirected to a website where you see a short video of someone typing in your question on google.com and you see the result combined with the question: Was it really that hard?

That was both uncomfortable and helpful for me. From then on, I never asked such extremely simple questions to colleagues again. Especially not ones that I could solve myself in the same time it took me to write the question. Doing so shows a lack of effort on my part, and a lack of respect for my colleague's time. Today I am not sure if I was just too lazy or if I just wanted their attention. I'm afraid it's the latter. Once you are aware of this small difference between someone who needs help and someone who just wants your attention, you can handle it much better. My colleague Hanno made it clear to me in a funny way that I shouldn't bother him with these little things and that his time is valuable. If I had a real problem I could come to him, but I should come prepared first.

When you raise a child, you usually want it to become a self-supporting member of society, able to confidently master life's problems. The educational sciences largely agree that a child needs freedom to develop a healthy independence. If one does everything for the child (as helicopter parents) then independence is actively subverted, as parents reward dependence, and a burden on society is created.

In the long run, dependent employees can destroy a team if there are too many of them in the company. Even the whole company could falter. They pull the energy of the high performers out of the system and prevent them from moving the company forward.

Maria Montessori, an Italian physician, reform educator and philosopher developed the Montessori education system. She became known for the guiding principle *"Help me to do it myself. Show me how to do it. Don't do it for me. I can and will do it alone. Have patience to understand my ways. They may be longer. I may need more time because I want to make several attempts. Allow myself to make mistakes, too, because I can learn from them."*.

I can't help but notice that this is the core of my management activity today. When you control every detail for your colleagues or employees, it is commonly called micromanagement. A word often frowned upon in management circles, but something that comes up very often in employee surveys.

A 2002 study by Sandra K. Collins and Kevin S. Collins entitled "Micromanagement - a costly management style"[25] concludes that *"the costs associated with long-term micromanagement can be exorbitant. Symptoms such as low employee morale, high staff turnover, reduction of productivity and patient dissatisfaction can be associated with micromanagement. The negative impacts are so intense that it is labeled among the top three reasons employees resign."*

So, looking at the facts, it makes perfect sense to help people learn how to solve problems, but no sense to solve their issues for them. I know that there are occasions where micromanagement can be beneficial, and they are also mentioned in the above quoted study but these are rare occasions.

And there are even larger areas in which the principle is important, for example, development aid. The guiding principle of helping people to help themselves has become a fundamental component of development aid. Whereas a few decades ago money was simply transferred from richer to poorer countries, without input from local communities. After all, they had already

---

[25] Collins SK, Collins KS. Micromanagement--a costly management style. Radiol Manage. 2002 Nov-Dec;24(6):32-5. PMID: 12510608.

failed, so they needed "our help". It became clear relatively quickly that these funds mostly just seeped into dark channels or were invested in unethical things like wars. One has gone to invest money instead in projects that give poorer countries education and training to enable them to solve their problems themselves.

Whereas in the past the money was a means to purchase a good conscience, an increased commitment to real development has led to an increase in the benefits of the investment that can be measured.

In this area, things are certainly still not perfect. Development aid urgently needs to be restructured from the ground up and that takes time and constant effort. The successes are not measured vigorously enough, and the mis-investments are not always documented and punished.

Poorly paid and under-trained staff at non-profit agencies will perform poorly, and waste funds. I do not want to dwell on this topic, but it illustrates the points from Zarathustra very well.

In summary, a good leader must distinguish between those who need help and those who seek pity and attention. Help the first and isolate the second. Just as my colleague Hanno showed me that personal attention problems have no place in this context.

There are trends in western society that discourage managers from honest feedback. Some managers are afraid. In the era of microaggressions, where challenging feedback is seen as an attack, clear words are rare and honest and sincere feedback is thin on the ground. If you are a racist, or a sexist, you should be afraid. But if you can look deep inside yourself, and know that your guidance is sincere and helpful, then you have nothing to fear. Ignore the pressures that society has placed upon you and follow what you know: constructive criticism is helpful to anybody who is willing to listen. Only you can know your motives, and their motives are unpredictable. Building trust and consistency will protect you.

We shield ourselves from the truth, forming a cocoon of positivity around us that makes it impossible to see that our request for help isn't actually a request at all, but just a silent cry for attention. The same disastrous habit that occurs with dictators who only surround themselves with people who flatter them, which we covered in the chapter "The Flies and the Marketplace".

"So the devil once said to me: "God also has his hell: that is his love for mankind.

And recently I heard him say this word: "God is dead; God died of his compassion for men.

So be warned against compassion: from it still comes a heavy cloud to men! Verily, I understand weather signs!"

The Priests

"And once Zarathustra gave a sign to his disciples and spoke these words to them:

"Here are priests: and though they be mine enemies, pass me quietly by them, and with sleeping sword!

Among them also are heroes; many of them suffered too much: so will they make others suffer.

Wicked enemies they are: Nothing is more vengeful than their humility. And easily he defiles himself who attacks them.

But my blood is kindred to theirs; and I will have my blood honored in theirs also."

Zarathustra's dislike of the priests stems from the fact that he sees them as the worldly leaders of the faith. We have already discussed his aversion of the supersensible or otherworldly, but that is not the point here. Here it is about the fact that the priests are synonymous with someone who explains to us that all we need to do is sacrifice something by living according to someone's laws. We need not strive any further.

It is about putting up an invisible barrier that prevents us from wanting to advance. The energy we spend following guidelines could be better invested in something to advance society itself. Instead of adhering to the values of an institution, we should tear down its walls and create new values. Zarathustra recognizes that even the priests are prisoners in this world. Or as Morpheus explains to Neo in the movie "The Matrix", all people who are connected to the system will always serve and defend it. So in short, he wants the people who take care of things in their realm to put all their energy into the here and now and to things that are achievable on our own.

Zarathustra states that even though he sees priests as his enemies, he doesn't want to fight with them. They are the generals of the faith and the leader of the missionary efforts, the commanders of the otherworldly - why would he not actively engage them in open debate to convince them or at least their listeners to turn their back on religion?

I once had a manager who was a brilliant workaholic who was totally dedicated to the company. On top of that, he was friendly and empathic. Usually, a great combination and a good base for a fast and steep advancement. But he never really moved forward. One or two promotions, but then he got stuck. His problem? He fought every battle possible. As a way to shine, he never missed an opportunity to put people outside of his team down. He made his superiors and even their superiors look stupid when they made what he thought were mistakes. If he had a solution, he would not directly put it forward but wait for the best moment to shine alone. He could never let his superiors stand in a good light or share successes with them.

Instead of just taking responsibility in a meeting and saying, *"All right, let's do better next time,"* or *"I'll take it with me and we'll analyze where the mistake came from and make sure it doesn't happen again"* he invested a tremendous amount of energy to prove that he and his team were not to blame. It was always his supervisors or other departments who had made mistakes in planning. He has never understood - although we often told him - that he must choose his battles carefully. Fighting every battle possible is a waste of energy, especially when all you try to do is shift the blame. All this energy could have been used to solve the actual problem. People who are seen as problem solvers are in a much better position than credit-seekers and blame shifters.

Eventually, he lost all support from the management and was sidelined as a troublemaker. This was also a huge loss for the company, which did not make maximum use of a great resource.

Instead of sleeping swords, he waved and jingled all the weapons he had at his disposal and constantly had a herald running around singing songs of praise to him and mocking songs to everyone else.

Sun Tzu, a Chinese military general, strategist, philosopher said in his famous book - The Art of War: *"He will win who knows when to fight and when not to fight."*

This book is often cited in management books and for good reason. The Art of War focuses mainly on how to best avoid war.

And so should you. Some battles are worth fighting, but most are not. Your energy is limited, and all energy invested into an argument, a forth and back email chain or an escalation call needs to be worth it. If you are in such a situation, take a step back, rest a moment, count from ten down to zero, whatever helps you calm down. Maybe even wait for another day and discuss it with your partner or a close friend. Lay down a strategy and calculate if it is really worth it. If not, let it go.

I once had another manager who was the master of the art of constraint. We were at a meeting in Luxembourg, presenting a white paper about a major pan-European project. The paper was sound, but not showing the results our VP had hoped for. Ignoring all the data, our VP freaked out and bashed us. My manager stayed calm, smiled and said something like: *"Good catch, we will double check the data and come back as soon as possible with a revised version."* We rephrased the points that had set the VP off and handed nearly the same paperback. It went through. He had quickly assessed what our VP was looking for and how to phrase the data in such a way for the VP to easily understand it. He knew that the VP was probably just having a bad day. So why fight?

Now one could say that facts and only facts should count, not prosaic formulated papers. That's true, but if the person who makes the decision in the end needs that, you can either start an argument in every meeting or relent and change your writing style slightly and get a lot more done.

On the other hand, there might be people looking up to you as the person who finally stands up to the boss and doesn't put up with everything. Someone who stands up for the rights of the oppressed and downtrodden and the compliance of the white paper writing rules - a real martyr.

The only problem is that all the martyred have something in common: They are dead. Spare yourself this pointless waste of energy as long as it is not absolutely worthwhile or necessary.

"And if one goes through fire for his teaching,-what does this prove! It is truly more that one's own teaching comes from one's own fire!

Sultry heart and cold head: where this meets, there arises the effervescent wind, the "Redeemer".

There were truly greater and higher-born than those whom the people call redeemers, these ravishing effervescent winds!

And even greater than all redeemers were, you, my brothers, must be redeemed, if you want to find the way to freedom!"

The Virtuous

"And in this way almost all believe to have a share in virtue; and at least everyone wants to be a connoisseur of "good" and "evil".
But Zarathustra did not come to say to all these liars and fools: "What do you know about virtue! What could you know of virtue!"-.
But that you, my friends, would get tired of the old words, which you have learned from the fools and liars:
Tired of the words "reward," "retribution," "punishment," "vengeance in justice"-
Tired of saying, "that an action is good, that makes it, it is unselfish."
Ah, my friends! That yourself be in the action, as the mother is in the child: this is your word of virtue to me!"

For Zarathustra there is no good and evil. These qualities are always subjective and apply in each case only from the viewpoint of the observer. That is why he has so many problems with the term morality. What is bad for you may not be bad for me, and vice versa with good. The chapter is once again a reckoning of Zarathustra with the people who think they have the truth for themselves. They think that they can define what is good and evil and then punish their evil or reward their good.

They derive their definition from their virtues and call themselves the virtuous. But all too often, these very virtues are only used as cover for a hidden agenda or to conceal their own inadequacies.

According to Zarathustra, these very people only hide their true nature and adapt themselves to gain the goodwill of as many people as possible.

As we have learned, the consensus of the masses is unfortunately only a convergence to the average. Now, if someone is very disruptive and thinks ahead of everyone else or pushes the boundaries of science, this person will always deviate from the average and thus violate the consensus of the masses.

The socially conforming "virtuous" people cannot help but regard disruptive people as not virtuous and thus deny them virtue in turn.

What is worse is that social conformists see themselves as representatives of the masses and think that they are entitled to speak for them and to make judgments. To punish and to reward.

A very good example is the set of values around the role of women in society in the early 20th century. A woman had little to do in business and was not expected to run a company. The few who fought for equality were seen as troublemakers, revolutionaries or even criminals. Today it is fortunately normal that women can choose a career of their choice. The general access to additional people and, moreover, the access to very intelligent people in leadership positions is priceless and the economic value for the companies of this change in values is undeniable.

To become a great leader, you have to understand this fact first, to understand this context, to understand why people act the way they do. This is especially important if you are the kind of person who likes to be disruptive and doesn't understand why you always get into trouble with colleagues and superiors. At least subconsciously, one is always perceived as not virtuous if one violates the prevailing consensus of virtue.

Just imagine you spoke for women's rights at a time when the mass of people saw it as an attack on society. Imagine being the person who advocates for renewable energy at a time when the masses see it as an attack on the country's economy. Imagine you are the person who says that Saddam Hussein had nothing to do with 9-11 while your whole country "knows" he holds weapons of mass destruction. Those who advocate for peace in times of war are outcasts. The masses, indoctrinated and inflamed by the guardians of virtue, will at best ignore and silence you. Expect, however, that you will be met with open contempt or even pure hatred.

On the other hand, you can also take advantage of this circumstance. You can and should avoid these falsely virtuous people.

Employees who make it their priority to monitor and pursue the virtues of their colleagues cannot spend this same energy on the core business. These behavioral police have an incredibly corrosive impact on morale and thus on engagement.

Of course, I know where the behavioral police came from. They were a response to intolerable conditions. Women in particular faced constant sexual harassment in the workplace. Minorities were eliminated from all but the most menial jobs while others with half their skills were promoted based on a privileged birth. So many people were robbed of their human dignity, and this went on for centuries, and continues to this day. All this is unacceptable. Many companies in the past had rules on the books that supported these outrages. And there are still company cultures, even if not written into their bylaws, that discourage and diminish groups of people. However, it is not the company as in the legal entity, but always the managers who behaved in this way.

One hopeful sign comes from the market. If there is no good and evil, then it must be the market that determines the rules of behavior. So a company in which women are still disadvantaged will have such serious disadvantages in recruiting employees that it will not be able to survive in international competition and in a society that is increasingly turning into a society of meaning. The company management therefore has an absolute interest in not employing anyone who creates such a climate.

Every company must carry out an annual or even semi-annual performance appraisal of all employees that follows the 360° principle. This principle requires feedback from employees, colleagues and superiors, thus ensuring that managers who create a negative working environment are rigorously exposed and culled.

But importantly, it has to be a process that is systematically integrated into the whole company and not trusted to an individual person as a kind of police force.

So, the golden rule is not to look at the virtues of others but to concentrate on living the virtues you expect from yourself and show or communicate them to the outside world.

Remember the key distinction between selflessness and selfishness. A good virtue is one that does not expect anything in return - a selfless virtue. As Zarathustra says in his example, imagine parents and children. The parents do not expect anything in return for protecting, nurturing and providing for their child. So, if you are evaluating a colleague or employee over their virtues- STOP. We do not do that. We only evaluate our own virtues, and these with the simple guideline: Am I doing this because I expect something in return or am I doing it simply because it is what a great leader would do.

And also importantly, both are okay, even if your virtues are selfish, but then you can't hang them out and pretend you're a virtuous person.

So, the story is not really that hard with social conformity, you can conform to social norms, but then you must recognize the drawbacks of holding an incredibly average opinion. Average views will almost never change the world. Choose your fights, following the norms when it doesn't matter, and standing out against them when it does. And secondly, social conformity is something that is directed outward, so by our definition it cannot be virtuous.

So be yourself the mirror that shows you your virtue, because most virtuous people then and now have never stood in front of a mirror.

"Truly I have taken from you a hundred words and the toys dearest to your virtue, and now you are angry with me as children are angry.

They were playing by the sea,-then the wave came and swept away their playthings into the deep: now they weep.

But the same wave shall bring them new playthings, and shall pour out before them new colored shells!

Thus they shall be comforted; and like them, you also, my friends, shall have your consolations-and new colored shells!"

The Rabble

"And this is not the morsel at which I choked most, to know that life itself has need of enmity and death and crosses of torture:-

But I once asked and almost choked on my question: how? does life also need the rabble?

Are poisoned wells necessary and stinking fires and polluted dreams and maggots in the broth of life?

Not my hatred, but my disgust ate hungrily at my life! Ah, I often grew tired of the spirit, when I also found the riffraff witty!

And I turned my back on the rulers when I saw what they now call ruling: bargaining and marketing for power - with the rabble!"

As I write these lines, Twitter is being taken over by Elon Musk. I have never really engaged with this medium before and was only registered there for the topic of NFTs. In the meantime, it looked as if the takeover would burst, but in the end, Elon pulled through and took over one of the largest opinion marketplaces. He was rebuilding the company and doing so in a very public way. The topic also made waves in Europe, and I decided to get more engaged in Twitter and to watch the spectacle.

Let me say, it was just that, a spectacle. Zarathustra would say it's like watching the flies in the marketplace. A verbal bashing and haunting of the particularly deep category. A lot of people seemed to have nothing else to do than to rag on Twitter about Twitter, with the others then ragging on these people again and so on. A screaming and howling of the extra class. The comparison with this chapter immediately came to my mind. Twitter as the well, poisoned by the rabble. In his case, he bought a well, so to speak, and then the rabble came and poisoned it. Perhaps the well was already poisoned long before Musk bought it. And by "the rabble" I mean all those who participate and have participated in these campaigns.

Like the described maggots in the bread loaf with Zarathustra, these people took something beautiful ate it up and poisoned it. However, long before Musk took over the service.

Is this good news or bad news for Twitter and Musk? It certainly reads badly on first pass, but we come back to our basic pillar: Challenge drives innovation.

Zarathustra rightly asks, are these challenges necessary? And I say: yes!

I'll venture a prediction; Twitter will emerge from this spectacle significantly stronger than it went in. Right now, user numbers are climbing to unprecedented heights, and even the big media companies dropped their big-name Twitter blockades pretty quickly. Looking at this spectacle now, I can't help but notice how skillfully Elon Musk is exploiting this to reform this company. In my opinion, he is a genius who has absolutely understood how to deal with the herd to achieve really important goals.

What do we learn from this now?

There is a famous quote from Charles-Maurice de Talleyrand-Périgord, a French statesman who mainly did his mischief in the 18th century. The quote went something like this:

"*Smart and hardworking - doesn't exist;*

smart and lazy - I am myself;

stupid and lazy - still quite usable for representation purposes;

stupid and hardworking - heaven forbid!"

I cannot completely agree with that and think also Zarathustra would have had bellyache with the quotation. I would change it to: *Smart and hardworking - is as rare as a blue moon.*

There are smart people who work really hard. Perhaps Talleyrand was referring to hard physical labor. Talleyrand's time was still quite limited in terms of information flow, which is why the range of people he knew was quite limited, despite his busy life. So, he might not have known smart, hardworking people especially as he was spending most of his time in politics.

But much more interesting for our chapter are the latter two. Lazy and stupid, Talleyrand sees for representative purposes such as politics quite well suited because they do little harm and can be easily directed. And here I also see the kind of people Zarathustra calls "the rabble". I am not defining it in the way it is defined in today's time. Rabble are generally defined as a loud and out-of-control group of people. For the purpose of this chapter, we will refine or extend this a bit to: the lazy and stupid. While the standard definition fits the herd of people on Twitter as a large, noisy, loud and uncontrolled group, that description doesn't fully cover the people I mean. The "stupid" are not necessarily stupid in terms of a low IQ, it means in Zarathustra's context to not strive for creating purpose. These folks are not getting that the one greatest purpose is to push humanity and the planet towards a higher goal. All your energy needs to be focused towards this higher goal. If you are not doing this, you belong to the rabble and thus stupid in the context of this book. Let me clarify to avoid misunderstanding.

So, the "stupid and lazy", they are absolutely not productive and don't care. All the people who always criticize without having any idea of how much work and dedication went into the object of their derision. Who neither knows the connections nor would be able to understand them even if they knew them. People who, due to their laziness, simply do not have the stamina to reach a certain level of participation. For example, if I were to sit on a panel discussion on the development of tax law in Venezuela, I would simply be out of place. I would be too "stupid" to make a qualified contribution and I have to admit, I am too lazy to spend months of study to inform myself about something that is not central to my existence. I just don't have the drive to deal with the subject and will therefore remain ignorant. Now, I might still sit there well dressed and eloquently represent someone or some company, but even that would most likely not contribute anything substantial to the topic. So, in this context, I would be classified as "stupid and lazy." That's OK for some things I choose to ignore, but if you were to describe the whole of my person, these terms don't apply.

Dealing with people in stupid lazy people is incredibly time and energy intensive. This applies to both internal (as employees, colleagues or supervisors) and external (customers, users) dealings.

When I look back on my career, I have seen many managers fail precisely at this task. And for one reason only, they never saw this task as a challenge, but only as a burden. Nothing they could grow from, but only something that takes them off the path. They couldn't be more wrong.

Just as Elon Musk takes this huge pile of rabble and sees it as an opportunity to achieve his goals with Twitter, every other great leader must always approach it with exactly the same attitude.

"Rabble" is a word with a justifiably negative connotation. In the context of this book, rabble is used as a stylistic device to produce a vivid and shocking image, but if you define it via the quote from Talleyrand, and look at it value-free, then we end up with exactly what Zarathustra recognizes. After initial intense rejection of having to deal with the rabble and also a huge aversion in general to stupid loud lazy people, he comes to the conclusion that this rejection is his own laziness to take up the challenge.

He then turns it around and starts to see the interaction positively. Instead of looking into the poisoned well and getting upset, one should see the high goal and try with all one's power and energy to reach it. The lazy ones will not follow anyway, because they are too lazy. Those who only look down and scold will always be frustrated. But those who have fought their way up are rewarded. So again, see challenges as opportunities to grow from. And this is also and especially true for the people you consider lazy or stupid around you. See them as challenges that either develop you by overcoming them or by educating, training and engaging them. And never forget, in the majority of fields, you and I would also be considered lazy and stupid.

In the end, reference must be made to those Talleyrand called stupid and hard working. He calls them a real danger, and even from a manager's point of view, they are a danger to any company and its workforce. We are not talking here about a hard-working janitor who may not have been at the top of his class. That person is not stupid. People working to the best of their abilities are never stupid. We are talking about what the Gallup research calls the "actively disengaged." People who only do their 9 to 5 jobs but nothing more, or have subconsciously or consciously quit their job, but still collect a paycheck. These special people are the ones who actively work against you. They don't follow any higher goal or vision like your company's north star. They are not only disinterested, but actively set their minds against the company's vision. Usually, you would ask yourself why such a person should be in the company at all, but there are always people like this. They are either too lazy to seek or unable to find another job, or they are upset because of something that happened in the past and they want their revenge. The company owes them a living.

I once was launching a fulfillment center in Germany with a great team in a different warehouse. We got along quite well; the hired employees were for the most part great and highly engaged. Managers were performing well and getting into all the necessary topics. Our hosts were amazing and thus we learned everything we needed to successfully set up our own warehouse.

We had an employee gathering one evening where we constantly checked the mood of the people and right from the beginning, there was one loud employee raising topics and asking confrontational questions that were unrelated to our training. He put the leadership team into a bad light even though they had done an awesome job, paid all expenses and even organized continuous engaging activities. So that person had something weird going on. Also, the other employees were irritated and couldn't relate to his accusations. It was quite clear to me that this person wasn't here to work but rather to produce dissent and create a bad work environment. But why? When we eventually arrived at our new warehouse and started work, he was there and the first thing he did was to found a works council. I couldn't prove it, but for me it was clear that he was sent to us from the unions to do this. But not with good intentions, to improve the situation for our employees, but rather, just harm the company. And this guy was working hard to undermine the company. He put all his efforts into blocking initiatives, inciting other employees against the employer and their managers. The company and their employees suffered for four years with this person damaging the relationship between the company and its employees. In the end the company was able to get rid of him but what a hell of effort this was and how many hours of management work time went into this. It took the whole management team months to rebuild the trust this person destroyed. Overall employee engagement rose after this person left.

Here I need to take a short excursion on the topic of works councils. For all who don't know what they are, works councils are an elected representative group of employees that serve as a mouthpiece for the workforce and act as an intermediary between employees and employers. There are many forms of works councils in different countries. In some countries they have more rights and in others less. Germany, for example, is traditionally a country where works councils have very extensive legal protection and thus play an important role in the world of larger companies. In the U.S., organized employee groups are also regaining a stronger role.

I remember standing in the cafeteria with the management team of one of my employers over breakfast coffee and our vice president asked me my opinion of why general productivity in the UK is worse than in Germany. I thought about it for a moment and then answered that it was because Germany had works-councils. Everyone started laughing out loud because they thought I was joking. However, I was serious and went on to explain that a works council can certainly be an unpleasant thorn in the employer's ass, and in any case, we have had some incredibly counterproductive works councils in some of our plants, but basically they are nothing more than an additional challenge, which in turn drives innovation.

A manager who works in a company with a works council and wants to implement a project will think twice, three or even four times about whether all the legal requirements have really been met, whether the project will really benefit the workforce, and whether all the data protection issues have really been clarified. The manager knows very well that the works council will stop or block the project if no thought was given to this during the project planning phase. These additional thoughts alone mean that the project is bound to be better than the one in a company where the manager does not have to think about this.

This additional gatekeeper ensures that the quality of work is simply better, just by its presence. That means, when I hear company leaders who are afraid of a works council or otherwise organized employees, I can only smile. Take the challenge and be happy about it because it will help your managers and the company as a whole. But only if you have good managers who see it as a challenge and not a burden.

"What happened to me? How have I freed myself from loathing? Who hath rejuvenated mine eye? How have I flown to the height where no rabble any longer sits at the wells?

Did my loathing itself create for me wings and fountain-divining powers? Verily, to the loftiest height had I to fly, to find again the well of delight!

Oh, I have found it, my brethren! Here on the loftiest height bubbled up for me the well of delight! And there is a life at whose waters none of the rabble drink with me!

On the tree of the future we build our nest; eagles shall bring us lone ones food in their beaks!

Verily, no food of which the impure could be fellow-partakers! Fire, would they think they devoured, and burn their mouths!

Verily, no abodes do we here keep ready for the impure! An ice-cave to their bodies would our happiness be, and to their spirits!

And as strong winds will we live above them, neighbors to the eagles, neighbors to the snow, neighbors to the sun: thus live the strong winds.

And like a wind will I one day blow amongst them, and with my spirit, take the breath from their spirit: thus willeth my future.

Verily, a strong wind is Zarathustra to all low places; and this counsel counselleth he to his enemies, and to whatever spitteth and speweth: "Take care not to spit AGAINST the wind!"

The Tarantulas

"So I speak to you in parables, you who turn souls, you preachers of equality! You are tarantulas to me and hidden vengeful ones!
But I will already bring your hiding places to light: therefore I laugh in your face my laughter of the height.
Therefore I tear at your net, that your rage may draw you out of your den of lies, and that your vengeance may spring forth behind your word "righteousness".
For that man may be redeemed from vengeance: that is to me the bridge to the highest hope and a rainbow after long storms.
But the tarantulas want it differently. "This is what justice means to us, that the world may be filled with the storms of our vengeance."

Nietzsche rejects the idea of socialism and democracy because they put power in the hands of the masses and thus are, obviously, directly opposed to his idea of the superman.

His main argument here is that the idea that all men are equal will set society back. We have already mentioned that overly democratic structures do not correlate with economic success. Zarathustra seeing the motive behind the actions of the tarantulas is the main point of this chapter. Their drive is revenge. Revenge fed by envy. They are envious of power and since they know that they will not become powerful by themselves and are too lazy to tread the stony path that everyone who wants to become a great leader must tread, they prefer to pull the powerful down to their level with the excuse that all people are equal. When I would ask my employee: "What do you think your manager does all day long? The answers were fascinating, and surprisingly similar. For example, when I asked a shipping employee in a logistics location what the team lead did all day, I was always told that the team lead probably spent most of his time on the computer while the employees did the hard work.

When I asked the team leads what they thought the department manager did all day long, they said that the managers spent the whole day in the office on the computer while they worked their asses off to keep the employees happy. When I asked the department managers what the operations managers were doing, I got about the same answer, all the way up the chain. But if you skip one or more levels and ask the dispatcher what the department manager is doing, the answers vary widely. Some think that they work incredibly hard at that level, others think that they just have fun and drink champagne all day.

But employees very often feel negatively towards their immediate supervisors, even after you explain to them in detail what the supervisor is doing. The main reason comes from the conviction that one could do it better oneself - or expressed differently, simply envy. We don't want to admit it, but envy sits deep in almost all of us. We just can't get rid of it.

A 2020 study titled "The Role of Subjective and Objective Social Status in the Generation of Envy"[26] looks at the influence of status on the generation of envy.

The authors, Bolló and colleagues, divide social status into objective social status and subjective social status. Objective social status is mainly driven by material goods while subjective social status is driven by social factors. According to the authors there is not always a link between both, so that people with high subjective social status might have a low objective social status and the other way around. Important for us is that the person above me in the management hierarchy has both a higher subjective social status (as they are higher in the ranks of the company) and also a higher objective social status (due to the higher salary). So the line manager combines both kinds of status, and they can both conflict with each other. You might have heard people saying

---

[26] Bolló H, Háger DR, Galvan M and Orosz G (2020) The Role of Subjective and Objective Social Status in the Generation of Envy. *Front. Psychol.* 11:513495. doi: 10.3389/fpsyg.2020.513495

they don't understand why this person earns more than them while doing less. Envy is a critical driver for personal engagement and thus so important to understand. There is also good and bad envy. The first one motivates you to reach a higher status and the latter one motivates you to bring others down to your level.

Our tarantulas are malicious envious creatures. They scream for equality, but not because they want to work to elevate their social status. They want to lower yours.

The scientists introduce one of the main sources for channeling the direction of envy toward either malicious or good. This is deservingness. Has someone deserved to be where they are or not? If we have the feeling the other person has deserved to be where they are, we are more likely to get motivated to also reach this level. If we on the contrary have the feeling that they did not deserve it, then envy gets malicious. There are of course even further implications that determine whether someone sees an achievement as deserved or not, but this would go too deep here. Feel free to read this great study to get further along with the topic.

The main finding of the study was that subjective social status plays a more important role than objective social status because social advantage of the superior other causes the most painful envy.

For the working environment this means that it is not so important how much money the supervisor earns, but much more important if the person deserves to be the supervisor. Titles are also important. A company in which fancy titles are thrown around unnecessarily elevates the tensions caused by subjective social status, which in turn leads to negative envy. A company that does not promote based on performance but based on non-performance-related criteria such as nepotism, quotas, ass-kissing, or years of service to the company creates exactly the same negative envy. A trend that is becoming more and more prevalent today, driven by the general shortage of good managers, is that even fairly new managers put the gun to the company's head and threaten to quit if they are not regularly and quickly promoted. I have experienced this situation many times and in every case in which the company rewarded these demands, the resulting opportunity costs were so high that it would have been better to let the demanding manager go.

Opportunity costs refer to lost profits due to a different decision. If you make one choice that means you can't choose the other. If you make a million dollars on one path, and 1.2 million on the other, then the first path doesn't *make* you a million dollars, it *costs* you $200,000. There is more to consider than profits. For example, the chosen path could lead to lower profits, but it is safer. Opportunity costs must be included in the calculation of the project success.

Back to the demanding manager, promoting him or her against one's better judgment will have consequences that must be taken into account. For example, if another employee quits or loses engagement because they see the company as unfair, this will generate costs that must be factored in. Firing the demanding but underperforming manager will also create cost in terms of rehiring.

We once had a manager who led the technical teams of several countries. He was familiar with certain legal issues in his home country and did a great job there. In our country, however, he caused serious legal problems with several decisions. Fortunately, we were able to iron out the mistakes in time, but had we failed, things could have gone terribly wrong. Since his behavior did not improve with direct feedback, I, as the responsible manager of the country but not his disciplinary line manager, escalated the points and pushed for disciplinary and/or organizational changes.

Unfortunately, he was the only manager in the company who had the technical expertise in his country and, contrary to my demands, he was promoted instead fired. He had put the gun to the company's head and said he had a good offer from a competitor and demanded a promotion. His other colleagues knew that he had caused these legal problems repeatedly and then felt betrayed by the company when this guy was promoted. What are the company's values if they are not promoted even though they have not been guilty of any legal misconduct? The company has clearly lowered the requirements for managers for all to see, thus destroying motivation and the feeling of fairness. From now on, we received comments on this topic in almost every development meeting and a clear demotivation became visible and audible.

An employee who gets regular feedback and is therefore clear about where he stands in terms of personal development; an employee who also stands behind the vision of the company and believes in its goals and understands the current market environment because they are openly communicated… Such an employee will never make such a demand.

If someone threatens to quit if a promotion does not come, this indicates two problems. First, the employee's manager was not good at communicating that the employee is not ready yet or the employee is in the wrong place. This must have consequences for one or the other, but it must never lead to an unjustified promotion. The harm done by unjustified promoted people or in general people who are in a position undeserved, is tremendous.

I had a great colleague who was doing an amazing job. We both started our career nearly the same time and simultaneously progressed on our career ladder. While we were geographically going in different directions, we were regularly updating, guiding and helping each other. Sometimes we just listened to the other's problems. One day she called me and told me that the company wanted to promote her into a very prominent role. I was happy for her, but she told me that she had the feeling, they only wanted to promote her because they needed more women in higher positions. She knew that there was at least one colleague who was more deserving. But the company is pushing hard on getting female leaders into place even if that means passing over a better performing male.

She knew that the man she would be stepping over would know that she was just promoted because of her gender. She declined the promotion and was quite happy with her decision. Her colleague was promoted, and everything went well. The colleague quickly moved on and then it was her turn. The whole facility stood behind her because everyone knew it was her turn now from a performance - so deservedness - point of view. Had she taken early promotion, she would have diminished her reputation and reduced the engagement of the whole team. Lower engagement reduces productivity and all related factors. We had a long discussion to make sure that she had an accurate assessment towards her own and the performance of her colleague. She wanted to make sure that it isn't her modesty towards her own skills, or any form of anxiety related to the colleague.

I was impressed by her courage and honesty. More importantly, it did no harm at all to her career.

It is your job to not let negative envy arise amongst your employees. When it arises, it was your fault as manager. There needs to be a clear bar for all talents in your company. And this bar needs to be consisting of measurable KPIs and thus be an illustration of your performance and not the color of your skin, your gender, your haircut or your years of service.

A total emphasis on what is called "equality" kills the challenges we need. When we figure out who is the best person in any sports discipline, we let them compete against each other and the best performers will win. I let my managers compete against each other and promote the winners. With SMART goals and consistent feedback, with everyone understanding their current place in the race, you can predict your successor and know who is second and third in line. These goals can be related to everything, including your behavior as a manager in terms of culture and inclusion. As soon as you can measure it fairly and objectively you can base your promotions fairly by using everything that can be measured (and yes, the big companies of today can measure the outcome of manager behavior). So, it is again your damn fault if you can't get your team lined up and perform against tough goals and measure their success, not theirs.

"With these preachers of equality I do not want to be mixed and confused. For thus speaketh righteousness unto me, "men are not equal."

And neither shall they be! What then would be my love for the superhuman if I spoke otherwise?

On a thousand bridges and footbridges they shall crowd to the future, and more and more war and inequality shall be set between them: so my great love makes me speak!

Inventors of images and ghosts they shall become in their enmities, and with their images and ghosts they shall still fight against each other the highest battle!"

The Famous Wise Ones

"Free from the happiness of servants, redeemed from gods and worship, fearless and fearsome, great and lonely: such is the will of the truthful.
In the desert the truthful ones, the free spirits, have always lived as masters of the desert; but in the cities live the well-fed, famous wise men, the draught animals.
They always pull people's carts as donkeys!
Not that I am angry with them, but they remain servants to me and harnessed, even if they shine with golden harnesses."

Isn't it a high goal to be considered wise? As an expert and a welcome guest on talk shows. As a person who is constantly asked to give their opinion in well-attended public appearances, across all formats?

The only problem is that the media usually make their programs according to the motto made famous by Prof. Dr. Helmut Thoma, the German media maker: "The worm must taste good to the fish, not to the fisher." So, it's all about giving the consumers what they want. And that's quite often not what they actually need.

If you do not want to swim with the masses, be aware you are choosing a rocky road. The public opinion is made, just as my opinion was made in this book. Through the influence of various media, situations and people, the version of my philosophy of work has emerged. We are all stuck in our own heads and shaped by the times and experiences of our lives. Am I considered a wise one? This was not my goal. I throw my opinion into the ring to be discussed and challenged, and this dialog will help me and the people working with me. I am not doing this for fame or adulation. I am doing it for the benefit of others. To help people create better work environments and increase employment satisfaction.

Now in the age of information overflow, an avalanche of opinions hit us from every direction. We need filters on how we let these flow into us to process them into outputs.

The direction toward social conformity originated the same way, from inputs derived from all sources, valid and invalid. The important difference is that once the politically "correct" view is set into stone, there can be no debate. The masses determine the current acceptable virtues. In the chapter from Zarathustra, now two important points are addressed, namely first, who is the mass and secondly, who establishes social norms.

The masses are the opinion of the average and therefore not a bar to be sought after. As a great leader, you must strive for the highest bar and not align yourself downward with the masses and thus become average yourself. Also, one must never be deterred from publishing one's opinion, even if it does not correspond to the social norms of a specific time. Expressing one's opinion and constantly questioning the status quo is a quality of great leaders.

Now, there are always people who are uniquely qualified to speak for the masses. They claim to be the mouthpiece of a particular group or ethnicity or gender, professional group, workforce or political movement. They are quoted up and down in the media and their published opinions are used as justification and proof. They put themselves before their respective flocks and proclaim themselves as their representatives. Well-educated and articulate, they have become the "wise ones" who make speeches but are always scrupulously careful not to be too far outside the comfort zone of the masses. They have adapted themselves exactly to this mass and use it to their advantage. They eat as Zarathustra says from golden plates and enjoy the recognition and respect of the masses.

This is not what I want, and I advise you to be careful about who you follow. If too many people start to flatter you, then you have stopped challenging them and have thus gone astray. I know that flattery feels great, but the true feeling of appreciation for your leadership is not experienced after the backslapping team meal together, but after hard times fought together. After narrowly reaching the seemingly impossible deadline for which you really worked your ass off. These are the moments that show team spirit and leadership, not the skillful selection of the best type of coffee at the Barista bar.

People tend to take the easy way out. Don't listen to them and don't be afraid to take the hard way when you must. In the end, the success of your team is what counts. The team will give you the recognition you deserve, but only if you have shown the way, even against the current well-known paths. The masses will always revolve around themselves and thus always see a new side of themselves and be happy about it. But if you really want to be successful, then you have to break out and go new ways. Against the mainstream, against the current prevailing opinion, daring to tear down walls. Do not listen to the opinion leaders and people who claim they serve the masses. They are nothing more than quacks. Those who had to go through hard times to get to where they are today are mostly not the beautiful actors, but those who consistently had to work hard for what they have achieved. Struggle always leaves traces, physical or psychological.

"Honorably you stand there for me and stiffly and with a straight back, you famous sages! -You are not driven by a strong wind and will.

Have you never seen a sail sail across the sea, furled and billowed and trembling before the impetuosity of the wind?

Like the sail, trembling before the impetuosity of the spirit, my wisdom goes over the sea-my wild wisdom!

But you servants of the people, you famous sages, how could you go with me!"

The Night Song

"He who always gives is in danger of losing his shame; he who always gives has his hand and heart calloused with giving.

My eye no longer overflows with the shame of the supplicant; my hand has become too hard for the trembling of filled hands.

Where did the tear come to my eye and down to my heart? O loneliness of all givers! O silence of all shining ones!

Many suns circle in the barren space: to all that is dark they speak with their light,-to me they are silent."

Has everything ever been too much for you? Have you ever thought something like: I don't feel like it anymore, what am I doing all this for? This is too much responsibility for me, I don't want it anymore.

Any person that consistently pursues their challenging philosophy of work and keeps up this pressure, the demands on oneself and the speed, will inevitably get tired. Zarathustra becomes tired here and does not want to be the breaker of values but simply lives as a regular person. Constant giving makes you tired of giving.

Zarathustra actually has a cheerful nature. He likes to sing and dance and have fun, but at this point in his journey he realizes that he has almost no time for himself. He cannot pursue his joy of singing and dancing, at least not to the extent he wishes.

The chapter is an excellent metaphor for the topic of work-life balance. Again, I subscribe to Jack Welch's version of the work-life choice instead of work-life balance, according to which everyone should be allowed to work as much as they want. Balance implies a certain midpoint, but where you choose to prioritize things in your life is something everyone has to decide for themselves.

The important thing is to never forget some kind of balance that works for you. Similarly, you need to be able to say no when it becomes too much. You will not be a good role model if you are a wreck. If you can only meet your demands on cocaine or speed, then you are a danger to yourself and others. You are certainly not a high performer.

We all go through phases of doubt. If you never doubt yourself, then you are an arrogant sociopath. Questioning everything includes questioning yourself. What always helps me is a clear goal for the future and the certainty that I don't only have plan A, but also B and C. Again, a healthy social environment is worth its weight in gold on the hard journey, no matter where it leads. But a healthy environment will leave you if you don't invest energy in building and maintaining it. The flame goes out when it has no more oxygen.

I used to say, for example, that family should always be prioritized, and I use my own example as an example of what to avoid. I had to learn painfully what it means to give too high a priority to work. Family and work can be more easily combined nowadays and if you have a supportive partner or family, then it's much easier. A 2010 meta-study, "Social Relationships and Mortality Risk: A Meta-analytic Review"[27] looked into the impact of social relationships on mental health and analyzed the impact on morbidity and mortality. The study indicated *"... a 50% increased likelihood of survival for participants with stronger social relationships [then the comparison group]. This finding remained consistent across age, sex, initial health status, cause of death, and follow-up period."*

There is no doubt that strong personal connections keep us healthy, but what if you don't have strong relationships? What if you are alone and have to shoulder the whole burden alone? It is very easy to lose strength and motivation in such

---

[27] Holt-Lunstad J, Smith TB, Layton JB. Social relationships and mortality risk: a meta-analytic review. PLoS Med. 2010 Jul 27;7(7):e1000316. doi: 10.1371/journal.pmed.1000316. PMID: 20668659; PMCID: PMC2910600.

a situation, or even become depressed. The incredible costs that depression has on our working world - apart from the individual fates behind it - are hard to overstate. A 2000 study named "Cost of depression among adults in England"[28] concluded that: *"The total cost of adult depression was estimated at over £9 billion, of which £370 million represents direct treatment costs. There were 109.7 million working days lost and 2,615 deaths due to depression in 2000."*

But how do we get out of this valley when we become lost in it?

You must first recognize that you have a problem. The pure value-free self-reflection that we should always be performing is the first step to recognizing that one has a problem. And yes, depressive behavior is a serious problem. It is essential that you occupy yourself with things that you enjoy. If you spend all your time doing something that makes you unhappy, it will drain all the energy out of you without giving you anything in return. Get out of that situation as soon as possible! Routines and achievable goals are extremely helpful. Routines help us take "small steps to the goal", while in power mode we prefer big steps. Placing incremental goals into a routine and checking off your frequent accomplishments will work wonders because each of them will trigger the reward areas in the brain, which helps to drive away the gloomy thoughts that arise when we worry about a massive project.

My well-meant advice about alcohol may not apply to some of you, but if you are prone to depression, it is an absolute command. No alcohol, and no drugs! The relief you seek will elude you, and your chemical dependency will both increase and feed your depression in a vicious circle. Hand in hand with this it is also important to follow a healthy sleep pattern.

Never be ashamed to seek professional help. If you feel that something that you can't seem to beat has an impact on your life, get help from people who know what they are doing. There is no substitute for talking to trained professionals.

---

[28] Thomas CM, Morris S. Cost of depression among adults in England in 2000. Br J Psychiatry. 2003 Dec;183:514-9. doi: 10.1192/bjp.183.6.514

Examine your current and future environment closely. An empathic work environment is one in which colleagues can openly share problems and help each other. In these places, everyone takes pleasure in the accomplishments of their co-workers. Conversely, a toxic work environment is characterized by incessant turf wars and colleagues who exploit every opportunity to gain an advantage for themselves, often by putting others down.

I can't express my gratitude enough for the many great colleagues who have listened to my problems over the years. The many times I've struggled with my superiors, or suffered from the heavy blows of fate, either at work or at home. Life can be really hard, especially if you are alone. I don't necessarily mean that you all need therapy. You don't need a soul striptease in front of your colleagues either. But what we all need is the ability to simply discuss problems and see them from different angles. Get a second opinion from a colleague. Someone who can empathize by pointing to their own mistakes and moving forward. This is priceless help in bringing me further.

One of the things I always look for in a job applicant is empathy. It is among the core competencies of a good manager. For example, I might ask an applicant, "You've noticed a colleague or employee of yours isn't doing well. The peer is down and having trouble dealing with the workload. Can you give me a concrete example of such a situation and how you dealt with it?"

The answers reveal a lot about the candidates and their ability to deal with people. There is no one right answer. It depends on the situations and how the candidate deals with the further questions as they progress. You would not believe what you hear some applicants say. People who lack empathy cannot turn it on and off like a switch. It is a deficiency that they always carry that is almost impossible to invent on the spot.

The higher you get in a company; the more important people management becomes. In the highest positions it should occupy at least 80% of your working time. With your direct reports you need a direct conversation at least once a week, preferably face to face. We are talking about the fact that great leaders and their teams form a sworn trusting community that can handle challenging projects and achieve the greatest goals based on this trust. This incredible atmosphere attracts other talents and becomes a wheel rolling on its own. Creating this trusting environment is the task of a great leader, and that can only be done with empathy, not by "leading through fear" or toxic behaviors in general. If you want to work in a great environment, you must become a driving force of that community. You can't stand on the sidelines and hope that others will create that great environment. This is your job.

"'Night it is: oh that I must be light! And thirst for night! And loneliness!
Night it is: now my desire bursts out of me like a spring,-I long for speech.
Night it is: now all the jumping fountains speak louder. And also my soul is a jumping well.
It is night: now all the songs of lovers are awakening. And also my soul is the song of a lover."

The Dance Song

"And when I talked privately with my wild wisdom, she said to me angrily, "You want, you desire, you love, therefore alone you praise life!"

I almost answered evil and told the truth to the angry one; and one cannot answer more evil than when one "tells the truth" to his wisdom.

That is how it is between the three of us. By reason only do I love life -and, verily, most when I hate it!

But that I am good to wisdom and often too good: that makes it reminds me very much of life!"

In the dance song, for the first time, a conflict is clearly addressed that rages within Zarathustra - the conflict between life and wisdom. Zarathustra's life is characterized by the search for wisdom, he develops the philosophy of the superman in his hermitage and brings it to the people. He quickly realizes teaching is practically taking his whole life. Was this how he imagined his life? Preaching day in and day out and constantly looking for new disciples? No. He wants to live, free and carefree.

He will "sing more songs" and it becomes clearer over the course of the book that he does not want to be the preacher. He wants to live free, without all these burdens and troubles. The hostility and struggles, everything wears on him and wants to make his life difficult. The so-called spirit of gravity comes back with force, his greatest and worst enemy.

Have you ever felt that you just don't feel like doing the job anymore? Just leave the hamster wheel and live on a little island in the sun. Throw off all the responsibility and just switch off. If you know this feeling, then I'm sure your employees do too. Social media aggressively helps people invent ever more beautiful dream castles and read stories about people who have actually done just that - escaped. Is it possible? Is it real?

Well, there are people who live in Bali or tour the world as travel bloggers and share their great lives with everyone. But make no mistake, they work hard too, don't share their struggles with you. If you don't have enough money in your bank account to spend the rest of your life chasing the sun, it's going to be almost impossible. The vast majority of people will work as employees for most of their lives in paid employment until retirement age is reached and then you hope to have prepared to lead a dignified life until death. Quite depressing, isn't it? But there is light at the end of the tunnel.

I find it exciting that Zarathustra defines wisdom and life as two different things. Do the two have to be mutually exclusive?

We all need money to live, as society expects something in return for the services it offers. If I want to eat I must either grow my own food or pay the producer.

If my work is dedicated to the pure acquisition of knowledge, I do not have much to give except this knowledge. The possibility to earn money with knowledge is however limited, in any case clearly more limited than the possibilities with physical work to earn money.

In the 18th and 19th centuries, work was almost always hard physical labor. So many occupational fields have been added today that no longer cause back pain from too much lifting but rather, through sitting in the wrong position in front of the computer. These developments have clearly changed the world of work.

Today, the pursuit of wisdom can itself be life. There are many people who earn quite a lot of money by giving speeches or sharing their wisdom in many different forums. It might start as being a teacher at primary school or a professor at a university. A trainer in a big corporation or a consultant. If you are clever about it, there is still a lot of time left for living. This is not entirely different from construction workers who will toil all their lives building things, and sharing their wisdom in the form of the craftsmanship they leave behind in their work. Both can be happy or unhappy with their jobs and both can call their work their lives or a burden - independent of the time invested.

So how do we distinguish between wisdom and life? The Cambridge Dictionary defines wisdom as: *"the ability to make good judgments based on what you have learned from your experience, or the knowledge and understanding that gives you this ability"* and life as: *"the period between birth and death, or the state of being alive"*.

So looking at these definitions, you could state that wisdom is the fine art of living your life. Wisdom is part of the subset of life. You can have both, and I think that the qualities of life and wisdom are strongly correlated. You need great wisdom to live a great life. Limited wisdom leads to a limited life, and poor wisdom produces a poor life.

Following this logic, the determining factor for the quality of your life is wisdom. So your ability to make decisions determines the direction it will inevitably go. By the way, you don't need a high IQ to make good decisions. We've all made a really stupid decision that sends an unpleasant shiver down our spine when we think about it. And in some lives, one bad and/or wrong decision is enough to screw up your whole life or shift it into a direction that makes it really hard.

Most of the decisions that relatively successful people make are positive ones. There are people who continually sabotage their futures for one reason or another, consistently selecting the easiest choice, but the readers of this book are unlikely to be among them, since working to become a great leader is difficult. It is important that we are always aware that each of these decisions is our own responsibility. Although the starting points in life are grossly unfair, the "I couldn't help it" or "I had no other choice" talk is rarely true. Accept full responsibility for all your decisions in life and above all, try to avoid things that make it difficult for you to make decisions, like drugs, toxic people, or peer pressure, because that is also your responsibility. You are responsible for the people around you and you are responsible for the things that you stuff into your body - no one else.

While hammering on your responsibility here, it is interesting to note that neuroscientists believe that more than 90% of our decisions are made by our subconscious mind[29] and we are not aware of them. But this should not be used as an excuse. Many of these 90% are inconsequential (like, should I cross my right foot over my left, or the other way around), and we can shape our subconscious mind to some extent. The major decisions in life remain under your control.

I once saw an interview with Matthew Perry about his alcohol addiction. It was a discussion between Perry and Peter Hitchens. Matthew Perry is admitting that he is a drug addict and if he has a drink he can't stop. He states that he is in control of the first drink but not about the next ones. It just pulls him away like an overflowing river. He can't help and can't stop anymore. A lot of people will relate to this, and I fully understand.

But still, the first glass is his decision. Do I take the first glass when I know that it will hurt me? So don't take the first glass. You can use this sentence as a metaphor when in front of a similar decision. What will the outcome be? If you can't clearly assume it will be positive, then don't take the glass.

Wisdom is making decisions that produce good outcomes. Now you could say that Matthew Perry is not wise. His poor decision led to him having a poor life. Why is he doing it? Why are people making these bad decisions?

Normally, one would hope that every decision one makes is conscious and calculated to optimize the result. However, as we all know from painful experience, this is not the case.

When we are faced with an important decision, we have to evaluate it rationally and extrapolate many possible consequences and assess the impact on our lives.

---

[29] Susan Weinschenk's "Neuro Web Design: What makes them click?"; 2009, Berkeley

As an example, I just baked cookies and they are in the oven. My partner is on the couch playing PlayStation and I am writing a book. Everything smells like the delicious coconut macaroons I just took out of the oven. I want to get up and try one. Then another. Now the considerations go off, I should ask my partner whether she wants one too, so that she will think I am generous instead of selfish. Should I have just taken one, considering my new diet? Maybe I should never have made them in the first place. So many points to consider just related to these cookies.

This kind of decision tree has to be done before any action, but of course that can't work. My cookie example is relatively simple, but often the decisions we make are so complex that it is impossible to estimate all the consequences. The complex world requires shortcuts, and this task is done by our subconsciousness. If I care about my partner, I bring her a cookie without having to think about it. And once I decided to make them, I need not second guess myself about my diet. This subconscious mind in turn is influenced by emotions much more extensively than our conscious thinking.

Why Matthew Perry drinks the first glass, of course, only he can answer, but what I often see in conversations is that people are well aware that the next decision is not necessarily the best, but there is a stronger reason to make it anyway. Often it has to do with the short-term release of "happiness" hormones like Serotonin, Dopamine Endorphins or Oxytocin. People are not happy where they are and want to drown out this unhappiness with a short kick. Often these destructive compulsions for a rush of happiness hormones began with something relatively harmless.

Another example, a man is sitting in a bar while at home, his wife and two children are waiting. He knows it would be wise to go home now, but instead orders the next drink, and then another, and another. The trouble coming at home doesn't matter. Where does this come from? Among the many reasons, is a strategy of the brain to avoid a place where one is simply not happy. He had imagined life differently than a small house with an indifferent wife who pays more attention to the spoiled children than to him. But his salary did not permit more than the small house, his mother kept pressuring him for grandchildren. Wasn't it all just what grownups do? And so, one thing led to another. In his early 20s he had hoped to see the world and become a travel blogger. To experience interesting people and places and then eventually open a bar in Madagascar and chill in the sun all day and watch others surf.

The person is pigeonholed and conformed, maneuvered into an unhappy situation, whether subconsciously or consciously. He chooses the short-term kick.

Can Zarathustra's wavering between wisdom and life be interpreted as exactly this dilemma? The constant fight between emotions (life) and well thought through decision (wisdom). The human tendency for fun choices is in constant opposition to the striving for a happy life. On the other hand, wise decisions produce a happy life. So, we should all strive to educate ourselves as much as possible to make wiser and wiser decisions and minimize the influence of emotions on these decisions. Finding the right balance will lead to success.

If we succeed in capturing the "Wild Wisdom", we will also have the "Dear Life" bound to us.

The probability of living and dying happily is immensely higher when we focus on gathering knowledge to make wise decisions. The theme of the book is directly related to this. Our aspiration to become great leaders is fundamentally dependent on how wise we are and, by inference, how smart we are perceived to be. Many pillars are designed or converge on this very point. Knowledge is not just power; knowledge is the cornerstone of almost everything. Therefore: Read! Learn! Write! Expose yourself to as many situations from which you can learn as possible. Accept and embrace challenges. Surround yourself with smart people and celebrate each Eureka moment, and furiously work towards the next. True happiness comes from striving to be better.

"And when once life asked me: Who is this then, the wisdom?-then I said eagerly: "Oh yes! the wisdom!

One thirsts for it and does not get full, one looks through veils, one hunts through nets.

Is it beautiful? What do I know! But the oldest carps are still baited with her.

She is changeable and defiant; I have often seen her bite her lip and comb against the grain of her hair.

Perhaps she is wicked and false, and in all things a wench; but when she speaks ill of herself, that is when she seduces the most."

When I said this to life, it laughed maliciously and closed its eyes. Who are you talking about?" she said, "about me?"

The Grave Song

"There is the island of graves, the silent one; there are also the graves of my youth. There I will carry an evergreen wreath of life."
Thus resolving in my heart, I sailed across the sea.
O you, my youth's faces and appearances! Oh, all your glimpses of love, you divine moments! How you die to me so quickly! I remember you today like my dead.
From you, my dearest dead, comes to me a sweet smell, a heart- and tear-solving. Truly, it shakes and loosens the heart of the lonely shipwrecked.
Still I am the richest and best to envy, I am the loneliest! For I had you, and you still have me: say, to whom did such rose-apples fall from the tree as to me?
Still I am your love's inheritance and earth, blooming to your memory of colorful wild-growing virtues, oh you most beloved!"

With the funeral song Zarathustra expands the thought structure of the previous chapter. When we are young, we have dreams. One wanted to become an astronaut, another one wanted to become a firefighter or a police officer, some wanted to become a singer or a professional athlete. Whatever it was, an unrestricted imagination drives our young thoughts and dreams. For most of us these dreams are lost as soon as we realize that life is a lot tougher than we imagined as children. With school, then possibly an apprenticeship and everything changes. Dreams become goals and goals become target agreements and development plans. Until you realize that you are too old to become an astronaut or an athlete. Then we laugh about the crazy dreams we had as children.

Back then everything was simpler - have you ever heard that saying? I would say: Today everything is more complex. Back then everything was a little more manageable, but definitely not simpler.

Our life is like a boat ride in a canoe. We just dismiss our childhood dreams, but we have always been in this boat. This boat follows the river of life, this flows sometimes faster and sometimes slower, sometimes we get into the nasty rapids and even capsize. But it is always the same canoe. When the ride gets fast and scary, many people slow down, and want to drift slowly again as in our youth.

At these points, our river of life shows us that if we want to go in the direction of our dreams, we have to really go for it. We should, for example, take our education seriously if we expect to win our dream job. Now it's getting fast on the river, and we should really dig in and paddle.

But many people get scared or tired here and decide against it. Better not to take a risk and take small steps to smaller successes. This is of course a rational decision and makes sense, but should you really sacrifice your dreams in favor of lower risks and lower rewards?

Achieving big goals requires big efforts - everyone knows that. But to make dreams real requires more than big effort, it requires an unshakable will.

To stay in our metaphor of the canoe and the river - if you just want to get from point A to point B, you have to paddle, if you want to go much further, you also need good technique to sustain the effort. But really big dreams are only reached after you have activated your last reserves at the end of your strength. With unbelievable effort and good technique, you paddle past the sign "Last footbridge before the waterfall" into the unknown. You grit your teeth and tumble down the waterfall with a scream, dive deep into the basin, fight your way back up to the surface and continue along the course of the river that has never been explored. Full of amazement and pride, you build your footbridge at the place your dream had envisioned.

Zarathustra talks in the text about his enemies who always put obstacles in his way, spoiled his successes, darkened his ways and insulted his joys. Enemies await us all. Who they are is intentionally left open, because each of us has to fight with our own enemies. And for each of us there are other enemies who stop us. But it is important to understand that most of them live within us and work out of us. Again, as I learned to overcome my worst enemy, unhealthy egoism, I was able to clear the way for the next level of my personal development. Let me exemplify this with a personal story from my past. I was working in a project management team with a new supervisor. A lanky guy with a blow-dry haircut who was overly candid with his words. His "qualifications" seem to be only that had studied literature and I just couldn't explain why they hired such a guy instead of promoting me. I was pissed off at first and more or less uncooperative. He tolerated me which is all I wanted from him. Then when I had to submit an important paper, he asked me if he could review it. I politely but firmly refused. What could such a guy teach me? I went into the meeting and my paper was torn up and I had to write it again. Again, he came to me and asked me if he could take a look at it. I was annoyed, but relented and gave him the paper. He rewrote it and what can I say? It was in a different league. The paper passed the second review without any objections, even though the content was almost identical. As a literary graduate, he was a masterful writer, and his experience in one of the leading management consultancies provided him with comprehensive knowledge that I did not yet have. I was downright embarrassed at how egotistical and self-absorbed I had been. Instead of seeing the opportunities his attitude would create for me and looking for what I could learn from him, I was simply blinded by my pride and envy. I shared the story openly and honestly with him and he just smiled and made me understand that my open self-reflection was the most important thing I could learn. I am still grateful to him today.

In our development model from camel to lion to child, the station in which we live as a lion is the one in which many people feel that they have reached their goal. They can roar loudly and are proud of what they have achieved but forget that this is only half of the way. This is where the arrogance and unhealthy egoism comes in and obscures their view of what is still possible. To admit that there is so much more to come would be to make what they have achieved look smaller. But virtually every one of the most accomplished scholars will state that the more they learn, the more clearly, they see how little they know.

It would be easy to stop and enjoy the fruits of success. We could stop at the jetty in front of the waterfall and join all the others. Get a 30-year mortgage to buy a small house in our hometown. Buy a reliable car and raise the kids as best as you can. But you could also build your strength, check the equipment and then set off in the direction of the waterfall, that is the way to become a child. To admit that one is not yet at the end, that there is still something to explore, to invent, to experience, that is the way to great leadership. But for this, as Zarathustra says so beautifully, you need one thing above all, an invulnerable will. One must be willing in order to attain. And the stronger the will, the greater the dream can be.

From the Spanish painter Pablo Picasso comes the wonderful quote, *"Everything you can imagine is real."* I would like to add to this: *"and only your will can make it reality".*

It is important to mention that will is independent of knowledge and cognition. One does not have to know how it goes, but one must have the will to find out. Will is the way to knowledge and cognition and thus we close the circle of the three songs.

We alone are masters of our destiny and our ability to make wise decisions enables us to achieve what we want. But how do you recognize a wise decision? Confucius says: *"Man has three ways to act wisely: by reflection is the noblest, by imitation the simplest, by experiencing the bitterest."*

A strong will coupled with the ability to make wise decisions enables us to achieve nearly everything we have ever dreamed of and never lose the motivation to overcome all the obstacles that we ourselves or others put in our way.

"Yes, there is an invulnerable, ineradicable thing about me, a rock-splintering thing: that is my will. Silently it walks and unchanged through the years.

It wants to walk its course on my feet, my old will; its mind is hard of heart and invulnerable.

Invulnerable I am alone on my heel. Still you live there and are equal to you, most patient! Still you broke through all graves!

In you also still lives the unredeemed of my youth; and as life and youth you sit here hoping on yellow grave ruins.

Yes, you are still my destroyer of all graves: Hail, my will! And only where graves are, there are resurrections."

Self-Surpassing

"That is your whole will, you wisest, as a will to power; and even if you speak of good and evil and of the valuations. If you still want to create the world before which you can kneel, it is your last hope and drunkenness."

This speech of Zarathustra is the most important speech in the whole book. He describes here one of the cores - if not the one core - of philosophy and that is the will to power.

Now, according to the German philosopher and motivational trainer Dr. Christian Weilmeier, the will to power is not to be misunderstood as the will to rule or dominate, it is rather a life-affirming and creative principle that underlies virtually everything - a life force.

However, Weilmeier also points out that there is no universal definition of Nietzsche's concept of the will to power, but only different interpretations. This suits me fine. I have my own interpretation to suit our purpose.

To progress from camel to child you must destroy values and create new ones. One cannot be satisfied with living and working according to the same guidelines. To create something great, something great must be destroyed. Be it in the context of large companies, whose rise naturally resulted in the demise of the old industries, or new, more agile companies that push their old and rusty competitors out of the market.

Those who can impose their values are creators and destroyers in one. To do that, you need power. And to achieve this power, you need the will to power. From this follows that striving to create a better world is a clear expression of the will to power. The two are linked because ambitious goals require power.

Take the climate movement initiated by Greta Thunberg around Fridays for Future, whose goal was to trigger a change in people's thinking about climate change. They want to create new values and abolish old values. A revaluation of values, a destruction or overcoming of the old. But this is only possible if you gain power over the old values and can bring them down, figuratively speaking. The will to change is the will to power in this sense.

And this then also applies to those who want to implement disruptive ideas in daring ventures. Those who invest all their time and effort to achieve their goals and fight for the fulfillment of their entrepreneurial dream. This struggle is the expression of the will to power.

This constant cycle of destruction and renewal was strongly coined in the standard economic work "Capitalism, Socialism and Democracy" by Joseph Schumpeter a national economist and politician from Austria, which is experiencing an interesting revival because of its statements on the demise of capitalism.

The principle appears in many works, starting with Darwin and continuing to today. The idea of creative destruction is nothing more than that the appearance of a disruptive renewal usually results in the extinction of the old. For example, Darwin described that often the introduction of a new species into a territory in which it was not native will lead to the extinction of other native species there.

Schumpeter's thesis in an example state that every company will start very agile and therefore cost competitive but with growing and growing it gets a bigger and bigger overhead which drives up the cost position till it is no longer competitive. New companies will come and take market share due to their better performance and destroy the old behemoth. But that is not necessarily something bad as these new companies usually create even more jobs and more wealth. Inferring from this simple example, Schumpeter's bigger thesis is that capitalism as a whole must overcome itself at some point. According to Schumpeter, capitalism will merge into socialism. And the interesting thing is that it will be its own success, the ever faster turning flywheel, that will eventually destroy capitalism. We got an interesting foretaste of the so-called financial crisis with the bankruptcy of Lehman Brothers Bank and the resulting shock waves that rolled around the globe. However, still the flywheel turns and has not slowed.

Life itself is will to power. You can't bypass it. You must go straight through it. What usually happens in something like a battle.

Which company gives up its market share voluntarily? Which manager likes to voluntarily give up the job? A new leader seeks to put their own stamp on the team from the start. The old is overcome to create something new, and that is a good thing. One challenges the old values and creates new ones. Challenge drives innovation.

In a way, our metamorphosis of the mind is nothing more than overcoming the previous phase. A rediscovery of one's potential and a building up of the ego. To become better, we must shake ourselves and our egoism. We draw energy from this disruption and see it as an opportunity to grow.

In 1917, Sigmund Freud coined the concept of the mortifications of humanity. These mortifications are deep cuts in human self-understanding, usually driven by new scientific discoveries. Thus, an early mortification was the Copernican one, according to which the Earth is not the center of the universe. Another was the Darwinian one, according to which man does not have a special position among the living beings but is only a further development of the animal world. The third, was named after himself, the Freudian mortification, according to which the subconscious controls us and our control over ourselves is an illusion. Each of these mortifications was a big hit for our human ego.

Prof. Dr. Gerhard Vollmer lists and explains more, including the ecological mortification, which means that we destroy our own planet and the "computer model" according to which we can create intelligences that are more powerful than we are.

DeepMind, the AI company that was acquired by Alphabet 2014, beat the world's best Go player, Lee Sedol and Deep Blue, owned by IBM beat Gari Kasparov the (at this time) best chess player in the world are nice examples of machines that can beat the best of us. The last one according to Vollmer is the neurobiological one. Here the work of Musk's company Neuralink and others is to be mentioned which wants to lift us to the next evolutionary stage. We are all becoming cyborgs. Is this possibly the "superhuman" of which Zarathustra speaks?

But this will certainly not be the last one. The science will drive these mortifications incessantly forward and if we only think far enough, probably the final mortification will be when we discover that we are not the highest intelligence in the universe. Because if we find them or they find us, the probability that this ends well for us is quite small.

But following our logic, this must also turbocharge our will to power, for our overcoming of the self. To meet aliens who are smarter than we, will be our final challenge and demand everything from us. We will hopefully still have some creators of new values on the planet, and they will also find a way here.

The famous quote, *"What does not kill me makes me stronger"* is also from Nietzsche and a beautiful illustration of our theme.

Yes, leaders must grow by our mistakes, but this is reactive. We must also proactively create challenges for ourselves and our teams. We need to build the environment where all of us can develop and demonstrate their will to power, their creativity, their ability to destroy old values and carve new ones in new plates. We must build a world in which we are the fire for the furnaces in which the innovations of tomorrow are cast. A world that sees new values not as an attack but as an opportunity to evolve towards something higher. A world that does not fear for its old industries but is eager to evolve continuously. A world in which companies as well as countries can challenge each other in open competition and have to put resources into innovation and people to advance our species as a whole and ensure its survival. Only our will to power, our will to life will enable us to do so.

"Do you want a name for this world? A solution for all its riddles? a light also for you, you most hidden, strongest, unafraid, most of midnight? This world is the will to power - and nothing else. And you yourselves are also this will to power - and nothing else."[30]

---

[30] Nietzsche's documents which were published around 1885 in "Der Wille zur Macht" (The Will to Power)

The Sublime Ones

"I love the neck of the bull in him, but now I also want to see the eye of the angel.
He must also still unlearn his heroic will: he shall be an exalted one for me and not only a sublime one:-the ether itself should lift him, the will-less one!
He conquered beasts, he solved riddles: but he should also redeem his beasts and riddles, he should still transform them into heavenly children.
His knowledge has not yet learned to smile and to be without jealousy; his flowing passion has not yet become quiet in beauty.
Verily, not in satiety shall his desire be silent and submerged, but in beauty! The grace belongs to the magnanimity of the great-minded."

What is true greatness? That is the question underlying the whole concept of great leaders or great leadership. If you were to ask me to list the great managers I've had, that list is short. But a few have stuck. And if you were to ask me what it was that made them such great leaders, I can think of many, mostly different things. Each of them had something different that made them special.

Another way to look at it, what didn't they have? They had no negative egoism, they were not aggressive or violent (in speech or physically), they were not pretentious. They were no mystery-mongers. I could list a lot of other things that they were not, but I think you understand what I mean.

If you read it like this, then the image of the three metamorphoses of the spirit comes to mind again. Zarathustra talks about bulls and lions, animals that symbolize violence and power. Characteristics that every child and most people would initially associate as heroic. You know what an association test is, don't you? It's where you're given a word and you say the first words that come to mind, without thinking too much. I just did this test with my daughter. I gave her the term "hero" and she answered in this order: (1) strong, (2) intelligent and (3) fast. I frequently ask this question to people and usually get the same answer. Do the test yourself, with the people around you.

But that's exactly the point, the great leaders I was allowed to get to know, were exactly that not, at least not superficially. They were never loud, for example. They never had to roar like lions. In a loud meeting, they would never be the ones to outdo others with the power of their voice, no they would wait, listen and then lean forward. The room would go quiet all by itself, waiting for them to say something. You don't have to be proactively loud; people want to hear you and will be quiet for your sake. You don't have to flex your muscles and push people out of your way, when you enter the room people will make room for you. It is fascinating how powerful and deafening the relaxed and calm nature of these people is.

So, all great leaders I have left the lion phase of their development behind and entered the child phase. They do not radiate violence, but just the opposite, calmness. But in a way that everybody knows that this calmness has been learned the way a ship captain wrestles calmness from the sea after hundreds of rough voyages. Everyone knows that it is this calmness that can be relied upon. A calmness that can infect and bring down the hustle and bustle through the cape.

Have you ever tried to tense your muscles and keep them tense for a long time? For me it usually does not last long before I have to relax. Showing muscles is not a proof of strength. In our picture, the best proof of power is to use it with "casual muscles". We learn from Brad Pitt in the movie "Snatch" that you don't have to be afraid of the musclemen, but of those with the scars on their fists. The musclemen are usually slow, the others usually hard as steel and fast. Those who try to lead by force always lead by fear. But fear decreases with distance. The best employees can move to another place and will quickly put distance between themselves and this person or completely leave the company. The company can afford having bad managers as long as it is on top of the wave and has enough other motivating factors to keep its employees. But as soon as this wears off, as it always does sooner or later, the bad manager becomes an unparalleled force of decay. I have experienced two of these managers and they were among the motivations to write this book.

To be exalted, you have to be elevated. That means you can't do it alone, but the people around you have to lift you up.

There is no formula or universal guide on how to achieve this. But if there's one thing you take away from this book, it's that when you feel like a lion, bursting with pride over how good you are, you are only halfway to becoming a great leader. Hold up the mirror in your proudest moment. You will see that your greatest beauty does not come from pride in yourself, but with the pride in the eyes of people who created something because they had your support. Your impact through others is true beauty and what makes a great leader. Overcome your pride and then help others do the same.

As Benjamin Franklin once said, *"In reality, perhaps none of our natural passions is so difficult to overcome as pride."*

Benjamin Franklin was obsessed with self-improvement. He had defined thirteen virtues for himself (already at the young age of just 20) and wrote them down. But what was interesting is that he only focused on one of these virtues at a time. Just as Zarathustra described, he concentrated on being good at one thing and understood that it would take too much strength to be exemplary at all times and in everything. He also revealed in his own autobiography that no matter how hard he tried, he could not meet all the requirements he set for himself. The self-critical restraint that one of the greatest geniuses of his time maintained is impressive and illustrates the core of our topic. There was certainly not much more Franklin could hope to achieve in his life, and yet he remained modest. A true great leader.

"And from no one I want so as from you just beauty, you mighty: your goodness is your last self-overwhelming.

I trust you with all evil: therefore I want good from you.

Verily, I often laughed at the weaklings, who believe themselves good, because they have lame paws!

You shall strive after the virtue of the pillar: it becomes more and more beautiful and tender, but inwardly it becomes harder and more burdensome, the more it rises.

Yes, you exalted one, one day you shall be beautiful and hold up the mirror to your own beauty.

Then your soul will shudder with divine desires; and worship will still be in your vanity!

This is the secret of the soul: only when the hero has left it, the super-hero approaches it in a dream."

The Land of Culture

"I flew too far into the future: a horror overtook me.
And when I looked around me, behold, time was my only contemporary.
Then I fled backward, homeward, and ever more hurriedly: thus I came to you,
O present ones, and to the land of learning.
For the first time I brought an eye for you, and good desire: truly, with longing in my heart I came."

Zarathustra ventures a look into the distant future and sees that humanity is extinct. And so, he travels back quickly, the horror still deep in his limbs, and meets the scholars of the day. He has to laugh because he realizes why there is no one in the future.

He does not mean this physically, but rather intellectually. It is a metaphor for the fact that if one limits the future to things of the past, nothing new could ever be built. Regardless of the topic, people always derive the future from the past. We all know the saying: history repeats itself. And there is the well-known quote by Karl Marx: *"History always repeats itself twice - the first time as a tragedy, the second time as a farce."*

But why is that? Or rather, why does it seem that way to people? According to Zarathustra, this results from the fact that people avoid the difficult task of thinking ahead and prefer to look backwards. That is easier, since everything has already happened and we need only comment on it, rather than create. When we have a future directed way of thinking, we must struggle with not knowing what will happen. The decision trees are infinite and even if the universe is deterministic, our little mind can never grasp and process it all.

Again and again, I see projects fail and great ideas fizzle because the database was not good enough to prove that it was right to pursue them. But you never know, and although data based on experience always helps with predictions, sometimes there is no data. What then? Make assumptions! You can't know what's coming, so make assumptions and justify them well, and then go for it. When we talk about the future, everything is a guess. Our revered experts and the wise ones of our time are almost always wrong. We live in a time when weather reports are more reliable than economic forecasts. Taleb's Black Swans are a great example to refer to here. When we try to predict the future out of the past, we can copy the predictable, but never foresee the possible.

Don't listen to the preachers of yesterday, you must break the old values and create new ones to define the future. If you always look for what was good yesterday, you will always get what was good yesterday. Nothing will improve and nothing will become new.

Georg W. F. Hegel, one of the most important philosophers of the past, once said: *"From the history of peoples we can learn that peoples have learned nothing from history."*

Learning from history would mean that we can leave it behind us. That we can redefine and not get caught in the thinking of the past. We see how cultural creators move the world forward, but what we rarely see is how many stones are thrown in their way by those who fear the future. The mass of people is caught in this anti-intellectual cycle that turns them into easily manipulated consumers. If I know that someone will always behave the way they have always behaved, then it is easy to tailor my products and services to that behavior. The fact that most people do not want to rethink the future, i.e., do not want to take the hard way, is what Zarathustra recognizes and highlights in this chapter.

Dare it! Dare! That is what great leaders do. They dare to go new ways. There is no reliable data? Make assumptions and go for it. There is no well-trodden path? Then create it.

An interesting aspect is that many people will be skeptical about these new ways. So, it is always a good indicator when you face a lot of headwinds, even when it comes from the "intellectual elite", that you are on the right track.

I can still remember well how it was to help build Amazon in Europe. The media had ensured that the company had such a bad reputation that I had to justify my actions to my family and relatives. The question was, how could I work for the devil in good conscience?

News headlines about Amazon destroying stores and plunging the world into a maelstrom of unemployment were making the rounds. A retail apocalypse was even predicted.

Jeff Bezos once said that Amazon is not killing main street, the future is. The Schumpeterian cycle of creative destruction does not stop for anyone and therefore anyone who wants to keep a cherished standard forever is doomed. They hated Amazon, but in the end the customer wants convenience, and this must be taken into account, whether the brick-and-mortar economy wants it or not. And if they don't go along with it, then they'll just fall by the wayside. In business, most good managers know this. It gets interesting in branches like public administration, schools, politics in general, the military or state-run companies.

For the reasons mentioned above, people in these branches still believe that they can win "the good fight" as long as they firmly believe in it. Coming from the former DDR (East Germany), my family and I have been living in a more or less stable democracy for almost 33 years now. I have consciously followed the required developments and find that they are equal to that of a company. Let me explain what I mean.

A young democracy replaced an old system. Everyone was excited and enthusiastic about the start-up culture. Blooming landscapes were promised, and for the time being, that's where things were heading. Gradually, the overhead increased, and more and more people went into administration and management in general. Salaries and bonuses increased disproportionately to workers' incomes, and my country's government apparatus is now the largest it has ever had. The expenses that the Taxpayers Association (an NGO in

Germany) summarizes every year under the term "waste" are constantly increasing and now amount to about 5% of the total budget. Just like in an average company. The international importance is dwindling and the ability to defend is known to be close to zero. The country is no longer competitive internationally due to ever-increasing wages and other cost drivers, and self-imposed social restrictions have sidelined its leading politicians at international conferences. Again, everything is exactly like an average company - on its way towards recession.

What would be the solution now? To continue like this and stick to the current course? Or would it be time to dare something new? Now I know that a country similar to a large tanker cannot be turned on the spot, but a publicly invoked lack of alternatives will certainly not lead to long-term success. On the contrary, it will lead to young start-ups coming and shaking up the existing system in their disruptive capacity. And that is a good thing. We need innovation and movement at all levels of society. There can be no standing still, new things must be dared.

I am sure that most politicians go into politics with good intentions to want to change something. They have ideals and may have good ideas. But then comes the reality that the job depends on being re-elected every few years. And that the mass of people will always be afraid of change. Truly innovative politicians are marginal phenomena and when they are flushed to the surface by chance, they are quickly forgotten again, because the system has so many protective mechanisms built in that it is almost impossible to change anything. While companies are in mostly free competition, this is not the case with political parties. But also, here it needs constant innovations, otherwise we will sooner than later see a frightening twist.

So, Zarathustra comes back from his journey into the future and sees these losers in charge sitting there, the advocates of stagnation, painted with the signs of the past and starts laughing. He is convinced that he and his philosophy will push them out of business and new leaders will come to power with new values. The system will be iterated further and something new will flourish. Stop clinging to the old and calling it the only way. It will disappear anyway; the only question is when and whether we wait for someone else to overthrow our systems or whether we prefer to be prepared and do it ourselves in a controlled way. And I don't mean any revolutionists or terrorists. I mean in particular to prepare for the technology that is rapidly advancing. If we ignore it, we will soon be in a firefighting mode in which we can only react to the collapse of the house.

Let's be the creators of the future and actively test the possibilities and find the best way while we are still in the driver's seat.

"I laughed and laughed, while my foot was still trembling and my heart too: "Here is the home of all color pots!

With fifty patches painted on your face and limbs: so you sat there to my amazement, you present ones!

And with fifty mirrors around you, flattering and talking after your play of colors!

Truly, you could not wear a better mask, you present ones, than your own face is! Who could recognize you!

Written with the signs of the past, and even these signs painted over with new signs: so you have hidden yourselves well from all sign interpreters!"

Zarathustra is perplexed because he sees a system that is so perfectly self-contained that the occupants can no longer help but see themselves as the past, the present and the future.

I am not a politician and have no political ambitions. I think politics has a relatively low probability of affecting change for good. But that is the crux, it should be. Politics should be THE place where the brightest minds argue together to give the country and its people the best possible future. A lively debate of visions and innovations to give the best future possible to those we owe it to, our children. I am fundamentally an optimist, and I am absolutely sure that within the next hundred years the current systems will no longer be, because they can no longer be. My only fear is how our current political systems will change, and what they will become.

"But I found no home anywhere: I am restless in all cities and a departure at all gates.

Foreign to me and a mockery are the present, to whom the heart recently drove me; and I am driven out of father and mother countries.

So I alone still love my children's land, the undiscovered, in the farthest sea: for it I shall search and search my sails.

In my children I will make it good that I am my fathers' child: and in all the future-this present!"

Immaculate Perception

"This parable I give to you sensitive hypocrites, you, the "pure-recognizers!" To you I call chandeliers!

You, too, love the earth and the earthly: I have guessed you well-but shame is in your love and a guilty conscience-you resemble the moon!

Your spirit has been persuaded to despise the earthly, but not your bowels, which are the strongest thing about you!

And now your spirit is ashamed that it is for the sake of your bowels, and before its own shame it goes by stealth and lies.

"That would be the highest thing for me-so your lying spirit talks to itself-to look at life without desire and not like the dog with a hanging tongue:

To be happy in looking, with stifled will, without grasp and greed of self-seeking-cold and ashen all over, but with drunken moon eyes!"

"That would be the dearest thing to me-so the seduced man seduces himself-to love the earth as the moon loves it, and to touch its beauty with the eye alone.

And that means to me the immaculate knowledge of all things, that I want nothing from things: except that I may lie there before them like a mirror with a hundred eyes.

Oh, you sensitive hypocrites, you lustful ones! You lack innocence in desire: and now you slander desire!"

Many people see weakness in emotions. In the executive suites of companies, emotion is almost always equated with weakness. But if you listen to a company founder, especially at the beginning of the company, giving a speech to the employees, at a time when everything seems achievable, then these speeches are filled with pure emotion. Just a couple of weeks ago from writing this, I listened to a company founder giving a speech to employees. The company is a few years old but the start-up spirit still flows from every pore. The company is already the market leader in its niche and on its way to becoming a global player. It is now valued at several billion dollars and is no longer a small fish in the pond. The speech was rousing and emotional. He actually faltered a few times as he became overwhelmed, looking over the many employees who work their asses off every day with him for the success of the company. It was really nice to listen to him and the almost fanatical applause of the staff. Pure Emotion. He started slowly and you could see his uncertainty as he read from a prepared text. But the more positive figures he showed, the warmer he became. He gave increasing free rein to his emotions. He had given more than one hundred percent from the beginning and never left any doubt that this company and every single employee in it is really important for him personally. That the fulfillment of his life's dream is only possible with them and through them. That this world needs this company. That the hard times will be worth it. Not only financially, but that the work of the people will save this planet. Emotion combined with meaning. You could feel with every statement how honest this speech was, how much it meant to the employees and how much this moment also meant to him. It was fantastic and the best introduction I could have had to the company.

And yet, in normal business, emotions are not welcome. I have seen many managers crying in conversations about too many topics to list here. A great example I still remember was, when we had just finished our Christmas business, one of the most stressful times in my company at that time. We would double the number of employees to cope with the Christmas volume and then halve the number after the rush. We kept the best ones every year to compensate for attrition.

Every seasonal employee was expected to be retained, no matter how high their absenteeism was or how bad their social behavior. Self-reflection was rare. All employees had a temporary contract, and it was clear to all that they would have to leave at the end of the season. Nevertheless, they all hoped that they would be kept on. Chances were good for the very best, so we as managers established good relationships with these employees.

As the planning progressed this year, all managers made their plans for the respective departments and after tough discussions it was clear who we wanted to keep and who not. Everyone was more or less happy with the selections, or at least we could live with them. We all clearly understood that this plan must not be shared with employees under any circumstances, as it could still change. Nevertheless, some managers gave their favorite candidates smaller or larger hints that things would work out for them.

As the day approached, we received a new plan number from headquarters a few hours before the farewells began. The new plan contained fewer jobs and we all had to go back and take more colleagues off the retention list. Some managers had all but guaranteed their best workers a contract. I saw how some managers turned pale and how tears welled up in their eyes. How should they tell some of their best employees two days before Christmas that the promised job would no longer be there? The people who have worked hard in good faith for a permanent job. They had probably already shared the joyful news with their families at home. And now they would come home for Christmas and tell the family that they would soon be unemployed again.

I remember several managers who I had to take in my arms and comfort afterwards.

The stresses and strains of a management role are immense and, for many, completely new territory. You often find yourself in situations that demand everything of you. A great leader must be able to build up so much trust that the staff meeting is an outlet for these pent-up emotions. So, these meetings are often very emotional. It's bad when they embarrass the employees and make the whole situation worse rather than better.

It is the same with successes and failures. If these become a matter of course and are no longer celebrated or mourned, then the company and the people involved fall into a vortex of passionless indifference. Dead for every company and team.

I see emotions avoided regardless of gender and age - "men don't cry," or "if I cry as a woman, they think I'm weak and fulfill the stereotype." "Let's not celebrate this too soon, who knows what's to come."

Daniel Goleman, an American author and psychologist published his book "Emotional Intelligence - Why It Can Matter More Than IQ" in 1995. A huge success at the time, it is now part of the standard literature. But still many people are unwilling or unable to show emotions or to react appropriately to them.

It's not about breaking out in frenetic jubilation at every success and sinking into a sea of tears at every failure, it's about developing passion for the things we do. To approach our projects and tasks with passion and to fight our way through the shoals of work with the same passion. And then when we have mastered them, we can celebrate that. And when we have failed, we can lament that too. There is nothing wrong with that.

Frank W. Bond, an English Professor of Psychology and Management published several studies and books around this topic. In one of his studies entitled: "The role of acceptance and job control in mental health, job satisfaction, and work performance." he concludes that *"acceptance, the willingness to experience thoughts, feelings, and physiological sensations without having to control them or let them determine one's actions, is a major individual determinant of mental health and behavioral effectiveness"* [...] it also *"indicated that acceptance predicted mental health and an objective measure of performance above and beyond job control, negative affectivity, and locus of control. These beneficial effects of having more job control were enhanced when people had higher levels of acceptance."*

There are few things worse than a supervisor or co-worker you can't assess. And the ability to read emotions is one of the basic building blocks of our survival since the early history of humanity. Someone who closes emotions from us is (subconsciously) suspicious and we automatically limit our affection. The person is perceived as "heartless" or "cold as stone". At least the person will not win the medal as a favorite colleague.

"Where is beauty? Where I MUST WILL with my whole Will; where I will love and perish, that an image may not remain merely an image.
Loving and perishing: these have rhymed from eternity. Will to love: that is to be ready also for death. Thus do I speak unto you cowards! "

Zarathustra finds people who pursue their activity emotionless are hypocrites and he denies them any will to create. They do things for the sake of doing, but not to unhinge the world.

For us this results in two important things. First, we must not be ashamed to show emotions and second, we must create a work environment in which our employees feel free to show their emotions. According to Zarathustra, if you always repress your emotions within yourself, it eats away at your guts. For my part, I would rather have managers in my ranks who know how to celebrate when successes can be celebrated and who know how to vomit when things go wrong. After that, they all get their act together again and move on to the next round.

But employees will only share their emotions with you if they trust you. And that's why it's all about building trust! And we're back to the topic of "approachability". A great leader finds just the right level of approachability and professional distance. I've seen many managers go too far in one direction or the other. In both cases, it has usually been their undoing. If you are too close to your people, you will find it incredibly difficult to make tough personnel decisions, but they will always have to be made. If you're too far away, employees simply won't trust you, and that leads to serious consequences in terms of employee engagement, with the familiar consequences for productivity and all other KPIs. I'm not talking about the excesses known from the staff from "Wolf of Wall Street", where Jordan Belfort (played by Leonardo DiCaprio) was having excessive parties in the office. Or the coldness that comes out of many government agencies. Both are wrong and have severe negative consequences.

So celebrate successes without burning down the hut and mourn without smothering the corridor in tears. You also need to recognize individual differences in people's comfort in sharing emotions. Some people gush over every little thing while others keep their emotions to themselves. Neither is "wrong". Sustainability is also individual. A great leader can't help but know each of his employees individually to determine the right level of closeness they need. If you don't talk to your direct reports on a weekly basis, you can't know them as well as you should. As already mentioned, several times, the higher we climb the career ladder, the more important people management becomes. Engagement is the key. Silence is silver and talk is gold - at least in this case.

"For already she comes, the glowing one,-her love to the earth comes! Innocence and creator-greed is all sun-love!

Look how she impatiently comes over the sea! Do you not feel the thirst and the hot breath of her love?

She wants to suck on the sea and drink its depth up to the heights: there the desire of the sea rises with a thousand breasts.

It wants to be kissed and sucked by the thirst of the sun; it wants to become air and height and footpath of light and light itself!

Truly, like the sun I love life and all deep seas.

And this means knowledge to me: all depth shall go up to my height!"

Scholars

"As I lay in sleep, a sheep ate at the ivy wreath of my head and said: "Zarathustra is no longer a scholar.
It spoke and went away stuttering and proud. A child told me.
I like to lie here, where the children play, by the broken wall, under thistles and red poppies.
I am still a scholar to the children and also to the thistles and red poppies. Innocent they are, even in their wickedness.
But to the sheep I am no more: so will my fate-blessed be it!
For this is the truth: I have gone out of the house of the learned, and have thrown the door behind me."

This story of Zarathustra is the reckoning with the class of the scholars, which broke with Nietzsche early on and to which he never really felt a connection. An important reason for this will have been the following. Nietzsche had been appointed associate professor of classical philology at the University of Basel at the young age of 24. Philology is the field in various sciences that explores texts and, as linguistics and literary studies, contributes to the study of culture and history. He was, as one would expect, an outsider. Colleagues didn't accept the youngster, and some of the students were older than he was. Colleagues make fun of him, and he despises his students. His subject doesn't really fill him with passion either. He is said to have once said about philology: *"Thus I regard philology as a freak of the goddess philosophy, produced by an idiot...."*
So, no intrinsic motivation, no extrinsic motivation, where else should this end but in a deeply ingrained dislike for scholars in general.

For our book, we can learn from the acceptance of someone who has no practical experience. We all know the job advertisements of today looking for people who already have 10 years of work experience for a salary that is paid to a recent graduate. And I also often meet people who come into the job after graduation and immediately think that there is no one better to do the job and that there is not much more to learn.

Let's jump back to our model of the metamorphosis of the spirit. The camel, lion and child transformation could not be abbreviated. It takes a lot of time to explain the intricacies of this metaphor. Now college, then an apprenticeship, followed by the first years in the job squarely within the camel phase. Conversely, this means that regardless of whether someone comes from a university or an apprenticeship, they simply can't know everything and certainly can't score points with experience. They may have good plans, but as soon as these are strongly challenged, they usually fall apart. Then comes the real challenge. Intelligence is problem-solving competence, and this problem-solving competence is mainly based on the experience one has made and the security one has in implementing the solutions learned through experience. Problem-solving is usually not learned in the university but during the practical application of what you have learned. No university in the world can prepare you for what hits you with full force in practice. However, Nietzsche was absolutely sure that he, the child prodigy who came to the University of Basel with the highest recommendations, would only be met with admiration and recognition. As we know, what awaited him was different. The experiences he took with him in this situation are reflected in the Zarathustra of this chapter.

Now one could say that there is just a stubborn and offended child reacting to the scolding of his tormentors, but Nietzsche is not completely wrong. He had lived only in the intellectual sphere, so studied, then graduated, habilitated and then taught at the university. He had no practical work experience or any other experience he could reference to. Today we would say that similar people live in their intellectual bubble and settle there. They don't have to get out, because their theory will always beat practice - at least from their point of view. During my time in higher education, I learned that professors who had spent some time in practical professions, or generally came from the business world, could give a much more inspiring and exciting lesson. Their anecdotes were usually helpful, and they could insightfully pick apart a completely superfluous theory, explaining why it would fail in practice. These professors were automatically more credible, because they could test their theories in practice based on lived experience.

I can only appeal to all students that they approach the job with appropriate reverence and show some humility. That you don't know everything does not make you a fool. You become a fool by pretending expertise that you lack. Honest humility will suit you better than this ridiculous arrogance, which is usually laughed at by everyone behind closed doors.

I appeal to all managers not to take the storm out of the sails of the newcomers, but to bring them down to earth with a management technique that one of my previous employers called "Hitting the Wall". We show our true colors when something goes really wrong. So to both teach our new direct reports and expose their true colors, we can create challenging situations that they can't easily handle. They get stuck and have that "hit the wall" moment. How will they react? Do they take a run up, climb the wall and keep running or do they sit down and cry that everything is too hard? Or do they ask someone for a helping hand? Their choices will tell us how to best coach and train them. Weaknesses can then be sensibly corrected. And more importantly, we can accurately and quickly identify our best people. Incidentally, there is no need to do this surreptitiously and set nasty traps along the way. We don't do this for a laugh at others expense, or as a cruel form of hazing. That can quickly lead to disengagement and drive people out of the company as they doubt the leader.

I communicate this tactic openly and my direct reports usually take it well. Many then see it as a game and have fun with these challenges. A positive cycle is triggered and helps everyone. It helps to separate the wheat from the chaff. It also helps the employees by giving them experience with challenging situations.

Of course, this technique must not be applied too soon, before the manager knows the employees. Each person must be challenged differently and individually. The results must be followed up and processed in personal discussions. A separate plan is then developed and implemented for each person. But if you worry that this is very time-consuming, I have to say: Yes! Developing our employees is damn well nearly the only task we have as managers. Again, a great leader invests the absolute majority of their work in hiring, developing and engaging their people. If you can't do that, then get out of management and become an entrepreneur. Working alone, you can't do much damage by scaring employees away from a company because they can't deal with your (imagined or real) genius. The company relies on the performance of its people more than it needs your individual genius. This is not all about you: let people who see leadership as their purpose and fulfillment be leaders.

But most importantly, never let people lead who have only heard about leadership in theory. No matter what they claim, let them start small. Someone who has no practical experience cannot be hired as a manager of managers. We don't want to say that there is any group of people who does not wish to advance, and everyone must be given opportunities. However, some people, like high school students working at McDonalds, are just there for the money, and will not likely make a career of it. The higher people climb in their careers, the more individually they need and want to be promoted. The more intensive the demands on people management become. Someone who has not yet seen any suffering and has not experienced any human abysses or has had to endure them together with others, will easily find the task too much and will find the sensitivity and balancing of needs incredibly difficult. Lions are not good leaders - children own the power!

"So they muffled the sound of my steps: and I was heard worst of all by the most learned.

They put all people's faults and weaknesses between them and me: they call it "false ground" in their houses.

But still I walk with my thoughts above their heads; and even if I wanted to walk on my own faults, I would still be above them and their heads.

For men are not equal: so saith justice. And what I want, they should not want!"

Poets

"Since I know the body better,-said Zarathustra to one of his disciples,-the spirit is only as it were spirit to me; and all the "imperishable"-that too is only a similitude."

"Thus I heard thee say before, replied the disciple; and then thou addedst, "but the poets lie too much." Why did you say, after all, that the poets lie too much?"

"Why?" said Zarathustra. You ask why? I am not one of those whom one may ask why.

Is my experience from yesterday? It has been a long time since I experienced the reasons for my opinions.

Wouldn't I have to be a barrel of memory if I also wanted to have my reasons with me?

It is already too much for me to keep my opinions to myself; and many birds fly away.

And sometimes I also find an animal in my dovecote that is strange to me and that trembles when I lay my hand on it.

But what did Zarathustra once tell you? Do poets lie too much?-but Zarathustra is also a poet.

Do you now believe that he spoke the truth here? Why do you believe that?"

One of the qualities I love in a great leader is that they can laugh at themselves. Someone who can admit mistakes and not try to be perfect, or worse, try to cover up mistakes or flaws, is stuck in the lion stage. Like showing your emotions, a healthy sense of humor - especially about yourself, will make you approachable.

In this chapter two important things happen, firstly Zarathustra makes fun of himself and secondly it is emphasized that it's OK to change your mind. If I realize that I was wrong, then I admit my mistake and adjust my opinion. There is nothing reprehensible about it. Who can know everything and have everything from all sides fully considered? I hire people smarter than me so that I can learn and change my views. I hope that every person I meet and talk to will broaden my horizons and improve my philosophy of life and work. Someone who makes a mistake can be careless or unwise, but not dangerous, because mistakes are not intentional and can teach if we are willing to learn. But someone who holds on to a mistake against better knowledge is dangerous, because there is intention behind it. The intention to never be seen as wrong carries with it so much that is characteristic of bad managers. They care more about themselves and their image than reality, and ironically, will be seen as fools. We see this behavior again and again, from people, from whole companies or even states. Instead of reacting agilely to new information, priority is given to saving face. Expert opinions are ignored and in particularly serious cases, "alternative facts" are even generated and disseminated. Clear behavior of people who are destined to be stuck in the lion phase. People who have never realized that insight is the first path to improvement and that learning from mistakes and adapting means evolution. An iron principle of nature is ignored here. Many people fail to understand that agile people, companies and states are more successful. Holding on to old values is the exact opposite of creating new values and creatively destroying the old and rotten. Someone will come along anyway to sweep away these old systems, why shouldn't it be you? Why should you of all people wait for someone else to come and show everyone that it is possible?

Improving a flawed process requires first admitting that the process is flawed. And the "flaw" can be something about you or something you supported. If you can't fix it, the error is carried on and in the worst case it starts to multiply or affects other systems.

Credibility is the key. If you as a manager admit a mistake, then your employees will dare to do so. If you don't live an open culture of admitting and adjusting error, your environment won't be either. Errors are concealed and, in the best case, attempts are made to solve them under the table. If that doesn't work, they are simply left in the system, where they can wreak havoc until extra resources are required down the road, which is much more expensive than if the error had been tackled directly.

Zarathustra also deals with vanity. Vanity is the other side of the coin. Some people conceal their mistakes out of shame. Others don't even realize they can ever be wrong. They are so full of themselves that it doesn't even occur to them that they have made a mistake. They can't laugh at themselves, except at their own bad jokes. We must understand the difference between those driven by shame and those driven by vanity so that we can manage both groups of people correctly. Each of them needs a clearly different approach.

People who deliberately sweep mistakes under the table must be shown that the working environment in which they now find themselves is characterized by trust and that there are no (ultimate) negative consequences to admitting mistakes. Quite the opposite is true. Dealing openly with mistakes and the clever handling of them when eliminating errors is proof of skill and is rewarded. In my interviews I almost always ask the question about the biggest mistake one has made so far. The biggest mess you ever made that still sends shivers down your spine when you think about it. How did you deal with it and what did you learn from it? The day before yesterday I had an interview in which the applicant told me that the biggest mistake, she had made so far was not canceling an Outlook calendar invitation for an online meeting she could not attend. I asked how severe the consequences were and she explained that there were none. Now, of course, it's possible that the person is flawless, but what are the chances of that? It is more likely that she hides mistakes to look better in the interview. The same behavior will probably continue at work. Not a good first impression. Of course, this question is not the only one and a not so good first impression can still be turned around by strong performance. Perhaps somebody advised her to be on guard for this kind of question, and her answer was not a true reflection of her character. We must always be cautious about jumping to broad conclusions from a single anecdote. An interview is a stressful and unnatural situation. Consciously hiding mistakes is something that can be discarded as soon as you feel safe in a trusted work environment with superiors who see that mistakes are not problems but treasures.

The "hit the wall" method provokes mistakes. A great leader must consciously allow them. Not so easy, as I may remark from my own experience. If you know that the mistake the person under your supervision is about to make will produce a red flag in the weekly business review (WBR) and that top management will come around the corner with unpleasant questions, then it is also necessary to cushion this blow and take it. It is always a good idea to proactively inform your superiors and be open about it or sometimes just swallow the damn toad. If it means that you get to develop your employee to the next level, it's worth it. A great leader is not selfish, but about the success of the people. Just as parents see themselves realized in their children; a manager must take pleasure in the success of the team.

And then there are the others who are so blinded by the glamor of themselves that they can't see the beacon of personal development. They think that they have already reached their goal and can't even imagine that there are still things to learn. For them, mistakes only happen to others or are foisted on them by others. The reason for this toxic behavior is often buried deep in the psyche and was created in early childhood. To "treat" this is not the job of a great leader but of a professional therapist. Now, of course, you first have to find out which of the two categories the employee belongs to, and you must take care to get this diagnosis right. But as soon as you know that the employee belongs to the "conceited" category, and the first attempt at open dialogue does not bear fruit, then take them out. The poison of a toxic person, especially in leadership positions, permeates the entire company over time and destroys it. Not immediately, but little by little. Don't waste time here and protect yourself and your teams from this type of employee.

Who does not want to learn is already lost.

> *"Verily, their spirit itself is the peacock of peacocks and a sea of vanity!*
>
> *Spectator wants the spirit of the poet: should it also be buffaloes!*
>
> *But I have grown tired of this spirit: and I see it coming to tire of itself.*
>
> *Already I saw the poets transformed and their gaze turned against themselves.*
>
> *Penitents of the spirit I saw coming: they grew out of them."*

Great Events

"The earth, he said, has a skin; and this skin has diseases. One of these diseases, for example, is called: "Man."

[...] and always, when I heard overthrow and ejection devils speak, I found them like you: salted, lying and flat.

You know how to roar and darken with ashes! You are the best loudmouths and have learned the art of boiling mud.

Where you are, there must always be mud in the proximity, and much spongy, high-lighted, squeezed: that wants into the freedom.

You all like to shout "freedom" most of all: but I lose faith in "great events," as soon as there is a lot of shouting and smoke around them.

And just believe me, friend hell-noise! The greatest events are not our loudest, but our quietest hours."

Creators reject the demands of the masses. Now the small crowd of those willing to change is now splitting into two classes. The loud ones and the quiet ones. Whereby quiet is not to be understood literally here.

Zarathustra calls the loud ones the revolutionaries. People who develop an idea or join one and then want to enforce it with a lot of roar and smoke. They fight in the truest sense of the word. Political revolutionaries are well-known representatives. Subversives who try to overturn political systems by force. We see them in almost every system at almost every time and in every culture. They are mostly idealists who rise up against a dominant opponent and often go down as martyrs. You can observe these representatives not only in politics but also in companies, the military and many other areas.

A characteristic result of loud revolutionaries is the collateral damage and many victims on both sides. Zarathustra despises them and makes no secret of the fact that this kind is an absolute waste. But why? Don't we all love the romantic stories of glorified revolutions? Well, it depends on which side you were on.

History, as we all know, is always written by the victors and therefore the glorification of revolutionaries should always be taken with extreme caution. The point is that this kind of roar and smoke attracts those who seek only to roar and burn. Just making a ruckus. It is not about the sense or the goal of the renewal but about the hullabaloo around it. This hullabaloo (although hullabaloo is trivialized here, it can also be excessive violence) dilutes the goal, puts the creators in a bad light and takes away their credibility. The thought, the new, the higher is dragged down and sullied by the dirt of the battle hawks and riot tourists. They hang their little spirits on high goals and ideals and complicate their flight or even make it impossible. If you need yelling and noise to push your idea through, then it's not worth it or you haven't formulated it well enough.

But there is another class, so Zarathustra wants to highlight. People who do not win by force but by enthusiasm. People who do not use roar and smoke but wisdom and a kind of inner glow to implement their ideas. There are two ways to motivate your employees to top performance, with fear and with engagement. The first, as already written, is also very successful, but only in the short term and the second in the long term.

I know how hard it is sometimes to control yourself, but that's where the subtle difference lies. Zarathustra's fire dog could represent the inner restlessness and anger that slumbers in all of us and that would like to break through with every big thought. But Zarathustra says that the real, the true drive lies much deeper and is made of pure gold. This rage and violence that we feel in us, sometimes powerless because of the terrible things or bottomless stupidity that strikes us is only superficial. Much deeper within us all dwells the peace, the wisdom that enables us to see through the smoke and hear above the noise. This is priceless - made of pure gold.

A great leader will never start a revolution or an upheaval by making a lot of noise and smoke and bluster. Almost all great ideas start at the fringe. They are mocked or ignored as "wrong" because they contradict the accepted dogma. Advancements almost never come as flashes of brilliance that are immediately recognized for their own merit. Instead, they fight their way from the fringe to the middle, over weeks, months or even years. I love the quote, paraphrased by Max Plank, "Science advances one funeral at a time". The "fight" need not be filled with smoke and roaring. Persistent confidence will eventually win the day.

A weak idea must be adorned with much jewelry to give it weight. A brilliant idea shines on its own, like gold. Its gravity will by itself attract enough people and keep them under its spell. Where there is sound and smoke, there can be no great leader and especially no great event.

"*Not around the inventors of new noise: around the inventors of new values the world turns; inaudibly it turns.*

And only confess it! Little was always done, when your noise and smoke disappeared. What is it that a city became a mummy, and a statue lies in the mud!

And this word I still say to the overthrowers of image pillars. This is the greatest folly, to throw salt into the sea and image pillars into the mud.

In the mud of your contempt lay the image pillar: but this is just its law, that out of contempt it grows again life and living beauty!"

The Soothsayer

"- and I saw a great sadness come over the people. The best became tired of their work.
A teaching went out, a faith ran beside it: "All is empty, All is equal, All was!"
And from all the hills it sounded again: "All is empty, All is equal, All was!"
Well have we reaped: but why did all the fruits turn us rotten and brown? What fell from the evil moon last night?
All work was in vain, our wine became poison, our fields and hearts turned yellow by the evil eye.
We all become dry; and when fire falls on us, we are like ashes:-yes, the fire itself makes us tired.
All wells dried up for us, even the sea receded. All the ground wants to tear, but the depth does not want to snare!
"Oh, where is another sea in which one could drown": so our lament sounds - over shallow marshes.
Truly, we were already too tired to die; now we still wake up and live away in burial chambers!"-.
Thus Zarathustra heard a soothsayer speak; and his prophecy went to his heart and changed him. He went about sad and weary; and he became like those of whom the soothsayer had spoken."

Here Zarathustra is listening to a soothsayer. Read this text twice and recognize the oozing pessimism in it. Zarathustra is infected by it and lets himself be dragged down. He even falls into a terrible dream and needs a long time to fight his way out of it.

How often has this happened to you? I hope it never has and never will. The spirit of gravity is Zarathustra's greatest enemy, just as pessimism drains the fuel of creativity. If you really want to change something, sustainably and without violence, then it will be an incredibly difficult path. To accomplish this without the drive for your turbo is almost impossible. If you look at the real value-creators of today, then you will always notice their industriousness and their consistent progress. When that stops, their progress also dries up or their goal is reached. We must not allow ourselves to be dragged down. But who or what are the weights that slow down our step and make it difficult and even unbearable to progress? The answer is quite simple... We ourselves! The spirit of gravity is our spirit in us. Only we allow it to make us heavy, to make our goals far away and turn normally surmountable obstacles into deep insurmountable chasms. We tell our children that when they grow up, they can achieve anything. Why don't we say the same to our colleagues, friends and most importantly - ourselves? Have we lost faith in ourselves? Or does the spirit of gravity, our pessimism have us in its grip.

John Strelecky's bestselling book "The Why Are You Here Café" contains a beautiful story about a golfer who repeatedly dreams about having to make an incredibly difficult shot that is almost impossible. But the ball keeps rolling away from him. It is a nightmare for him. He lets it drag him down and it weighs heavily on him. Until he finds out that he can just take the ball and put it somewhere else. He is the master of the ball and not the other way around. The lesson to take from it is that if we control the situation, then the situation can't pull us down.

Zarathustra is the champion of a life-affirming optimism, even if only a few can see this from his texts. All of us who want to become great leaders must follow the path of optimism. Those who fall prey to the spirit of gravity have no chance. No one follows a mourning dungeon except to its demise.

So if you want people to follow you without fear or coercion; if you want your employees to go the extra mile and give your idea and your company the best they have; if you want your colleagues to support you with all their strength and without ulterior motives; if you want your manager to fight for you and lead the company or project to success together with you, then smile, laugh at yourself, and have fun with your mistakes. Be happy where you are, smile and say yes to life. To your life!

"Are you not yourself the wind with shrill whistling, which tears open the gates of the castles of death?

Aren't you yourself the coffin full of colorful wickednesses and angels' faces of life?

Verily, like thousandfold child's laughter Zarathustra comes into all dead chambers, laughing at these night and grave guards, and who else rattles with gloomy keys.

You will frighten and overthrow them with your laughter; fainting and waking up will prove your power over them.

And even when the long twilight comes and the fatigue of death, you will not perish in our sky, you advocate of life!

You let us see new stars and new night glories; truly, you stretched laughter itself over us like a colorful tent.

Now the laughter of children will always spring from coffins; now a strong wind will always triumph over all the fatigue of death: you yourself are our guarantor and soothsayer!"

Redemption

"One day, as Zarathustra was crossing the great bridge, the cripples and beggars surrounded him, and a hunchback spoke to him thus:

"Behold, Zarathustra! The people also learn from you and gain faith in your teaching: but that they should believe you completely, one thing is still needed-you must first persuade us cripples! Here you have now a beautiful choice and truly, an opportunity with more than One Scope! You can heal the blind and make the lame walk; and to him who has too much behind him, you could probably also take a little away:-that, I think, would be the right way to make the cripples believe in Zarathustra!"

Zarathustra, however, answered the one who spoke thus: "If one takes away the hunchback of a hunchback, one takes away his spirit-so teaches the people. And if you give the blind man his eyes, he sees too many bad things on earth: so he curses the one who healed him. But he that maketh the lame to walk doeth him the greatest harm: for as soon as he can walk, his vices run away with him."

This chapter is about challenges and motivation. Challenges drive more than just innovation. Almost all progress comes from challenges that nature or the environment impose on us. It starts simple as with evolution. By presenting each species with challenges, nature managed to separate the fit from the unfit, the wheat from the chaff. At the moment, it seems that some members of today's societies are doing everything they can to stop the selection process that allowed humans to dominate the earth. To suspend the challenging environment that has made us what we are today and relax. Prefer ready-made solutions over challenges. Conceived by smart people, pre-portioned and decorated so that everyone can find them good. And so that no one has to challenge the other. One should never feel attacked or offended. A ready-made society to comfort people who don't want to think for themselves.

But is that a good idea? One could even argue that we should stop or slow down evolution, because we have already reached the pinnacle of creation. Nobody likes to be selected against. Can't we all just admit that we have arrived?

We try to create an environment that is less challenging for all of us. Some who could never have survived in the dark past are now saved. We strive to include everybody. This is a great achievement for our society in general, but it should not be applied to the workplace. Just as competition drives every species to success or extinction, competition drives innovation in the workplace. As I write this book, I consider myself lucky to be healthy and in pretty competitive shape. But that could change tomorrow - knock on wood that it doesn't. Every organization carries its dead wood around, and I hope to stay useful. I don't want to live and work in a society where I have to worry every day about losing my job and therefore my life, so I can't afford food or shelter.

However, this does not imply a right to keep my current job after I am no longer able to fill it. I have no moral right to force my employer to keep me in a position for which I am not suitable, either mentally or physically. It is my duty to prove myself worthy of the job I am doing. I have an obligation to do everything in my power to be the best at my job. It is not the job of my employer to create a workplace that is adapted to my needs. The company has needs, and only those needs need to be met by creating a job that actually makes economic sense. This position needs to be filled by the most capable person. That is because this person is not only capable, but the best possible candidate. The company is in a constant struggle with new recruits, and even if there are none in sight at the moment, they are being created right now. Maybe in a country we don't have on our radar or in a niche that is hidden at the moment.

But there is a balance to be taken care of. Every company needs to make sure to attract the best talents and so the jobs need to be attractive. If you want to have the smartest employees working for you, you have to make sure that your work environment attracts them. For example, the cost associated with creating a barrier free work environment in the majority of office jobs is no problem at all and enables the access to a huge group of disabled people for the company. It would make no economic sense to forego the many talents that are available in the large group of people with disabilities.

In the last few years, companies have started to create jobs not for the best possible benefit of the company, but to look good in the eyes of the public. They carry around nonsensical jobs like feather ornaments and think that this makes them look more attractive. A great piece of work here is David Graeber's book "Bullshit Jobs: A Theory". It describes a set of jobs that is not adding any value. They are only there to make the company look better. And yes, they do, but to employees who do not have the company's success in mind but only their reputation and who in turn want to have the company's name on their resume like a feather ornament.

This idea of a highly integrative work environment in which every employee is treated equally, in which there are no more hard decisions but only cooperative compromises, in which the insufficient are not sorted out and the best are not promoted, runs counter to the principle of "challenge drives innovation". The harsh reality is that not every human child is born with identical talents, and as they grow, inequalities at birth are amplified by inequalities in education and upbringing. Children with nurturing parents who attend great schools get a boost. Those who don't must work extra hard to overcome their disadvantages, and indeed, some do. These people who have overcome obstacles to rise to the top are likely to be the best of all possible talents. But not every person will rise above every challenge. This translates to extreme differences in talent, initiative and qualification among the workforces. I can feel the furor already, but this has nothing to do with race or gender: every hypothetical subdivision of humans will have variations in talents *within* their group at birth. The idea that we are all equals is a utopian fantasy. Some of your workers are more talented than others.

To put it this way is probably very easy for a privileged person who is doing well at the moment. From another point of view, it would look different. Everybody has biases that cloud their objectivity. Everything depends on your point of view. This is mine. I was born with higher-than-average intelligence. Both my parents loved and cared for me. I went to great schools all the way through my development, and I have worked hard all my life. Yes, I was born privileged, and took every advantage that I could ever since. And so should you.

I used to be a competitive athlete. Even quite successful for my sensibilities. It was fun and I enjoyed the sport. I have been canoeing - always on the water since I was eight years old. But after a while, I lost interest and started partying and fooling around, as many people do in their awakening youth and after. As a consequence, my abilities declined and couldn't keep up anymore. I was eventually excluded from the performance group and assigned to the recreational group. Did I demand now that I should remain in the top group? No, of course not. I knew I wasn't good enough and I knew it was my fault. I didn't complain about unfair treatment because it was unthinkable to me to not accept responsibility. I wasn't good enough to fight my peer competitors anymore.

Another example would be Dan Truman played by Billy Bob Thornton in the movie "Armageddon" with Bruce Willis, Ben Affleck and Liv Tyler. He always wanted to be an astronaut but couldn't be due to a disability. He became an engineer because NASA only wants people in absolute physical conditions to go on their missions. During a discussion with Harry Stamper (Bruce Willis), Dansays:

"I went into the engineering program. Kinda had to. But boy, I wanted to go up there. I wanted to be one of those guys with a mission patch on my arm."

That perfectly makes sense as these space missions are exorbitantly expensive, and all risk factors must be minimized. To choose the fittest people to carry out these missions is a pure rational business decision. It's not meant to be discriminating. There is a place for everyone, and Dan Truman is still a Director in NASA and one of the most important people in the mission. Challenging each other is not the same as fighting each other or fighting for one's life in general. A challenge can also be intellectual, creative or athletic. We humans are like cars, we need fuel to drive, but we also need someone to push on the gas to accelerate. If you just want to just drive, then eat, sleep and have fun. But if you want to win at le mans, face every challenge that might prevent you from winning. The same goes for your employees. If you want them to do their normal job, pay them, provide an engaging and safe work environment and they will work for you. But if you want them to work hard and reach for the stars, you need to put the pedal to the metal by challenging them. Let them hit the wall and help them overcome it. Give them the tasks that no one else wants to do because they are considered nearly impossible and rejoice in the great results they will achieve. Make sure you reward those great accomplishments and make them feel appreciated. If you give them an impossible task, you can't punish them for failure, but rather, nurture them for the next fight. Sounds like a two-tiered society, doesn't it? That's exactly what it is. People are different, and you have to treat them differently. Treating everyone the same is always unfair to someone - always.

People who complain about the micro-aggressive or macro-aggressive environment simply don't have the right inner attitude towards personal development. They lack the willingness to rise above and reach for the stars. Nothing is free, we have to fight for the great things we want to achieve. If we want to make the world a better place for everyone, it will cost some dearly. If you want to renew yourself and thus grow, you have to be challenged or challenge yourself. And that always includes an environment that puts pressure on you. The talented ambitious must be treated differently than the competent but content. You can't challenge everybody the same way because people have different personal preferences and expectations of their employer. And that's fine, because in this case it's all about communication and staff alignment.

The best work environment is where everyone can achieve their desired work goals. Not the position or the salary, but the work environment. That is the beginning of any good employer-employee relationship. A great environment that has equality of opportunity, where everyone can choose whether or not to take advantage of them. We are talking about equal opportunities instead of equalizing outcomes!

Every company seeks to hire only the best talent, and most of the best talent wants to be CEO and, surprisingly, are convinced they can be. This is not possible and creates a lot of frustration for the employee, but also for the company, which usually leads to high turnover. High turnover means high costs. According to a report published by the Society for Human Resource Management (SHRM), it costs a company an average of six to nine months of an employee's salary to hire and train a new employee. A company that tries to offer the same results to every employee by promising that everyone can be a future CEO is bound to fail. Work environments are often characterized by scarcity, where fewer and fewer people can be promoted the higher, they go on the ladder. False promises lead to frustration among high performers, who despite their success, will never be CEO. To "solve" this discrepancy, these companies bestow nice sounding job titles in an inflationary manner. If they can't all be CEOs, make them all senior vice presidents or whatever. The result is a loss of functional authority and authority in general. In addition, a vacuum of responsibility and coordination is created. Since it is no longer possible to clearly assign who has which function, rights and responsibilities, there is a great loss of time and resources. This makes perfect sense: make one person responsible, and the job gets done. Make three people responsible, and each can defer to the other two and nobody is at fault.

If you clearly communicate from the beginning what the bar is for talent in your company, employees will feel that it's perfectly fine to meet the company's high expectations, and in return, the company will appreciate your hard work in the form of pay, appealing work atmosphere, and other benefits, but not in the form of promotions. If you want to be promoted, you have to be an exceptional talent, a superstar. You may think you are a superstar, but you probably aren't. (Yes, I know, you might be.) If you want to be the next CEO, you have to be willing to give everything you've got, while possessing all the talents required combined with the luck of being at the right time in the right place. It's not enough to just work, you also have to feel all the pain that these people go through. I like to compare these entrepreneurial ventures to the nautical adventures of the past. Every one of them was a gamble. The captains staked their entire fortunes, hired a daring crew, most of whom gave up everything they owned, and everyone hoped for the pot of gold at the end of the rainbow. As they sailed the seas, they battled the unbridled forces of nature and the depths of their own psyches. They suffered hunger and thirst, they wept and laughed - but above all they fought. They fought for every meter or centimeter above the sea. Maybe I'm being overly romantic here, but anyone who has started a business may have similar memories and can relate.

Are you ready for this journey with all the pain it will bring? If so, stop looking for the most relaxing and restful place to work, with a low number of hours, a 4-day work week, and a work environment where "family and friends" rule. This equates to a calm lake. The likelihood of finding great treasure here is not zero, but it's not great either. Desire the rough and open sea, the unknown depths and strong currents that can only be found where others dare not sail. For where other ships sink lie hidden great treasures for the brave.

Stop striving for work environments that promise full inclusion for every single employee. Not everyone can make it to the top. There simply isn't enough room up there, and not everyone is suited. But not everyone wants to get to the top either. Managing a company is rarely pure charity, but an attempt to earn money with the work and, in the best case, to create added value for the customer. The company needs professionals who can do this as effectively and efficiently as possible. Each in their place and each to their best use. Even if you run an organization that focuses on charity, you want people to get the goods or money to people in need as efficiently as possible.

Call on volunteers to get in on the wild ride and explain what the bar is for participation. Explain in detail to others how they can make life as easy as possible for the adventurers by supporting them where they can. And if someone volunteers and doesn't meet the requirements or fails along the way, give them a chance to join the supporters or help them find a better job outside.

Again, your best sailors should be volunteers and the best of all employees; a quota cannot solve this for you. You must be the person who selects the crew based on what you need and the best contribution they can make. There are times when the thing that is needed is a visible leader who can motivate everybody in the workforce, who happens to fit a quota. This is especially true if a workplace has a history of discrimination. But this is not a quota hire; it is a strategic hire that is meant to increase engagement of the team, and the new leader must be qualified (or the effort will backfire). A diverse team performs best, so everyone should always strive for a team with a wide variety of skills and values. Teams who don't seek diversity are simply being stupid and harming their own advantage and will have to pay for it in the long run.

But why is the chapter called "Redemption"? For Zarathustra redemption is not necessarily good. If you look back on your whole life until now, would you say: that's exactly how I wanted it? Everything is exactly as it should be? Probably not, because almost all of us have made mistakes that are embarrassing or unpleasant in retrospect. Most people, however, do not face these mistakes and instead explain that they actually intended everything to work out the way it did. This is a typical resolution of cognitive dissonance. Our brain does not want to admit that it has made mistakes. Rather it explains that it was actually good, that one wanted it this way. Deep inside, however, we know this is a lie and, according to Zarathustra, causes an inner resentment. And this resentment is the trigger of various unpleasant things like feelings of revenge, but alternatively, redemption for many. Rather than turn their anger and revenge on themselves, as they should they lash out against others. The lame man in the story wants to walk again. But Zarathustra tells him that he then only runs to his death. He should see his lame leg as a challenge and accordingly look for an activity that is best suited to his performance. He should stop crying in the figurative sense and finally make the best of it. There are no miracles - especially not at this time. This is easy to say when you are not the lame one. But in the end, it's no use waiting for a miracle. You have to make the best of your situation. You have to see every mistake as an opportunity, as a treasure that you can lift and learn something great from it and then make.

Or as Ludovici said in his comments on Zarathustra and this chapter: *"He who can be proud of his enemies, who can be grateful to them for the obstacles they have put in his way; he who can regard his worst calamity as but the extra strain on the bow of his life, which is to send the arrow of his longing even further than he could have hoped;—this man knows no revenge, neither does he know despair, he truly has found redemption and can turn on the worst in his life and even in himself, and call it his best"*

Manly Prudence

"This is my first human wisdom, that I allow myself to be deceived in order to not be on guard against deceivers.
But this is my other human wisdom: I spare the vain more than the proud.
But this is my third human wisdom, that I do not let your fearfulness spoil the sight of the wicked."

In today's society, where the marketing of the ego through social media has become incredibly important, individualism is very often confused with eccentricity. Only the person who adorns himself with as many colorful feathers as possible and wears the most radical outfit or has the most unusual identity or gender is truly an individual. Outward pretense counts more than quiet creativity. The reality is that those who follow a formula for being recognized by the masses as an individual tend to be ridiculous conformists.

The Cambridge Dictionary defines individuality as follows: *"the idea that freedom of thought and action for each person is the most important quality of a society, rather than shared effort and responsibility"*.

Freedom of thought and action is something great, something comprehensive. Something that applies to everyone regardless of confession, political opinion, skin color, or sexual orientation. To be eccentric for recognition is a joke. It wants to be different for the sake of being different. They are actors, and nothing more. In the narrative in which one has to stand out through the magnifying glass of social media, the boundaries are unfortunately all too often blurred.

The western world has become a theater in which the masses no longer sit in the audience but stand on the stage. Only those who can't afford to dance dressed up on this stage still sit enviously in the stands. But I prefer to sit in the stands. I prefer to sit between those without the means or just don't feel like making an ass of themselves. But only for a short time. I prefer to walk outside the theater in nature. Because there are also those who simply do not have time to be an actor, or to follow them. Those who use their time sensibly to bring this society fundamentally forward. Those who turn the wheel and keep everything going so that the lights don't go out in the theater and all the vain peacocks suddenly wake up and stream out of the theater onto the street to realize how stupid they actually look in the light of the real sun.

Don't get me wrong, I too love to wear nice clothes and share my most beautiful vacation experiences with my friends on a few social platforms. I long for platforms that can finally bring people together instead of apart. I wouldn't advise anyone to be just a gray mouse among many gray mice. But arrogance and vanity are not real adornments but distractions. Once you shine through performance, you don't need to wear a golden dress.

I have seen it so often that people have come into leadership positions simply because they look great and speak with an inflated vocabulary, but when it came down to it, they failed. When shit hit the fan and required action, they failed. I can only appeal again and again to hiring managers, don't be dazzled. People who really have it are generally reserved. They are less conspicuous, and immune to pretentious eccentricity. They do not concentrate their time on their jewelry, but on their task. They will not be constantly pushing for being at the big stage, but will stand on the sidelines and tinker, brainstorm and write. They will not indulge in vanity but smile at the vain and take care of important things. They will not let themselves be frightened by others but will make their own experiences.

Those who call themselves "the good and the righteous" are usually neither. They think out of their context without ever questioning it, because they cannot.

Great leaders do not see themselves as good and just, they simply are. The great leaders will not point out at every opportunity how good and just they are, the process of the decision these leaders make will clearly show if the decisions were good and just. Because to judge this is not up to the doing but to the receiving. If you think something is good, it may be true from your point of view, but not from the point of view of many others. Good and just is not ultimate but individual.

That what Zarathustra defines as the superman, that - so he recognizes now - most would consider to be wrong. They would not understand the new values and the new ways that they are not able to think of them, that they can see only their own point of view as the good and just.

My appeal to all great leaders out there, all those who have transcended the lion phase, pull through and do not let yourselves be distracted. Success will prove you right, even if it takes a long time for others to catch up.

"Oh, I was tired of these highest and best ones: from their "height" I longed to go up, out, away to the superman!

A horror overcame me when I saw these best ones naked: then my wings grew, to float away into distant futures.

To more distant futures, to a more southerly south, than any sculptor ever dreamed of: to where gods are ashamed of all clothes!

But disguised I will see you, you neighbors and fellow men, and well dressed, and vain, and worthy, as "the good and the just,"

And disguised will I myself sit among you,-that I may forget you and myself: for this is my last human wisdom."

The Stillest Hour

"Don't you know who does the most for everyone? He who commands great things.
To do great things is difficult, but the more difficult is to command great things. This is your most unforgivable thing: you have the power, and you do not want to rule."
And I answered, "I lack the voice of the lion for all commanding."
Then it spoke to me again like a whisper: "It is the quietest words that bring the storm. Thoughts, which come with dove's feet, steer the world.
O Zarathustra, thou shalt go as a shadow of that which must come: thus shalt thou command and go forth commanding."
And I answered, "I am ashamed."
Then it spoke to me again without voice: "You must still become a child and without shame."

Zarathustra realizes that he has to leave. He realizes in this last chapter of the second part that he is not yet the great leader he would have to be to make his philosophy accessible to the broadest masses. He is wise, can speak well and can attract disciples. But the way to the superhuman is yet to be discovered. He has traveled so far and said so much, but he is still far from his goal. As in the first part, he realizes that the problem is not the world but himself. He must return to the solitude of his cave and continue to hone himself to become the great leader he envisions.

Personally, I think it's great to know that even a genius has doubts. It's even greater that there is deep self-reflection on these doubts and that they're dealt with openly and honestly.

That is our final lesson in this book. I want to share one more story with you that brought home something important to me.

I was a department manager in one of the largest companies in the world, running the day shift. Normally, between shifts, we would have a short break where the employees of one shift would leave, and the other shift would slowly gather. The shift always started with a kick-off meeting, which had to be short and crisp but also enthusiastic so that the employees were engaged in their day's work. I usually watched the meeting led by my colleague and had a short chat with him afterwards.

One day I watched the starting meeting and everything was good, employees were engaged, all the important news was delivered so the shift could start. All the employees dispersed to their workstations except for one. One little woman stopped in the middle of the area and started crying. I watched the situation from a distance of about twenty meters. My colleague went to her and talked for maybe thirty seconds. Then he turned around and went to his computer and started typing.

But the employee was still standing there and crying. Other onlookers began to look questioning and a little helpless. I was puzzled and decided that I should go and help her.

I asked her what had happened, and she looked at me and told me that she had just come from the doctor. She was diagnosed with stage 4 cancer. She had to start therapy immediately and now she didn't know what to do. She didn't get a sick note and didn't know if she should go or stay. She cried even more.

I was shocked. I took her off the shopfloor and brought her to our HR department. My HR person immediately stopped what she was doing to help us get her into professional hands. We clarified that of course she could go home immediately and take paid time off. I was relieved that we could help - and suddenly got incredibly angry. Angry at my colleague who had left the poor woman crying alone to hide behind his computer.

I was so angry that I went straight back to him. I found him at his place, still typing on his damn computer. I built myself up in front of him and gave him -

let's say - very direct feedback. I have to say that I am quite tall and broad and have a loud voice that was used to drown out a big warehouse at that time. I talked my anger out of my soul because of this inexcusable stupid behavior. And I was loud, so that the surrounding colleagues noticed and looked to the floor in embarrassment. Somehow, they all felt complicit. My god I was so angry at him.

But then I noticed that my colleague did not react at all. He just stared at his screen. I stopped my rant and looked at him. Awkward silence came up. I asked him if everything was okay, and he looked me in the eye - like the employee before him - and told me that his mother had died of cancer two weeks earlier. When the woman told him her diagnosis, he almost collapsed on the spot. To avoid bursting into tears and sinking to the floor he had managed to escape to his desk to avoid making things worse for her. The memory was too painful. He couldn't stand the talk and had to run from his responsibilities. He felt terrible but knew he wouldn't be of any help.

There was never a day when I felt as bad as I did at that moment. It was like a scale from my eyes how stupid I had been. I was so convinced that I was an exemplary manager who always took good care of his employees. I wanted to show him that he was bad, and I wanted to shout it out in front of everybody there.

I didn't even try to put on his shoes and look at the situation neutrally before I snapped. I was just an asshole in true lion fashion.

I always thought that we had a good relationship, my colleague and me. But if he couldn't even tell me that his mother had died, our relationship couldn't have been that good. Even today, so many years later, I shudder when I think of that situation.

But not because it is still unpleasant for me, and I am ashamed of myself. But because I know that this was one of the most important moments of my career. I learned so much about myself and broke with my pride at that desk at that moment. I was loud the last time; I was arrogant towards a colleague the last time. I looked at a situation superficially the last time and drew my conclusions. I went home to my cave. I withdrew and reinvented myself.

"Oh my friends! I still have something to tell you, I still have something to give you! Why don't I give it? Am I stingy?"

But when Zarathustra had spoken these words, he was overcome by the force of pain and the nearness of parting from his friends, so that he wept aloud; and no one knew how to comfort him. At night, however, he went away alone and left his friends."

The End

The book "Thus spoke Zarathustra", goes even further. We have gone through the first two parts but there are two more. After Zarathustra separates from his disciples again after the second part, he goes on the search for the supermen in part three and four. Everyone reading will get something different for themself. My book is only what I shamelessly stole from Nietzsche's book and interpreted for myself. You might find something completely different. And that is good. I hope you enjoy your own journey of discovery.

It is an inner concern to me to point out again that I have already read countless books and my philosophy of work and life is a conglomerate of many books, films, discussions, experiences and so forth. I would like to encourage you to read as many interesting and even boring books as possible, to experience as much as you can and to challenge yourself as hard as you can to develop your own philosophy. I look forward to your feedback on this book, but also to the suggestions that may be an inspiration for another book.

I summarized the pillars again in the appendix and am happy to be challenged on them as well.

I have added a list of all the books I mention in the text. I think all of them are worth reading and I hope that one or the other will help you broaden your view of the world.

For further recommendations I am at your disposal. And I always like to receive book recommendations. You never stop learning.

Please get in contact with me via my website: www.philosophyofwork.org where you can also find all details and news summarized again.

Our world is at the brink because the masses want to consume as relaxed and conveniently as possible while also looking with envy at those who create that wealth. Instead of cheering and supporting them, they actively or subconsciously work against these people. What we need here is great leaders who play the role of mediating between the masses and the creators while eventually being creators themselves.

The wealth created in the western world was mainly built on environmental pollution, violence, cruelty and especially at the cost of our nature and other countries. The outcome was tremendous. We are living in a safe and comfortable world that is relaxed and convenient. But we know it can't continue like this. We need smart people who can develop ways of working that create wealth without degrading the earth as we have in the past. We need people who write in blood the plan to success and execute them.

Today we work 8 hours a day, usually 5 days a week. That is amazingly low compared to the past. In 1830 the average working time per week ranged between 70 hours (North America) to 82 hours (Germany) and we came down to an average of 40 and below sometime in the 20th century. During the last 200 years, the average number of hours people work per week has halved and a lot of people argue that this is still too much. This trend creates the impression that there is a correlation between working less and an ever-accelerating economic growth. A kind of invisible hand that enables more people to escape poverty and incredibly bad working environments. There is no invisible hand, but a tirelessly working community of creators that push humanity from one invention to the next. We need to make sure that these people are found and attracted to our teams and that we are able to make use of them. That we do all in our power to help them do what they are best at - creating the future.

In the current world of economics, we see an ever-increasing competition between especially China, the US, India, Russia, Japan and Europe with parts of Africa and South America pushing fast as well. The companies are more and more international and serve customers around the globe. I see an ever-increasing need for great leaders in these companies who want to lead humanity into a brighter future.

While in the western world the expectation of our new generation of managers is that a 40-hour workweek is already too much, India is still at 54 hours on average and China still at 47 hours per week. A manager in India is working on average 50% more than a western manager. I agree that this is not necessarily equal to delivering 50% more as more work is not equal to more results and mental health needs to be taken into account here. But 50% more time spent on your development and the development of your company, is an incredible advantage. Elon Musk's says that a highly successful person needs to work 80-100 hours per week. Do 13 hours working per day in a 6-day work week sound as something you would like to go for? If your answer is no, you should seriously think if the path of becoming one of these incredible successful persons is really the right one for you. Of course, the chance is not zero, but the likelihood shrinks. And you rather plan for an incredible workload and be happy if you don't need all this time because of your great self-organization, IQ or sheer luck than if you try several times and wonder why all the other folks are more successful than you. Like one of my former managers loved to say: *"Talent over hours."* It is not about hours, but your willingness to go the extra mile. It's about your ownership, your curiosity, your passion, your commitment - in short, it's about you.

The challenges of the near and distant future will push us to the limits of what we are capable of enduring. To accomplish that, we need great leaders to make sure we fight together, not each other.

I hope you are one of the few who are willing to join in and make this world a better place for humanity by making you a better self. Keep that chaos within yourself to be able to give birth to many dancing stars.

"I tell you: you must still have chaos within you in order to give birth to a dancing star. I tell you: you have chaos within you."

Note of Thanks

Countless people have inspired me on my way so far. I thank my great wife for understanding that I have sacrificed our time together to write this book and of course for the good discussions on topics inside and outside the book. Your opinion means more to me than you can imagine.

To my daughter whom I love dearly and who gave me a childlike perspective on some of the issues. I will always make sure you can keep your chaos. May you turn the world upside down.

I thank my whole family for their spiritual and moral support on the way to completing this book.

I also want to highlight my colleagues at work, supervisors and people who have worked with me and/ or are still working for me. The many sometimes really emotional conversations mean a lot to me and I look forward to every further conversation. To list them all would go beyond the scope of this book, but I would like to express my gratitude from the bottom of my heart to all those with whom I have been able to experience and suffer through so many crazy things.

Special thanks also to all the people who supported me with proofreading the book and giving so much valuable feedback. Monika Kohlmann, Christopher Schnell, Alica Friedrich-Salomon, Nour Mansour - you are the best.

Marija, Dennis and Ben I would like to thank in particular, because our conversation was the bone of contention to write this book. Thank you for your trust and here's to seeing you soon, wherever that may be.

All artworks are done by George Miroshnichenko, thanks a lot for all the great brainstorming and drawings.

The cover artwork by Jessika Musigk - #dietattootrulla

For Hanno and Julchen - I1 forever

Principles

The whole concept is based on five simple pillars and our development scheme. Below there are all of them summarized again.

<u>The three metamorphoses of the spirit: Camel - Lion - Child</u>

Your life is a lifetime of learning. You start as a camel and load up all the knowledge and experience you gain in the first and most important learning stages of your life. This includes school, university, apprenticeship, and the first years of work. But also, everything that comes along the way like the first love, the first crisis and life's ups and downs.

After you have built up enough knowledge, you become a lion and realize that on top of all this knowledge you can now build something functional like a family, a career, and a business. You are proud and you take credit for your accomplishments, which are now visible to everyone. This is a stage marked by behavior. At a certain stage, you act strong and confident. You collect recognition not for its own sake, but rather, because you are kicking ass, and doing great things. A lion is already a leader. And often even a good leader. They can attack but also protect. They can roar loudly and state their opinion, and they are heard. They separate from the mass and are counted into the pool of the creators. They don't accept that something needs to be done as it has always been done and can think outside the box. They lead to new lands and conquer new worlds. But this stage is where most people get stuck and fail to progress - unfortunately.

Because the last stage is the most important. Here you become a child again and learn that all the pride is trivial. You rather pass on your knowledge so that many more people can benefit from it. You share and give away credit, and the knowledge you have built up before. You drop the old ballast and burdens and unnecessary things you have surrounded yourself with over the years. Your ego subsides and you are no longer driven by strategic ingratiation or bound by social conformity. No more leading through fear or rank. Leadership now feels natural. A child is a curious person that creates for the sake of creation, a person who researches only to learn, who lives for the sake of life and experience. The child is defined according to their own system of beliefs, values and ideas - their own philosophy.

Challenge drives Innovation

We have learned two ways to approach this principle in the book. Challenge drives innovation and Hit the Wall. Challenge is fundamental for every great leader. You have to challenge yourself to rise above, and the same applies to your colleagues and employees.

These challenges will inevitably lead us to run into walls that we can't get past. Our reactions to challenges define us. Do we sit down and cry or do we accept the challenge and climb over the damn wall? It's OK to ask someone for help. The main thing is to get over the wall.

Once we get over that wall and celebrate our success, the next wall will come and present us with the next challenge. With each wall we overcome, we will become more alert and better in our personal development. We learn and build our experience. This process should never stop, because it keeps us and our brain young and fit.

Don't speak to the dead

There are always people out there who either won't or can't understand you. The former are driven by conscious or unconscious prejudices and the latter are held back by their own possibilities. The question now is how much time you spend on them. How much time and energy do you invest in convincing them of an idea? I suggest you make this decision quickly but carefully. Quickly because time is precious, but carefully because if you are seen as capriciously dismissive, your work environment will suffer. As hard as this might sound now, it's not your job to fix the gaps in basic knowledge within your audience. If you realize that they are not capable of understanding you, make adjustments. Revise your language and arguments and try again or stop talking to them. Albert Einstein once said, "If you can't explain it easily, you haven't understood it well enough," so do some soul-searching and come up with a tactic, but again, don't waste your time. Time is the only thing we are given in this life, and how you choose to invest it will determine how far you will go.

There is a thin line between explanation and excuse

Some people confuse excuses with explanations, and there is a fine line between the two. But the distinction is clear, and dependent on your internal attitude. An excuse is meant to deflect blame away from yourself while an explanation is meant to provide information. An apology can contain elements of both: Insincere apologies shift blame while sincere apologies acknowledge responsibility. An explanation is a clear statement of what happened.

Take responsibility. This is hard and is one of the first things to practice on the way to becoming a great leader. It is hard because we have to accept that we are not perfect and there is no higher authority to blame for our mistakes.

Don't make excuses to deflect. You did it on purpose, and you have to stand by it. Never apologize for what you are. Whether you are black, white, a woman, a man, tall or short, fat or thin, it's nobody's business because it's you. Any assessment must depend on your performance and if the company and the employees do not value your performance, you need to work harder on yourself or the company is the wrong one and you should leave it.

You need to be happy where you are

You need to be happy where you are, whether it's in your professional or personal life, in your role, or in your relationship. If you are not happy where you are, your brain will develop avoidance strategies to keep you from going where you are not happy. Why would you want to be in a place that makes you unhappy? This contradiction, that is, voluntarily putting yourself in a situation that is unpleasant for you, creates a cognitive dissonance. That is, a discrepancy between what is expected to happen and what actually happens. Your brain can't resolve this discrepancy for the time being and slowly goes into defense mode. Every brain handles this differently, and some start a real fight. And there you go, you're in a mess. That's why it's so important to take care of your mental health by making sure you're happy where you are. Remember that where most people are is not necessarily where you're happiest. Go your own way and find your own place. Don't let anyone tell you that here or there is better or worse. Don't just listen to your brain, listen to your gut.

If you write, write in blood

Of all that is written, I love only that which someone has written with his blood. Write with blood, and you will find that blood is spirit. Says Zarathustra right at the beginning of the chapter and this is for me one of the deepest wisdoms in his book. If you want to do something, do it with passion and full dedication. Do it as if your life depended on it and don't let anything stop you. Then you'll be pure inspiration and you'll sweep other people away. Don't talk, do.

Literature

I highly recommend these books for your reference. The list is far from exhaustive, and some, like "The Black Swan" were not mentioned in the book.

Author	Title
Martin E.P. Seligmann	Authentic Happiness
Ben Kimura-Gross	How we connect
Ben Horowitz	Hard things about hard things
Jack Welch	Winning & Winning 2
Sadhguru	Inner Engineering: A Yogi's Guide to Joy
Ray Dalio	Principles
G. Michael Hopf	Those Who Remain
Hans Rosling, Ola Rosling, et al	Factfulness: Ten Reasons We're Wrong About The World - And Why Things Are Better Than You Think
Tim Urban	The Cook and the Chef: Musk's Secret Sauce
Steven D. Levitt & Stephen J Dubner	Freakonomics
Adam Grant	Give and Take: A Revolutionary Approach to Success
Oscar Wilde	The Soul of Man under Socialism

Jim Collins	From Good to Great
Stefanie Stahl	The Child in You
Fränzi Kühne	Was Männer nie gefragt werden: Ich frage trotzdem mal
Ayn Rand	The Fountainhead & Atlas Shrugged
Sun Tzu	The Art of War
Joseph Schumpeter	Capitalism, Socialism, and Democracy
Daniel Goleman	Emotional Intelligence- Why It Can Matter More Than IQ
Prof. Dr. Matthias Sutter	The Discovery of Patience - Perseverance Beats Talent
David Graeber	Bullshit Jobs: A Theory
John Strelecky	The Why Are You Here Café
Malcolm Gladwell	Outliers